BEATLE MANIA

An Unauthorized Collector's Guide

Courtney McWilliams

Schiffer Publishing Ltd ®

4880 Lower Valley Road, Atglen, PA 19310 USA

Dedication

I would like to dedicate this book to my son, Julian, who is a beautiful person in his own right and to my best friend in the whole world, Mary Berry (and her husband Steve). Thank you both, Julian and Mary, for all of your support through life's ups and downs and, Mary and Steve, congratulations on that new baby, Ethan Thomas. He is beautiful.

I would also like to thank my mother, Kay Upfold, for always encouraging me to pursue my dreams, Kent Stoaks and Roberta Barlowe for their encouragement, and my grandmother, Jonna Upfold for always being there for me when I was growing up. I love you all. I would also like to thank God for placing stepping stones strategically in my path throughout my life. It was these stones that helped me to stay afloat through the roughest of seas ...

Copyright © 1998 by Courtney McWilliams
Library of Congress Catalog Card Number: 98-85864

All rights reserved. No part of this work may be reproduced or used in any form or by any means—graphic, electronic, or mechanical, including photocopying or information storage and retrieval systems—without written permission from the copyright holder.
"Schiffer," "Schiffer Publishing Ltd. & Design," and the "Design of pen and ink well" are registered trademarks of Schiffer Publishing, Ltd.

Designed by Bonnie M. Hensley
Layout by Randy L. Hensley
Typeset in Seagull Hv Bt/ZaphHumnst BT

ISBN: 0-7643-0657-X
Printed in China
1 2 3 4 C

Published by Schiffer Publishing Ltd.
4880 Lower Valley Road
Atglen, PA 19310
Phone: (610) 593-1777; Fax: (610) 593-2002
E-mail: Schifferbk@aol.com
Please write for a free catalog.
This book may be purchased from the publisher.
Please include $3.95 for shipping.

In Europe, Schiffer books are distributed by
Bushwood Books
6 Marksbury Avenue Kew Gardens
Surrey TW9 4JF England
Phone: 44 (0) 181 392-8585; Fax: 44 (0) 181 392-9876
E-mail: Bushwd@aol.com

Please try your bookstore first.
We are interested in hearing from authors
with book ideas on related subjects.

Contents

Preface

This book is very special to me because it gives me an opportunity to introduce you to my family. My partner and soul mate, Douglas Jay Hastings, did the fabulous photography of most of the items you will see pictured in this book. Doug and I share a multiplicity of life interests, of which the Beatles are only one. He was born in Ft. Collins, Colorado, and has lived in Colorado for most of his life. He spent quite a bit of time in Europe in the late 1970s, traveling all around. He settled in Frankfurt, Germany, for three years before returning to the United States.

Doug studied logistics systems management in college, but found it too confining. Once he started to look at the world from an artist's point of view, he started to realize that photography was a way to breathe life into some of his ideas, which ultimately got him started on a Beatle quest of his own. Thank you Doug, for being my life mate and for stopping to pick hyacinths for my soul.

I would also like to introduce our son, Julian, who is already very dear to us. Julian, all that I ask is that you have a vivid imagination, a thirst for knowledge, and the courage to always pursue your dreams. You are the light of my life and the fuel for my hopes and dreams...

Acknowledgements

Our very special thanks go out to Dennis and Connie Dailey for letting us photograph a portion of their fabulous collection and for welcoming us into their home. We had a blast. We would also like to thank Dennis for his tireless help and expertise in the field of Beatles collecting. He was instrumental in helping to make this book as accurate as possible. Dennis is a very knowledgeable collector and owns one of the largest collections in the world. You can reach Dennis at CONDAI@NQUE.COM

A special thanks also, to Dana Haas of Colorado Springs, Colorado, for allowing us to photograph his collection and turn his home into a studio for awhile. We would also like to thank his wife, Beth, for letting us borrow him for awhile, after they had been married for such a short time.

I would like to thank my best friend, Mary Berry, for her help and encouragement all the way through this project, despite the fact that she was about to be a new mother any minute. And God bless Ethan, the newest Berry, who came just in time to get his name in the book.

I would also like to include a very special thanks to all of the doctors that helped me through rehabilitation, and continue to inspire me today. Without your help and encouragement I might never have soared up to reach my dream. Thank you Dr. Miles Yeagley, Dr. Jack Rook, Dr. Leppard, Dr. Bjork, Dr. Garrison (my doctor at Capron Rehabilitation), Chris Bauer, and Patti Janitell.

We would also like to thank Gene at D & H Camera Repair and Sales of Colorado Springs, Colorado, for always keeping our cameras going, no matter what. If you would like to see what Gene can do for your photographic equipment, you can reach him at 4587 Austin Bluffs Parkway, 719-587-0336.

I would also like to thank Kathy Childers: singer, songwriter and rhythm guitarist for the City Zoo band out of Seattle. Her music has been tremendously influenced by the Beatles and it shows. I appreciate her allowing us to publish photographs of her collection in this book. Go see the band. It rocks!

And a very special thanks to Mark Lapidos of Mark Lapidos Productions Ltd., for featuring our book in his Beatlefest catalog of mostly new memorabilia, with some older memorabilia mixed in. The catalog also gives dates, locations, and ticket information for the various Beatlefest conventions around the United States. You can reach Mark at: Beatlefest National Headquarters, P.O. Box 436, Westwood, New Jersey, 07675-0436. Or you can call 1-800-BEATLES; or contact him through his website at www.beatlefest.com.

I would like to send out an extra special thanks to my readers in the United Kingdom , where my publisher assures me that my first book is doing quite well. I would also like to thank the people who took the time to write to me to share their thoughts and stories about their own personal Beatles quest. I am very interested in trading information as well as memorabilia from the United States with someone in the United Kingdom for British memorabilia. If you are interested you can e-mail me at my website or write to me at my P.O. box address in the front of the book. I'm looking forward to hearing from you. I would also be interested in doing the same sort of trade with people from other parts of the planet. E-mail me, we'll talk.

A very special thanks goes out to Tony and Jane Cox for all of their help, support, and understanding in matters of friendship, Beatles, and spirituality. I believe that God brought us all together for a reason. May he bless you both. We love you guys.

Extra special thanks to Christine Knauer for being such a great friend and all around wonderful person. She is the rare type of family that a person chooses for themselves in life. No one could ever take her place in our hearts. The three of us love you more than you could ever know, Christine. We are so proud to number you among our friends. Most of all, thank you for believing in us...and making us all feel so special.

Special thanks to my dear friend, Russell Dreismeir, who I met in rehab after being hit by a drunk driver. You encouraged me and kept me going in the early days and gave me a little nudge here and there, when I needed it. Thanks Russ, for being such a wonderful friend and I apologize if I was a bit reclusive during the writing of this book. I just wanted you to know how much the three of us appreciate the fact that we have a friend like you. We love you, man. You always help bring me back down to earth. I hope we can be the kind of parents to Julian that you have been to Jenny. You have raised a very fine human being. You should be very proud.

I would also like to thank David Freed for hooking me up with some of my first Beatle sources in the state of Colorado. I just want you to know how important it is to me that you were in my life, and that it did make a difference. I will never forget you.

And last, but certainly not least. a special thanks to John Hesch, the best Neuromuscular therapist in Colorado Springs, and possibly the world. Thanks for helping me work out the kinks through all of this. If you would like to experience one of the best massages of your life call; 719-592-0787 and tell him that you saw his name in my book. -

Introduction

I would like to begin by thanking my readers for their wonderful response to my first book. I have received a substantial amount of mail from all over the world in response to my work and I really appreciate all of the feedback. However, your response has been so great that I have addressed many of the questions posed to me in this edition. I will continue to strive to provide my readers with pertinent and timely information by any means possible. Our new website should serve to greatly expedite this process. If you would like to reach us, you can e-mail us at www.beatles-collectibles.com

Speaking as a self-confessed Beatlemaniac and avid collector, I get really excited over the fact that there are other people throughout the world who share my passion for all things Beatle. In an effort to further this community of interest, we will be launching a website in conjunction with the publication of my second Beatles value guide. The site promises a lot of exciting and creative information for Beatles collectors. In addition to that, we will offer the opportunity to purchase signed editions of the book as well as information as to when future editions will be available. Also, we would love to hear your comments and suggestions regarding both this book and the earlier edition, *The Beatles, Yesterday and Tomorrow*. Please join us on our website. We'd love to have you.

When you add a piece of Beatles memorabilia to your collection , the condition of each item is of the utmost importance when considering its value. However, an item's value can only be determined upon completion of the transaction between buyer and seller. The amount agreed upon between these two parties can, and does, fluctuate from market to market and time to time. By its very nature, the value of any collectible is influenced by a variety of factors that affect the dynamics of the marketplace. This tends to facilitate price movement and variation across markets. However, a strong community which deals in Beatles memorabilia has developed, which provides data on transactions throughout the world and gives us an indication of the value of an item.

As is inherent with all good research, sometimes miscalculations in the availability of an item occur. In my quest to be as accurate as possible, I must bring an important miscalculation to your attention. Specifically, be cautious when purchasing some of the more recent newspapers (i.e. not from the 1960s). Further research has indicted a significant over supply of papers from the era surrounding the death of John Lennon that wasn't originally anticipated. This has served to significantly depress the value of many of these newspapers. As is true with all investments, reference material is only a starting point. In the end, it is ultimately up to the buyer to research all investments before deciding to make a purchase.

Whether you are a collector just starting out or a super collector who has been at it for years, I sincerely hope you find this value guide series a useful resource in your collecting activity. Thank you and good luck.

About the Price Codes

It is important, at this juncture, to explain my coding system for the condition of a piece. I use the abbreviations G, E, and NM when referring to items in the book. The G, or Good, code is for merchandise that has been used by the current or previous owner(s)and show some signs of wear. This can include tack holes or small tears in posters, hairline cracks in plastic and ceramics, or some general wear on a record. This wear should be minimal and not immediately noticeable from across the room. In other words, the item should remain generally intact.

My E, or Excellent, code refers to merchandise that is still in very fine shape, but which may not include the original packaging, promotional stickers, etc.

The NM, or Near Mint, code refers to merchandise that still retains its original packaging. I call it near mint because I believe that very few items on the market today that date back as far at the 1960s can still be in absolutely perfect condition. Also, as car companies have proven many times, even when an item is fresh from the factory, it can sometimes have a few flaws. This is still the highest rating that I give for merchandise and it should be as nearly perfect as possible.

Chapter One
A Day InThe Life

The Beatles were quite a phenomenon in the 1960s. I think that you could honestly say that their music inspired a generation and helped us to expand our minds. If the sixties taught us anything, it taught us how to be individuals and stand up for what we believe in. In some ways that is certainly ironic as most of us referred to the Beatles as John-Paul-George-and-Ringo. They were allowed very little individual identity once Beatlemania swept the world. It caught them up in a huge wave of revolution and change and virtually swept them away in it.

In 1963 the Beatles came to grips with their fame in Europe and learned to deal with their rapidly multiplying fans. The boys played at a local carnival in the Liverpool suburbs in July of that year and had a taste of what it was like to be adored. The group had to flee the stage right after they had played their last note to avoid being mobbed by the audience. The show went very well and Tom McKenzie, the band's emcee for the evening was just finishing up a few things when he heard some strange noises coming from the men's room. He went in to investigate, only to find George slumped over the toilet: "I'm sick as a bloody dog." he said, looking up at him with big, sad eyes.

"You're also stuck here because the other boys have already left." Tom replied.

A barely audible moan escaped George's lips as he sat there considering his plight. McKenzie decided to help him, but they had to think fast. He left the men's room to see if the coast was clear, only to be mobbed by a large group of screaming young women who were dying to get a glimpse of a Beatle. When they spotted McKenzie, they seemed rather let down. They rushed past him into the night air seeking their idols while Tom made his way out into the parking lot. It was there that he ran into a bus driver who was waiting to take some fans back into Liverpool. That was just the sort of break he had been hoping for. He asked the driver if he would like to meet George Harrison in exchange for a small favor. Of course the driver leapt at the chance and was soon ushered backstage where he switched clothes with the forlorn Fab. Then McKenzie led Harrison outside and straight through the milling crowd.

The year 1964 had to be one of the most exciting and action-packed years that the Beatles ever had. There were increasing demands from their fans for an American tour. They were all very pleased about that because many of their own music mentors had come from the States and the Beatles were really looking forward to meeting some of them. The American tour was set to begin in the summer of 1964. It was then that a most staggering event took place at London's Heathrow airport. Hoards of Beatles fans watched the sun come up as they waited for the boys to arrive. They had set up a sort of camp, complete with sleeping bags and transistor radios to keep them posted on the status of the Fab Four. They came from every corner of the United Kingdom and filled the airport and the tarmac outside to overflowing. The British bobbies were totally overwhelmed by their first glimpse of Beatlemania. They had never before experienced a crowd quite like this one. It swelled to a mass of thousands. England had never seen such a fuss made over any other group and it was a bit bewildering at first.

When the Beatles did finally arrive on the scene, they were totally in awe of the situation. By this time airport officials were positively frantic. It became difficult to distinguish the fans from the passengers. Many passengers were frightened and confused as well. They wandered around in a daze, trying to figure out what was going on. It must have appeared to some as if some sort of political uprising was going on. While it was definitely an uprising, it had not yet become political.

The Fabs got out of their car and were immediately swept away in the crowd. They managed, finally, to make their way to a private airport lounge. The noise from the lobby was deafening. Everyone was screaming their hearts out for the Beatles.

When it was time for their flight to take off, officials quickly and secretly ushered the boys aboard through the dark infrastructure of the airport. It was quite a harrowing experience, but at last they stood on the steps to the airplane, waving and shouting to the screaming throng. As soon as the door closed, they began to celebrate their success. They were really pumped up, as you can imagine. Their manager, Brian Epstein, broke open a case of champagne and the party was underway.

A very long flight later, the plane touched down at Kennedy Airport in New York City. The reception that the boys had received in their native England was certainly equaled by the reception that they received from American fans. The screaming of the fans actually drowned out the roar of the jet engines, for the first few moments. The Beatles were totally blown away by this show of affection. In their experience, even royalty had never been greeted like this. It fulfilled the Beatles wildest dreams of acceptance from the United States. Even New Yorkers were in awe of the power of this scene. Of all the madness they had ever witnessed, this was certainly the most memorable. That wasn't the end of it either. Fans lined the streets around their hotel, making it almost impossible for them to get there. They stood screaming and waving banners and Beatles memorabilia in their excitement.

Once again, the police had their hands full, trying to deal with crowd control. And once again the Beatles were forced to hide in their rooms when they weren't playing, to keep from being torn limb from limb by the adoring mob of teenagers.

Security at the hotel was on guard day and night to protect the Fabs and their entourage. There were security guards posted at the door of their suite as well as around the elevators and every other conceivable entrance or exit to the place. Some of them were even armed.

The Beatles really broke open the American market when they appeared on the *Ed Sullivan Show* on February 9, 1964. When word got out that they were going to play Sullivan, the show received over 60,000 requests for tickets. Unfortunately, the studio only had enough seats for 700 very lucky fans. More than 73 million people watched the Beatles play that gig on Sullivan. The Beatles didn't know it yet, but they had reached another goal that they never expected to achieve. The largest number of tickets demanded for a show, previous to that, was 7000 in 1958, when Elvis Presley played the show. The boys had drawn a bigger audience than "the king" and they certainly were astounded. That performance served to seal the fate of the Fabs. They had now become famous beyond any of their wildest dreams.

In 1964, John also began to experiment heavily with unusual sounds in recording. He was the first person to ever use guitar feedback on a record. It can be heard at the beginning of his single *I Feel Fine*. This opened up the way for much more exploration by Lennon/McCartney as well as paving the way for acid rockers like Jimi Hendrix. The Beatles really did revolutionize the art of recording music.

The year 1964 also saw the Beatles break into film with *A Hard Days Night*. The movie was originally to have been called *Beatlemania*, but was changed toward the end of production. Brian Epstein was the one who cut the deal for the picture because he saw how successful the Elvis movies were and he thought the Beatles would also do well. Sadly, when he made the initial deal, the Beatles had not yet moved into a good bargaining position in the industry. In October of the previous year, Brian had been approached by an American film producer named Walter Shenson, who had the financial blessings of United Artists to sign the Beatles to a movie deal. Brian agreed to a meeting with Shenson and Bud Orenstein and executives of United Artists in Great Britain, despite the fact that he had no experience with contracts in this area. In fact, the manager was so inexperienced in this area that he made a serious faux pas. Instead of waiting for U.A. to make the first offer of a percentage, he spoke up and told them that the boys couldn't possibly take less than seven and a half percent. U.A. jumped on the deal as they had been ready to offer a twenty-five percent cut.

Brian didn't realize it at the time, but United Artists had found a glitch in the contracts that the Beatles had already signed with EMI and Capitol. Neither company had thought to cover movie soundtracks in their contracts and U.A. had certainly not missed this. United Artists was actually more interested in the soundtrack to the movie than it was in the film itself. They knew that even if the film was a flop, they could make a fortune from their percentage of the record sales. To make matters even worse, Epstein agreed to a three picture deal in which all rights to the movies would revert back to Shenson after fifteen years. All in all, it was a business disaster.

By the time production started on the movie seven months later, the Beatles had become international stars. At that point they really should have renegotiated their contract. But Epstein

wouldn't hear of it. He maintained that a deal was a deal, and so everything continued as planned.

After the second day of filming, George invited Patti Boyd back to the Beatles' trailer for a cup of tea. She actually turned him down when asked to go on a date and he seemed rather impressed by that. George wasn't prepared to give up that easily, and on the third day of filming he asked her out again. She told him that she was an old-fashioned girl, and wasn't prepared to jeopardize her relationship with her boyfriend for a few nights on the town with him. George was again impressed by her attitude, and told her that he wanted to try more than "a few nights on the town." He asked her out to dinner later that same day and she finally accepted. George had met her parents by the end of the week, and the couple had started looking for a house to share.

George and Patti got married on January 21, 1966 at the Epson registry office in Surrey. Paul ended up being the only other Beatle at the ceremony, but John and Ringo each sent their congratulations. The couple spent their honeymoon in Barbados. George and Patti even posed for some rare photographs on the beach.

Their next retreat was to be in Ireland with John and Cynthia. They made up an elaborate scheme to keep their vacation plans a secret. John and George decided that they would disguise themselves by wearing fake facial hair, hats, and sunglasses. They then chartered a small plane and reserved a suite of lavish rooms at the Dromoland Castle Hotel in Ireland. The problem with the scheme was that the two couples failed to keep their composure whilst they were traipsing through the airport at Manchester. What other people in the airport witnessed was two rather badly disguised guys who were being followed by two hysterically giggling women. Not quite the effect that they had in mind when they started out. Despite their failed performance, they made it to the plane without incident.

The first day at the hotel was wonderful. They were greeted by total peace and quiet, a respite from the screams of their fans. In fact, that day went so well that they let their guard down a bit and started to relax for the first time in a long time. By sunrise, the phone was ringing off the hook and the couples discovered that a mob of fans had surrounded the castle.

They had to rely on the hotel management to help them ease out of there without being mobbed by admirers. The press still had its heart set on getting pictures of the newlyweds, but George and Patti did not want to be photographed together, so they decided to split up. Besides, Patti and Cynthia figured that the fans were mostly after John and George, so the Fabs took off for the airport on their own. The management then arranged to smuggle the Beatle wives out of the hotel in a laundry truck. Most of the staff contributed something to this covert operation. A couple of the chambermaids loaned their uniforms to the Fab wives so that they could remain inconspicuous. The plan was for Patti and Cynthia to carry a huge wicker laundry basket down to the entrance for "pick up." But instead of carrying laundry, the girls climbed into the basket and were themselves loaded onto the truck by the staff.

The original plan was for them to remain in the basket only until they were safely in the vehicle. At that point they were supposed to be released, but that is where the plan started to go terribly wrong... The problem arose when the press somehow got wind of the plan and were headed their way. At that point the two employees who were carrying the basket panicked, tossed them roughly into the truck and sped away. The basket tipped over and pinned them inside. That is when the girls started to panic. They screamed for help, but to no avail. For what seemed like an age, the truck sped down the road, rounding sharp corners and tossing the girls about like rag dolls. Eventually they did reach the airport and the driver set them free, so everything worked out aside from a few scrapes and bruises and some badly cramped muscles from being all curled up together in that basket.

The premiere of *Hard Days' Night* was held in London at the Pavilion Theater in July of 1964. The movie was the talk of the town and everyone was tremendously excited by it. Once again, the streets in the area surrounding the theater were lined with fans. Traffic actually had to be re-routed because of the huge traffic jam that was building in the area. At first the Beatles didn't realize that all the commotion was over them. When Brian informed them of that fact, it blew their minds. All these people were here just hoping to catch a glimpse of them on their way to the opening.

American film critic Andrew Sarris dubbed *Hard Days' Night* the *Citizen Kane* of juke box movies. *Newsweek* said, "The legitimacy of the Beatles phenomenon is inescapable."

After the opening, Brian held a party for the boys at his Belgravia penthouse. The party actually took place on the roof and it took five days for Epstein's people to prepare the setting. First, a giant white marquee was erected to cover the top of the building. This was then formed into a white canvas tent the size of a small circus structure. It was fitted with wooden sides and French windows around the perimeter so the guests had a good view of the city while they were eating. A raised floor was built over the tar roof and covered with red sisal carpeting. A bandstand was erected on top of it with a hardwood dance floor. Several thousand carnations were ordered to build centerpieces for each of the tables. The center pole of the great tent was covered in Spanish moss which was intertwined with 700 carnations in the shape of a palm tree. A caterer was hired to prepare filet mignon, cold duck, and lobster as well as a selection of kosher foods for Brian's family. A small orchestra was hired for ambiance.

The party arranged by Epstein soon became the most widely talked about social event of the season. Engraved invitations were sent to the reigning stars of London. Hundreds of people lined the streets just to watch the guests arrive. Two uniformed guards stood at the door of the building, demanding to see invitations. Later that evening, one of the security guards came up to tell them that there was a lady downstairs wearing a mink coat and insisting that Brian had invited her to the party just the night before. The lady turned out to be Judy Garland and, of course, she was escorted to the party.

It was around the period following the release of their first movie that the merchandising of Beatles memorabilia really began to take off. Anything associated with the group became valuable. In fact, after their concert in Kansas City, a couple of guys paid $1000 for the bed linen that the Beatles had slept on. These bed clothes were then cut into 150,000 one inch squares and sold to the public for ten dollars apiece. Many of these and other bed sheet pieces are still floating around out there, but I assure you that those little scraps of cloth are now worth at least ten times the amount that they originally sold for.

Over the next few years licensing deals for Beatles products began to spring up with the help of New York businessman Nicky Byrns. He created the SELTAEB Ltd. logo (which is Beatles spelled backward), which was also affiliated with Brian Epstein's own NEMS Enterprises Ltd. (North End Music Store) out of London. By the time of Epstein's death from an accidental overdose in 1967, he had listed 234 different products under these two marks. A Beatle bingo game along with ladies panties and other clothing were some of the licensed items. One of the more bizarre products that never made its way onto store shelves was the Beatles sanitary napkin. There were four different styles of napkins per box. Each Fab had his image on one. A Chicago firm even went so far as to market "canned Beatles breath" to the public.

Musical Instruments

The "Big Beat Bongo," made by Mastro. The cylinder portion of the bongo is made of hard plastic and features a group photo decal on each side. It measures approximately 6" high, The drum heads are made of a stretched cream colored skin. This item is extremely hard to locate and a rare find. If the original box exists, double the values given: G: $3,000 E: $4,500 NM: $7,000.

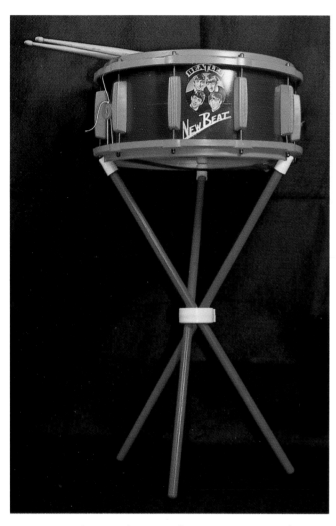

This photo shows the "New Beat Drum" drum head. A copy of Ringo's autograph can be seen along the top edge of the drums surface. The top measures 14" in diameter and has snares all around the side.

"New Beat Drum" with a copy of Ringo's signature on the drum head. This drum was manufactured by Selcol. As you can see in the photo, it came with drumsticks and a tripod stand. Additional original paraphernalia includes the instruction booklet and a tuning key. Made in the United Kingdom. If the original box and its accessories are present, add $400 to the listed values: G: $700 E: $800 NM: $900.

"Big Beat" guitar was made in the United Kingdom by Selcol. It is a four-string model and is 21" long. A sticker appears on the bottom left hand corner of the guitar body featuring the group's faces, along with copies of their signatures (first names only). The signatures can be seen across from the sticker. The original box is similar to those pictured previously. If the original box is present add $300 to the listed values: G: $500 E: $600 NM: $700.

This is the box that the "New Beat Drum" came in. Note the sticker with the Fab Four's faces and copies of their signatures (first names only). An additional sticker says "Drum Set" on it and has a copy of Ringo's full signature.

The "New Beat Guitar" was manufactured in the United Kingdom by Selcol and measures 32 1/2" long. It has a sticker with the Fab's faces on the upper left hand corner of the guitar's body, along with copies of their signatures (first names only) in the lower left hand corner. This is a four-string instrument and comes with the box shown here. The sticker should be in place on this piece in order for it to retain its full value. Add $300 to the listed values if the original box is present. G: $400 E: $500 NM: $600.

"Four Pop Guitar" was made by Mastro. It is a four-string guitar and is 21" long. This particular model was manufactured in two different versions, in the printing that appears on the instrument. The "Four Pop" is the one shown in the photo, but another version was made as the "FOUR POP." The Beatles faces appear on the neck of the guitar, as well as on the body, and it comes with the instruction booklet seen here. Values: G: $500 E: $600 NM: $750.

"Big Six Guitar" is very similar in appearance to the "New Beat" version, although there are some subtle differences. This guitar is also 32 1/2" long and is made in the United Kingdom by Selcol. This model has a six-string design rather than four. The packaging is identical to that of the "New Beat" except for the model name of the instrument, which appears on the sticker that is affixed to the box. Add $300 to the listed values if the original box is present. G: $400 E: $500 NM: $600.

The "FOUR POP" guitar was also made by Mastro. This guitar measures 21" long and is very similar to the Four Pop guitar. The original packaging consisted of a cardboard back with the instrument sealed in clear plastic. The Beatles faces appear on the cardboard back and an instruction book was also included. The value given here is only for the guitar sealed in original package. Otherwise, refer to values listed for the Four Pop. NM: $2,200

The "New Sound Guitar" was made in the United Kingdom by Selcol. It is a four-string instrument and is 23" long. The Fab's faces appear on the body of the guitar along with their first names. The original packaging consisted of a cardboard back with the instrument sealed in clear plastic. If the original packaging is present, add $300 to the listed values: G: $450 E: $550 NM: $700.

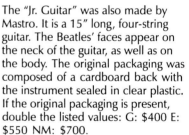

The "Jr. Guitar" was also made by Mastro. It is a 15" long, four-string guitar. The Beatles' faces appear on the neck of the guitar, as well as on the body. The original packaging was composed of a cardboard back with the instrument sealed in clear plastic. If the original packaging is present, double the listed values: G: $400 E: $550 NM: $700.

The "Beatle-ist" guitar was made by Mastro; it measures 30" long and has six strings. The Fab's faces and copies of their signatures appear on the main body of the guitar along with "The Beatles Beatle-ist Guitar." It originally came packaged attached to a cardboard back with shrink wrap. If original packaging exists, double the values given: G: $650 E: $850 NM: $1,050.

"Beatles Jnr." guitar, made by Selcol in the U.K. It measures 14" in length. This guitar is a rather difficult model to find. Because of this, it is worth quite a bit more than previous models, despite its small size. It also has only four strings. It was packaged with a cardboard back and shrink wrap. If the original packaging exists, add half again to the given values: G: $2500 E: $3000 NM: $3500.

"The Beatles" mini guitar. Made in China, it measures 8" long. This guitar has four strings and to this point, it was undocumented. It looks old, but I was not able find any references to prove if it is authentic. Therefore, the value is not as high as the other guitars. G: $30 E: $40 NM: $50.

"The Beatles Harmonica" box was made in Germany by M. Hohner. The box measures 5" long and there were two variations available in this harmonica box. The Beatles' faces appear on the top of the box along with copies of their signatures. If you look closely you will see that Paul McCartney and George Harrison's names have been switched on the left-hand box. The box on the right has the correct name paired with the appropriate face. The harmonicas that came in the boxes had no markings. Value for incorrect version: G: $40 E: $50 NM: $70 Value for correct version: G: $75 E: $100 NM: $150.

"Beatles Guitar String," made by Hofner, Selmer of London in the United Kingdom. Each package contains one guitar string and there are six variations available. The string comes in a 3 1/2" square package. Value is for string with the package: G: $65 E: $80 NM: $95.

Electronic Items

Beatles record player. This item is a rare one, only 5,000 of these are known to exist. It has four different speeds and when the lid is open a group photo can be seen. The serial number can be found on a strip of cardboard attached to the inside top of the lid. Within the past year the value of this item has increased immensely. The original box is so hard to find that if you can find it be prepared to pay a fortune! Value for record player only: G: $2,400 E: $3,600 NM: $4,800. Original box value: VERY RARE!

This photo shows what the top of the record player looks like.

"Beatlephones," from 1966, made by Koss Electronics Inc. The box, insert, and warranty (shown here) are a very important part of the value for this item, as well as the Fab Four's face stickers on the side of each earphone. Value for headphones with stickers only: G: $300 E: $400 NM: $500. Value for all items shown in the above picture: G: $2,000 E: $2,500 NM: $3,000.

Dolls, Figurines and Cake Decorations

"Bobbin Head Display Dolls" were made by Carmascot. They stand 14" tall and they were used as a display to help sell the smaller 8" size dolls. They are made of composition and at the base of each Beatle is a copy signature of that Beatle. These dolls are extremely hard to find due to the fact that they only produced them for display purposes. Values given are for the set of four: G: $10,000 E: $12,500 NM: $15,000.

These Paul and Ringo rubber figures were made in Mexico. These figures stand approximately 6" to 8" tall. Ringo is seated behind his "The Beatles" drum and Paul holds his guitar. These figures are dated 1966. Values given are per each: G: $235 E: $355 NM: $475.

"The Beatles" figurines put out by Subuteo Ltd. stand about 2" tall and are made of hard plastic. They were sold originally in a rectangular shaped box with a clear plastic front to make them appear as if they are on stage. Double the values given if original box is present: G: $75 E: $95 NM: $125. Set of four.

"Mascot Doll," made by Remco. This doll is a stuffed cloth doll measuring about 30" long. It originally sold with a string tag attached and a cardboard guitar. The string tag reads "The Beatles Official Mascot Doll". As with almost any collectible, tags, guitar, inserts, etc. are very important when considering values. Double the values given if the string tag and cardboard guitar are present: G: $185 E: $250 NM: $375.

"The Swingers Music Set" cake decorations are made of plastic, and each of them have their own instrument. If original box is not present, subtract half of the given values: G: $125 E: $175 NM: $200. Set of four.

Beatles rubber dolls put out by Remco. Each of the four dolls came with its own musical instrument. They stand about 5" tall. Values listed are with the instrument. If the instrument is not present, subtract $25 from the given values: Paul, George and Ringo are: G: $70 E: $90 NM: $110. The value for John is: G: $95 E: $125 NM: $155. The dolls seen in this picture each have their own box. In general, the boxes are valued at: G: $75 E: $100 NM: $125 each.

This photo shows what the Remco dolls look like outside of their boxes.

"The Swingers Music Set": made in Hong Kong by Katat. These cake decorations are made of hard plastic and their heads are made to be moved around. They stand about 4" tall. As seen in the photo, these cake decorations originally were sold attached to a cardboard back with plastic. Values are cut in half if the original packaging is missing. G: $125 E: $175 NM: $200. Set of four.

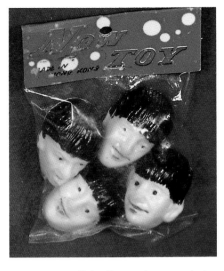

Cake Decoration, made of hard plastic; the faces are embossed so that they stand out from the blue background. An interesting piece to say the least! Values: G: $55 E: $75 NM: $100. Set of four.

Cake Decorations, made in Hong Kong. These are made of a hard plastic material. The Fab Four's heads would be placed on top of a cake for instant popularity. Original packaging doubles the values given: G: $25 E: $35 NM: $45. Set of four.

TOILETRIES

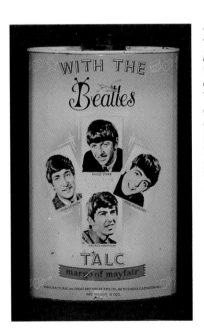

"With The Beatles" Bath Talc was made by Margo of Mayfair in the United Kingdom. The container stands 7" tall. This tin bears a picture of the Beatles' faces on one side. A full body pose of the group is on the opposite side. This is the front of the tin. Values: G: $350 E: $400 NM: $500.

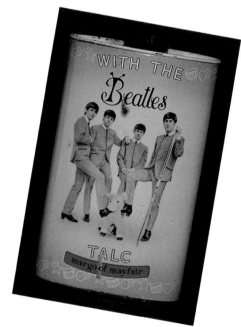

This is the back of the "With The Beatles" bath talc tin.

"The Beatles Hair Spray" was made by Bronson Products, Copyright NEMS ENT. Ltd. 1964. Licensed by Seltaeb. The Beatles' faces appear on the front of the can along with copies of their signatures. This aerosol can is 8" tall. Values: G: $800 E: $900 NM: $1000.

"Beatles Hair Spray": this can of hair spray is believed to be authentic; however, at the time of this writing it is undocumented. This can stands approximately 4" tall. Although, I have never seen another can of it, through talking to other super collectors the general consensus leads me to believe that it is authentic. Values: G: $750 E: $900 NM: $1000.

"Beatle Hair Brush" made by Belliston Products. They were made in a variety of colors. Inserted into the original packaging was a black & white wallet card featuring their faces and copies of their signatures beneath each appropriate portrait. The Beatles faces are engraved in the hard plastic on the back of each brush. If the original packaging (shown here) is present then double the values given. G: $20 E: $25 NM: $30.

Comb Set, made by Valex Products of Blackpool. This set is undocumented up to now. The gold lettering on the packaging reads, "Valex Products Pic of the Stars, Tear - a - comb". This set was purchased by a well known super collector at an auction in Liverpool. Value is per set: G: $150 E: $200 NM: $250.

This Genuine Autographed Beatles Jumbo Comb was made by Lido Toys. It is made of hard plastic and measures about 3" x 14". This item was produced in various colors and has the Beatles' faces, as well as copies of their signatures, across the top front. G: $100 E: $150 NM: $200.

This is a view of the back of the Jumbo Comb.

Headbands, Bows, Hair Pomade

Headband. This is an Australian product made by L and C Vincent Industries PTY. LTD. Beetle bugs are pictured with guitars across the headband's surface. It came in several different colors and features the Beatles' faces and copies of their signatures along the top edge of the card that it is wrapped around. Double the values given if the original packaging exists: G: $125 E: $150 NM: $200.

Headbands were made by Better Wear Inc. and were manufactured exclusively for Seltaeb Inc. Each band had the phrase, "Love The Beatles" on it. While only five colors are shown here, this product was manufactured in eight different colors. Double the values given if the original packaging is included: (as shown here) G: $25 E: $35 NM: $45.

"The Official Beatles Hair Bow" was made by Burlington. The phrase, "I Love the Beatles" appears over and over again across its surface. Beatles wallet photos appear at the bottom with instructions for the buyer to cut them off. Copies of the Beatles signatures appear at the bottom of the card. Double the values given if the original packaging exists: G: $150 E: $175 NM: $200.

Hair Pomade packet, made by H.H. Cosmetic Lab in the Philippines. It came from a box that would display a total of 50 packets per box. Value given is for one 2 1/2" x 1" packet: (shown here) G: $75 E: $100 NM: $125.

Bubble Bath, Soap Boxes, "Living Beatles", Band-Aid

"Beatles Bubble Bath" containers, Paul and Ringo, put out by Colgate in 1965. They were originally packaged in a pink cardboard box, in which their heads would pop out from the top. They measure 9" tall and only Paul and Ringo were produced. The values given are without the original box. If your bubble bath has the original box add $100 to the values given: G: $125 E: $165 NM: $200.

These Lux soap boxes advertise the Beatles inflatable dolls. They were put out by Lever Brothers Co. in 1965 and came in a few different colors. Values per box: G: $175 E: $250 NM: $275.

Original *Help!* Band-Aid with original packaging. It consists of a white Curad Band-Aid with "HELP BEATLES" printed across it over and over in red letters. The wrapper is also white with red lettering which says "BEATLES HELP BEATLES" and "CAPITOL". 1965. Values: G: $15 E: $20 NM: $25.

"Living Beatles" Grow Your Own Beatles Hair. Contains a 5" x 7 1/2" sheet of cardboard that can be divided into four pieces , one for each Beatle. The instructions inform you that if you place each respective Beatle in a glass of water, your favorite Fab will soon grow green hair. Values: G: $200 E: $250 NM: $300.

Lamps

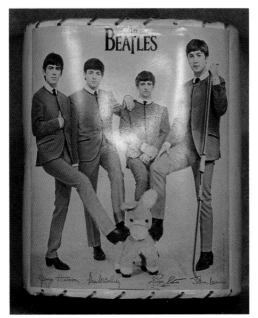

This Beatles wall lamp has a group photo on the front of the rounded paper shade. The lamp would be attached to the wall with hardware on the back of the lamp. Values: G: $650 E: $750 NM: $ 900.

Beatles table lamp, the shade on this lamp is made of paper and the faces of the Beatles go all the way around the shade. The black base is made of porcelain and includes a guitar that has been painted in gold as decoration. Values: G: $800 E: $1000 NM: $1200.

Beatles table lamp. This table lamp is very similar in design to the wall lamp; however, it has a different group photo on the paper shade and metal legs to stand on. Values: G: $650 E: $750 NM: $900.

CHRISTMAS ITEMS

Christmas stocking: this stocking contained Beatles memorabilia and other doodads. It is uncertain as to who produced these. Value for stocking with contents: G: $165 E: $185 NM: $210.

The Christmas ornaments shown here were made in Italy. They came in several different colors. These decorations are also hand blown, making each one unique. They are missing their instruments, and so value given is without instrument. Add $50 to each ornament if instrument is present. Value per each: G: $225 E: $250 NM: $300.

Christmas ornaments, made in Italy. A complete set of four in gold, without instruments, but are in their original box. Ornaments are hand blown and therefore each set is unique. They are, thus far, undocumented and unlicensed. The value given is for each ornament without the instrument and without the original box. Add $50 if the instrument is present and $100 if original box is present.. Value for each: G: $225 E: $250 NM: $300.

CARRYING CASES, RECORD CASES, ETC.

"The Beatles Kaboodle Kit" is made of vinyl. It was put out by Standard Plastic Products Inc. This kit was put out in a number of different colors. Value: G: $800 E: $1000 NM: $1200.

Beatles carrying case, put out by Air Flite. This case is getting hard to find, and the value reflects that. Also, this carrying case came in a number of colors, and measures 6" x 9". A group photo appears on the front of the case. Value: G: $400 E: $550 NM: $700.

This picture shows some of the different colors of "The Kaboodle Kit".

The Beatles Hatbox/Overnight Case was produced by Air Flite. This case was put out in black or red only. The case is made of vinyl. It has a hand strap to carry it by and a picture of the Fab Four on the front. Value for each: G: $450 E: $500 NM: $550.

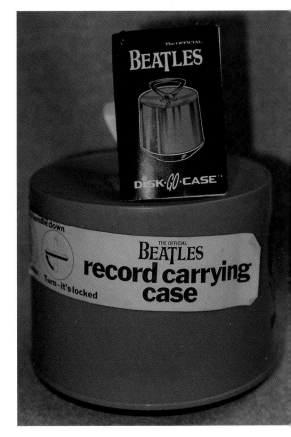

This photo shows the many different colors that the record carrying cases came in.

The "Disk Go Case" was made by Charter Industries. This particular case shows the hang tag and the sticker that were originally sold with it. These cases are made of plastic and held a number of 45 rpm singles. It has a picture of the group on the front.(shown in the following photo) As with almost any item, the value is raised when the original tag and sticker are present. Value given is for the case without either the tag or sticker; if they are present then add 1 1/2 times the value given. G: $175 E: $225 NM: $300.

This Record Case was put out by Air Flite. It has a group picture on the front along with copies of their signatures. The case is made of a strong cardboard material, and would carry 33 RPM records. Value: G: $550 E: $650 NM: $800.

Record Cases: these are 45 rpm cases. Other than the size, all the information is the same as for the 33 rpm cases, except the value: G: $450 E: $550 NM: $700.

Record Carrier, made by Seagull Ent. This case would carry 45 rpm records and has plastic dividers to separate the records while carrying them. Value: G: $185 E: $215 NM: $250.

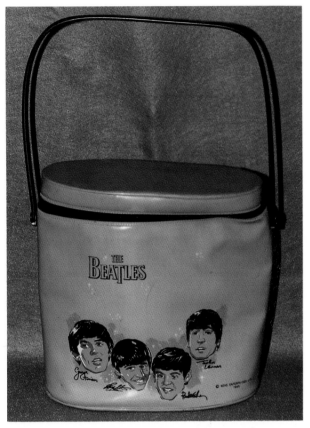

Beatles Brunch Bag. A light blue vinyl tote made by Alladin. The 8" brunch bag sports a wrap around zipper at the top along with a black carrying strap. The group is pictured on the front, along with copies of their signatures. The thermos originally came with this item, but is valued separately. Value is for the brunch bag only: G: $325 E: $450 NM: $575.

Alladin blue metal thermos with a plastic top. This is the companion piece to the brunch bag. The measurements are 7" tall and 3 3/4" in diameter . This particular piece is a dual collectible for both lunch box collectors and Beatles collectors. Thermos value: G: $125 E: $150 NM: $175.

Toys, Puzzles, Etc.

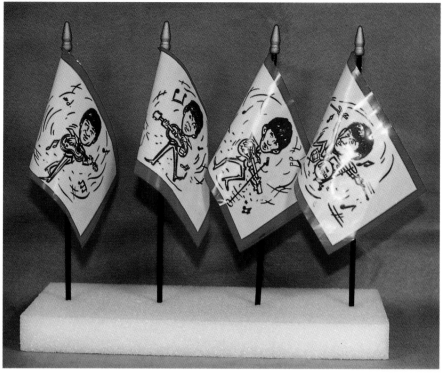

Bicycle flags came in a plastic bag; there were 5 flags in the bag—along with a metal piece that attached to the handlebars, so that all flags could be displayed at the same time. If the original package is included, add $150 to the values given. Value given is for each flag: G: $125 E: $150 NM: $175.

"Beatles Balloon," put out by United Industries. These balloons were made in a variety of colors, the packaging consisted of a plastic bag with a group pose on it. Value given includes the original package: G: $75 E: $95 NM: $120.

"Beatle Twig," the maker of this toy is uncertain. This toy came wrapped in a plastic bag. The packaging included an insert with instructions and a photo of the Beatles' faces along with copies of their signatures. The actual toy is composed of two red wooden sticks and two plastic discs. This toy is unusual to say the least, and values will reflect this. Values given include the original package: G: $200 E: $250 NM: $325.

"Spatter! The Toy with the Beatle Beat" was made by "The Spatter Toy Company Inc." Cuba, MO. The packaging has a yellow card marked, "Twirl with the Beatles." On the same card are instructions for using this toy. Value given includes the original packaging: G: $45 E: $65 NM: $90.

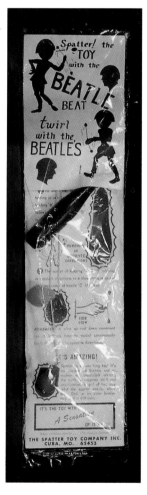

24

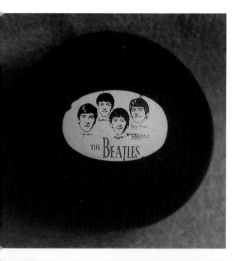

Black rubber ball: it has "The Beatles" printed inside an oval white shape on the ball that also shows their faces and copies of their signatures. The ball is marked NEMS Ent Ltd. This is a rare find. Value: G: $475 E: $700 NM: $900.

Rubber Toy Figures. These toy figures are shrink wrapped to a cardboard back. There is a group pose on the cardboard back, along with the red ink phrases, "HEY KIDS!!! We're Here!!!" They originally sold for 10 cents. The value given is for toy figures in the shrink wrapped package. G: $25 E: $30 NM: $40.

8 mm Newsreels With Projector: originally came with four 8 mm newsreels. The value given is for everything shown in this photo: G: $200 E: $225 NM: $275.

This 8 mm Newsreel Footage has a colorful orange and white box with one of The Beatles most famous poses on the front. This newsreel was originally put out as a silent movie and sold for a whopping $2.50. Those were the day's!!! Value in the original box. G: $275 E: $400 NM: $550.

"The Beatles Cartoon Kit, A Colorforms Toy." This toy was put out in 1966, and is extremely colorful, hence the name "Colorforms." Instructions on how to use this kit were included. It is very hard to find this item. If you have it, consider yourself fortunate. The value given is for the complete set: G: $425 E: $625 NM: $800.

This Airbed item was put out by Li-Lo of the U.K. When the mattress is fully inflated, it measures 3' x 6', all four of the Beatles' faces can be seen along with copies of their signatures on the pillow section of the bed. Values: G: $385 E: $550 NM: $775.

These Beatle Bugle mega-phones were put out by Yell-a-Phone. They have embossed Fab faces and copies of their signatures on front. They only come in the three colors shown here. Each megaphone has a metal rim and chain to hold onto. The megaphones are made of hard plastic and they stand about 7" tall. Value given is for each. G: $625 E: $750 NM: $975.

Model kits, John and Paul. These models were put out by Revell. Models came with instructions for assembly. Each model would be assembled to match the figure on top of the box. The box and the instructions are important components when considering values. Value for complete, unassembled model in the original box is: (John) G: $325 E: $450 NM: $525, (Paul) G: $175 E: $275 NM: $375. Models already assembled, without the box and instructions, are 1/3 of the values listed.

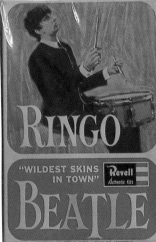

Values for Revell's models of George and Ringo are the same as for Paul.

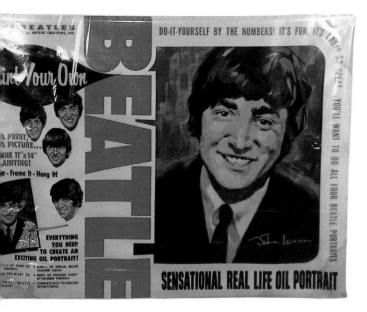

"Paint Your Own Beatle", put out by Artistic Creations. You would paint by numbers to complete John's portrait. Enclosed in the box were the necessary supplies to complete your own 11" x 14" painting. Value is for box with contents: G: $475 E: $650 NM: $850.

"Paint Your Own Beatle", put out by Artistic Creations. Paint George by the numbers! Enclosed in each box were the supplies needed (such as brushes, paint, etc.) to finish painting "Your Own Beatle." 11" x 14" Beatle portrait. Value is for box with contents: G: $475 E: $650 NM: $850.

Jigsaw Puzzles

A 340 piece jigsaw puzzle made in the United Kingdom. This puzzle put together measures approximately 17" x 11" and shows the Fab Four on stage. Value is for complete puzzle in box: G: $160 E: $200 NM: $240.

Variations of The Beatles Jigsaw.

Jigsaw puzzle, "The Beatles Illustrated Lyrics Puzzle In A Puzzle". This puzzle came with a full color poster and had 13 Beatles song titles hidden in the picture. The puzzle has 800 pieces and when complete, measured 33" x 18 1/2". It was put out in 1970 and is very colorful. Value given is for box, jigsaw puzzle, and puzzle solutions which were included in the original package: G: $85 E: $135 NM: $195.

Portraits/Pictures

"Full color oil portrait, The Beatles". These portraits were reproduced by Nems Ent. Ltd. for the Beatle Buddies' Club. (Card attached here.) This picture of the group measures 20" x 16" and was painted by Leo Jansen. Value is for painting in original package: G: $50 E: $75 NM: $100.

"4 full color oil portraits—the Beatles." These portraits were reproduced by Nems Ent. Ltd. for "The Beatle Buddies' Club." These portraits measure 12" x 9" and were painted by Leo Jansen. Take notice of the header card shown (front and back). Value given for full set of 4 in unopened package: G: $160 E: $185 NM: $210.

Additional copies of "4 full color oil portraits—the Beatles."

Portraits by Resco Products—shown here are John and Paul. These portraits measure 12" x 12" and are all black and white. There was more than one way to get these portraits; either by mail order (shown here) or through retail stores. These portraits came by mail in a manila envelope. For retail they were packaged in plastic. Values are for each picture: G: $50 E: $60 NM: $75.

Portraits of George and Ringo by Resco Products. The values for each portrait are the same as those for John and Paul.

A set of six, full color picture portraits. There are two group photos and a shot of each Beatle included. These portraits were produced by J.M. Distributors and originally cost 59 cents for the package. Each measures 8" x 10". Value given is for all six pictures in original package: G: $60 E: $90 NM: $125.

This is the mailing envelope which was used to hold the four black and white Resco Products portraits. Value given here is for all four drawings and the envelope: G: $275 E: $315 NM: $375.

"Beatles Giant Colour Pic!" was put out by Pyx Products. This item has many wonderful color photos. Also included was a giant poster. Values given are for the complete book: G: $50 E: $70 NM: $90.

"The Beatles Punch-Out Portraits." This book of punch-out photos was put out by Whitman. There were lots of fun items to punch-out, such as mobiles, colorful punch-outs of the group, etc. Value given is for an unpunched book: G: $75 E: $115 NM: $150.

Candy, Collectors Cards, Etc.

Candy stick boxes, made by World Candies Inc. These boxes came in a variety of colors and each held two sticks of candy. Each box has an animated drawing of a Beatle and his first name. Although these boxes are rather small, 2 1/2" x 1 3/8", the value is somewhat high due to availability on the secondary market. Value for each: G: $40 E: $85 NM: $115.

"Beatles Color Photos" display box with unopened single package of trading cards. The display box would contain 24 packages of trading cards with bazooka gum. This display box has all four of the Beatles side by side in bust poses. Value for display box only: G: $125 E: $175 NM: $250. Value for unopened package of trading cards: G: $20 E: $40 NM: $60.

Licorice record candy display box, and licorice record with all the Fab Fours' faces on it. These were made by Clevedon Confectionery in the United Kingdom. The display box contained 36 licorice records and measured approximately 10" x 5" x 2 1/2". The licorice record itself measured 4" in diameter and had a sleeve that was orange, white, and black that read, "The Beatles." Value given is for display box only: G: $375 E: $500 NM: $625. Value for licorice record and sleeve: G: $40 E: $50 NM: $60.

Licorice candy records with sleeves. This photo shows that records were put out for each member of the band. Value given is per record with sleeve: G: $40 E: $50 NM: $60.

"Beatles Movie *A Hard Day's Night*" trading card display box with original wrappers. The display box would contain 24 packages of trading cards with bazooka gum. The box has a film strip design across the top with one of each of the Fab Fours' faces per clip. Value for display box only: G: $175 E: $225 NM: $300. Value for wrapper only: G: $10 E: $20 NM: $35.

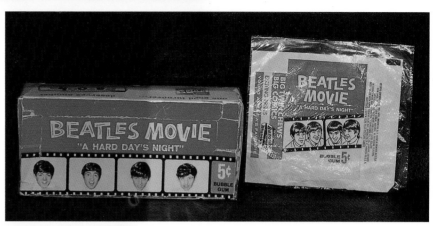

"New Series The Beatles" display box with original wrapper. This display box would contain 24 packages of trading cards with bazooka gum. This box shows the Fab Fours' faces on the top and side. Value for the display box only: G: $125 E: $175 NM: $250. Value for the wrapper only: G: $10 E: $20 NM: $25.

"Beatles Movie *A Hard Day's Night*" rack pack, United Artists release. This package contained 30 individual cards for 29 cents. Value given is for 30 cards with the header card in the original package: G: $80 E: $120 NM: $175.

"Beatles Autographed Photos" unopened package of trading cards. Put out by A&BC Chewing Gum Ltd. This package contained two black and white trading cards with gum. Value for unopened package: G: $20 E: $40 NM: $60.

"Beatles Color Photos" rack pack, put out by Trading Card Guild. This package contained 30 individual trading cards for 29 cents. Value given is for 30 cards with the header card and the original packaging: G: $80 E: $120 NM: $175.

"Ringo" candy rolls came out in a number of flavors. Undocumented to this point, it is believed that these are original memorabilia. Value given is per roll: G: $20 E: $25 NM: $35.

Beatles Plaks cards series. These cards came in a package with gum. There are 55 cards in the series. These cards interlocked with one another and would hang from the wall that way. These Plaks cards were not on the market for long and their values reflect this. Value per card: G: $5 E: $7 NM: $10.

More Plaks cards.

Yes, it's the last of the Plaks cards!

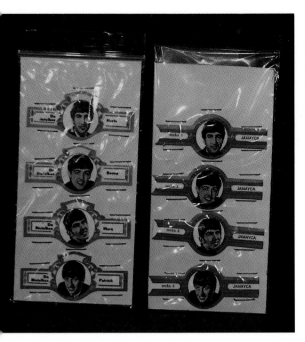

These two different sets of cigar bands came in a number of colors. These bands were made in Holland. Each set of four features one Beatle per band. Please notice that the names are incorrect on one set. Value given is for a set of four: G: $25 E: $30 NM: $35.

Wallets & Coin Purses

This photo shows the interior of the Standard Plastic Products wallets.

Wallets made by Standard Plastic Products. The Beatles group pose appears on the front. Originally these wallets came with a mirror, comb, nail file, and even a place to hold coins. These came in a number of colors. (As seen here). Value given is per wallet: G: $90 E: $125 NM: $150.

These coin purses came in red or black, were made of hard plastic, and had to be squeezed to put in coins. Each purse measures approximately 3" x 2" and is decorated with "The Beatles", their faces, and their first names on the front. Value for each purse: G: $20 E: $30 NM: $35.

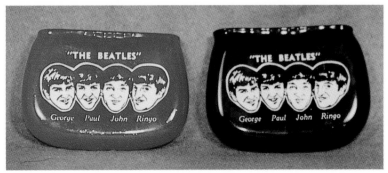

These vinyl character coin purses of John and Paul have no manufacturer's markings; however, they are believed to be original memorabilia. Each purse has a zipper on one side to insert coins. Value for each: G: $15 E: $25 NM: $30.

These vinyl character coin purses of George & Ringo are made in the same way, also lack manufacturer's marks, and have the same values as the red suited John and Paul character purses.

School Supplies, Notebooks, Binders, Etc.

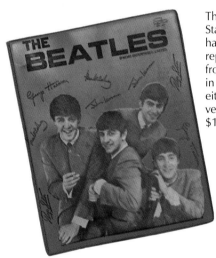

This blue binder, made by Standard Plastic Products, has a group photo with repeating names on its front. These binders came in a number of colors, in either two or three ring versions. Value: G: $75 E: $100 NM: $125.

Beige binder: this binder was made by New York Loose-leaf Corporation and has the same design as the Standard Plastic Products binder. It is a three ring binder. Value: G: $50 E: $75 NM: $100.

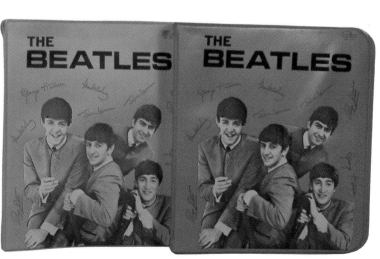

Pink and red binders, made by Standard Plastic Products, have the group photo with repeating names on the front. Value for each: G: $100 E: $125 NM: $160.

34

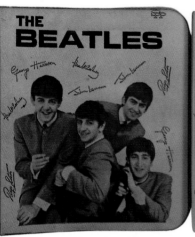

Beige binders made by (SSP) Standard Plastic Products. Here are two different versions, with very subtle differences including rounded edges and the placement of the SSP logo on front cover. Value is the same for each: G: $50 E: $75 NM: $100.

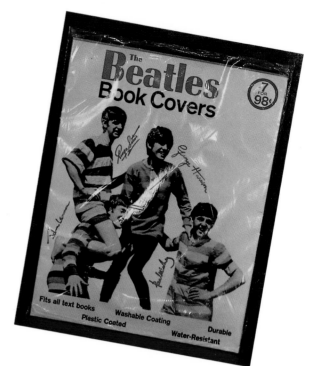

The Beatles book covers. This sealed package contained seven covers and was made by Book Covers Inc. Value given is for the sealed package: G: $50 E: $60 NM: $75.

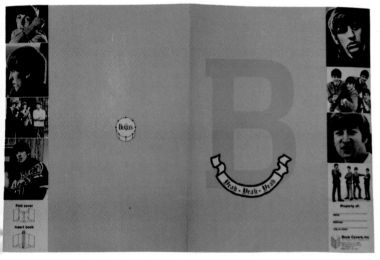

This book cover, made by Book Covers Inc., measures 13" x 10", has photos down each side flap, a large B with "Yeah, Yeah, Yeah" in a ribbon at base of the B, and "The Beatles" inside a drum logo on the other side. Value for a single book cover: G: $5 E: $8 NM: $10.

"Assignments and Notes" book "Beatles Approved", made by Select-O-Pak, has the Fab Fours' faces on a card tucked under the clear plastic protector. These came in a number of vinyl colors. They measured 4" x 6 1/2" and the inside pages have Beatles on the top. (Accompanying photo.) Value for complete assignment book: G: $125 E: $175 NM: $225.

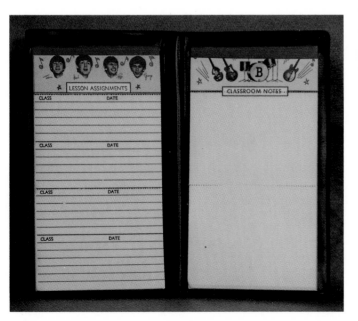

This photo shows the inside of the "Beatles Approved" assignment book.

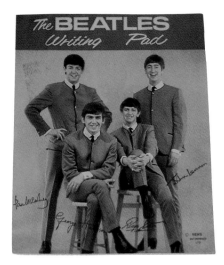

"The Beatles Writing Pad" by Nems Enterprises Ltd. has a photo of the Beatles on the front along with copies of their signatures. Value is for the pad with paper: G: $100 E: $150 NM: $185.

Pencil case, beige, made by Standard Plastic Products. The case has a photo of the "Fab Four" on the front along with copies of their signatures. A zipper across the top allows pencils and pens to be inserted. It measures 8" x 3 1/2". This case came in a number of colors. Value for the case: G: $80 E: $110 NM: $150.

School bag by Nems Enterprises Ltd. and Burnel Ltd. The school bag is beige and has a plastic handle, or can be carried with shoulder strap. It also has a brass clasp that can be locked. The bag has a group photo on each side of the front and copies of their signatures in the center. Value: G: $575 E: $775 NM: $975.

Plastic school bag made by Select-O-Pak; this bag has a paper insert of the Beatles in the spotlight, with their Pierre Cardin style suits on under a clear plastic protector. The bag has a zipper to allow things to be inserted into the bag and measures about 15" x 10 1/2". Value: G: $135 E: $165 NM: $215.

Pillows

Pillow, by Nordic House: this pillow shows the group from the waist up with instruments for John and George. "The Beatles" is enclosed in a circle in the upper right. Copies of their signatures appear across the bottom. Value: G: $110 E: $175 NM: $225.

This pillow, made by Nordic House, has a carrying strap on the upper left corner. It also has original tags sewn on. The pillow is also adorned with a bust group photo and signature copies across the bottom. The strap and tags are important when considering the value: G: $175 E: $225 NM: $300.

Pillow, also put out by Nordic House: this pillow shows the group in an head to toe pose. Each Beatle has his instrument. "The Beatles" on a drum shape appears on the bottom left. Also has copies of signatures across the bottom. Value: G: $200 E: $275 NM: $350.

Stamps

"Beatle Stamps Are Here!" banner: this is a display banner for the Hallmark stamps. The banner measures 2 3/4" x 20" and would be placed above the stamp booklet display box. Value: G: $35 E: $45 NM: $60.

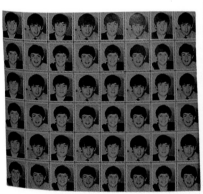 

The "Original Beatle Stamps" on the right were put out by Hallmark. They came in a booklet of 100 stamps. Five different pages contained 20 stamps per page—one page for each Beatle and one group page. This booklet measures approximately 4" x 7". A number of these have recently hit the market value: G: $20 E: $25 NM: $35. On the left is the original box that held these booklets of stamps and could be displayed in this box. Value for the empty display box: G: $25 E: $30 NM: $35.

"Beatle Photo Stamps" with the display box. The stamps came in sheets of 48 black and white stamps that could be attached to almost anything. The display box has red lettering to promote the sheets of 48 stamps. Value for each sheet of 48: G: $20 E$25 NM: $30. Value for the display box only: G: $65 E: $80 NM: $100.

Miscellaneous Items

This vinyl material, made in the United Kingdom, was originally sold by the square yard and could be used for a number of things, including picnic table cover, drapes, and shower curtains. This vinyl material has a repeat pattern of individual Beatles, a group pose, and copies of their signatures. Value given is for a square yard of material: G: $65 E: $95 NM: $125.

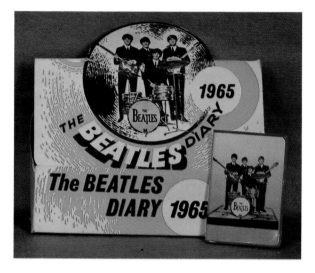

"Make a Date With The Beatles" desk calendar, made in the United Kingdom. The calendar has a photo of the group with a red background and guitars. It is octagon shaped and has knobs on back to change the date, month, and day. Value: G: $165 E: $245 NM: $325.

Diary and display box put out by H. B. Langman Co. "The Beatles Diary 1965" display box has a black and white photo of the group on an album. The diary has a photo of group standing on stage, on the cover. Value for the display box only: G: $125 E: $175 NM: $250. Value for the diary only: G: $30 E: $35 NM: $45.

Sunglasses, made by Solarex, are made of plastic and have decals of two of the Beatles' faces on each side. Value for glasses with stickers: G: $75 E: $90 NM: $110.

The cardboard coaster has the faces of all four Beatles on it. Also appearing on the coaster are the title "With Love From Me To You", a guitar in each corner, and the names of additional songs along the sides. "The Beatles" appears at the base. Value for each coaster: G: $8 E: $10 NM: $15.

The napkin shown here, put out by the Rolex Paper Co. from the United Kingdom, originally came in a package of 50. The folded napkin measures about 6 1/2" x 6 1/2". This napkin pictures the Beatles, each on his own stand, with copies of the Beatles' signatures. Value given is for each napkin: G: $15 E: $20 NM: $25.

Bamboo plates, made by Bamboo Tray Specialist, Co., came in three different sizes (shown here)—small 6" diameter, medium 11 1/2" diameter, and large 12" diameter. The scene on these plates is all the same—the famous haircut scene from *A Hard Day's Night*. Value is the same for any size: G: $90 E: $110 NM: $130.

Hors d'oeuvre picks—plastic picks with a heart flasher on the top of each—made in Hong Kong. The heart shape flashes back and forth from a heart to two different Beatles' faces per heart. Value given is for a complete package of six picks and the back card: G: $80 E: $95 NM: $110.

Chapter Two
YESTERDAY

The Beatles continued their meteoric rise to success. They were very much in demand and didn't have time to play all of the venues they were offered. In 1965, they were destined to make their second film for United Artists. The film was tentatively called *Eight Arms To Hold You*, but in the final stages it was called simply *Help!* Production costs for this film were three times as much as they had been on their previous venture, it took twice as long to shoot, and *Help!* only received a third of the critical acclaim. The opening scene shows the Fabs each entering a front door in four identical terrace houses. The camera pans inside to the communal living space with four separate entrances. It is equipped with vending machines, a sunken floor, a carpet made of grass, and a cinema organ. *Help!* was meant to be a parody of high tech spy movies like the James Bond series. The plot centered around a mad scientist and a Hindu religious sect in search of a valuable ring that just happened to end up on Ringo's finger. When asked what his opinion of the movie was, John made it known that he had felt as if the Beatles had been cast as extras in their own movie. Critics called the Fab Four the new Marx Brothers despite this fact.

Early one morning in the summer of 1965 Paul woke up with a terrific idea. He went to the piano and proceeded to write an entire song in one sitting. He called the song "Yesterday," and it became the most highly acclaimed Beatles song ever written. It was also the first Beatles song to capture the hearts of the older music buying public and was a very good indication of Paul's prowess as a composer. "Yesterday" was destined to become the single most recorded song in history. Paul called it, "A miraculous creation, like an egg; seamless, flawless, a wonder in itself." It was not included on the American release of *Help!*, but did appear on the British version. Capitol later released it as a single in America in September of 1965.

John's aunt Mimi came to the opening of *Help!* and stayed with John and Cynthia in Weybridge. Lennon then bought her a new house because too many tourists were turning up at the old one and he feared for her safety living there alone.

In 1965 the Beatles extended the boundaries of music once again with their *Rubber Soul* album. This album featured the use of unconventional instruments to create a new and exciting sound. This was prompted by George's suggestion that they use a sitar. George had developed a deep and abiding interest in India and the Indian culture; music became a natural extension of this. While the group had used a sitar once before, on *Help!*, it proved to be less effective than their use of the instrument in the song "Norwegian Wood," a very powerful song that John wrote about the beginnings of his relationship with Yoko Ono.

Rubber Soul was a breakthrough album for the Beatles in other ways too. It was the first album on which they took control of the cover design. John was great at coming up with new and unique ideas to call attention to their work. It was his idea that they take the cover photograph and distort it to really give the illusion that makes *Rubber Soul* a reality.

John took his unconventional way of thinking a step further when he came up with the idea for the butcher cover for the Beatles *Yesterday and Today* album in 1966. It made a very strong statement about how the Beatles felt about their songs being butchered or cut up, rearranged and recycled onto a sterile bit of fluff called an album, just to make more money. At first Capitol allowed some of the record covers to be produced. On it the Beatles wore white butchers smocks covered in blood. They were surrounded by randomly mutilated pieces of meat and dolls with no heads or appendages. It did make a very strong statement about how the Beatles themselves were being treated like pieces of meat. The reaction to the new cover was immediate and strong. DJ's started attacking it as soon as it was released. It was pronounced repulsive and in bad taste. When word got back to Capitol, it pulled the record and pasted another cover over the original so they could get it back on the market as soon as possible, thereby proving the groups point in making the cover in the first place. They also threw away 750,000 of the offensive covers. Capitol did later produce the new cover without pasting it over, but the statement had already been made. For more information about the "Butcher" cover, please see the first volume of what is going to be a three volume set eventually, *Yesterday and Tomorrow. the Beatles: a collector's guide to Beatles memorabilia.* This volume addresses the value of the album in each of its four states. Of course, the "Butcher" cover in its original state has always been considered the most valuable, but due to well peeled paste overs, this may soon be changing. Technology in this area has advanced so much that some albums have been so expertly peeled as to be sold as original "Butchers." Please be very careful in this area as a peeled version has actually been greatly devalued. So many people get the paste overs and peel them, that the un-peeled versions are becoming more and more scarce. Because of this and the story behind this album, I feel that someday the paste overs may actually become worth more. How can you tell if your album has a paste over cover without peeling it? A reputable record dealer can help you. When in doubt about a pieces' origin, always get at least one expert opinion.

The Beatles took their music even further on the *Revolver* album in 1966. This album was presented as a sort of continuous narrative performance, which had never been done before. It turned out to be so technologically advanced, in terms of sound quality, that the Fabs were unable to perform any of the songs live. The electronic distortion and the sounds made by synthesizers were impossible to duplicate in a live performance. For instance, in John's version of "You're Only Sleeping," the yawning sound was created by taping a guitar passage and then playing it backward. Because of this, none of the songs from *Revolver* were performed on the American tour. This was another gigantic achievement in music, however, and prompted the Beatles to get more involved in producing the sound quality and diversity that could only be found on an album that was totally designed in the studio.

The *Revolver* cover was another artistic masterpiece. It consisted of a black and white line drawing with a kaleidoscope of photo fragments encased in hair. The Fabs faces appear in the middle of this frame of hair.

The statement that Paul makes on this album is one of profound sadness with songs like "Eleanor Rigby." When asked what he was thinking about when he wrote the song, he replied: "At first I thought it was a bit like 'Annabel Lee' ..." —a classic poem written by Edgar Allen Poe about his girlfriend who passed away, but not so sexy. Perhaps he was mourning the loss of his own lady love...

Their new sound made the Beatles even more popular with the youth of the world. So much so, that when *Newsweek* did a poll of students on thirty-eight college campuses, in 1967, the Beatles proved to be the most popular non-ideological idols in America. At least one of the Beatles's names tended to come up when the students were asked who their leaders and heroes were. As the leader of the group and, later, a champion of peace, John's name was mentioned slightly more often.

By 1967 Paul had decided that he had met the girl of his dreams in Jane Asher. On Christmas Day he asked her to marry him. He presented her with a diamond and emerald engagement ring and she said yes. They were planning on getting married sometime in 1968.

The couple first met in 1963, after the Beatles had made an appearance in London. Paul really fell hard for Jane. They met at a party that was held after the show. At that time the vivacious redhead was an established actress of stage and screen as well as being both intelligent and beautiful. She was also sweet and refined. After hanging out at the party and talking to everyone for awhile, Paul and Jane went off alone together into the bedroom. To everyone's great surprise, nothing happened. The two of them simply talked. It turns out that Miss Asher was still a virgin and Paul was so taken with her that he actually respected her for it.

Over the next few weeks the couple became inseparable. Jane's mother adored Paul and asked him to move into the family home with them. He happily accepted. Even though Paul and Jane were now living in the same house, they still maintained separate rooms. In fact, the famous bachelor was very cognizant of the fact that Jane's parents wanted her reputation to remain spotless. No small feat when you are living with a Beatle.

Brian was less than happy that the heartthrob of the group was joining the ranks of the spoken for. Paul basically told Brian to mind his own business. Jane, on the other hand, tried to help Brain to maintain the group's image. In 1964 she even told the British teen magazine, *Fabulous*, that she and Paul were not, in fact, engaged. Because of what had happened with John and Cynthia, rumors were flying that the couple had been secretly married, which was not true. Asher denied it publicly in the article.

Paul never became a big fan of the stage; however, he still made it to most of Jane's opening nights and backstage parties. Paul was intrigued by the lifestyle of the theater group though, and he actually asked Jane Asher to teach him to be more refined. After all, he was moving up in the world and it was his wish to be respected as such. His thirst for knowledge was very impressive, yet he never lost his sense of humor about his background. When an interviewer told him that he was currently reading *Naked Lunch* by William Burroughs, Paul replied that he was, himself, reading *The Packed Lunch* by Greedy Blighter.

As an actress, Asher really didn't have to worry about her professional life bleeding over into her private life, but this was hardly true for Paul. He was constantly being pursued by enthusiastic female fans who would have liked nothing better than to be in Jane's shoes. The problem for Asher was that McCartney was eating up the attention.

Needless to say, this sort of behavior did not exactly endear him to Jane. Still, she tried to understand that he loved her and this type of thing was only to maintain his Beatle image.

As Paul's success continued, he and Asher bought a townhouse in St. John's Wood. Jane did most of the decorating herself. She spent her days picking out wallpaper, carpets and paint. Her excellent taste was evident in the understated finery of the home. It was really beginning to look as though the couple would be married. They were already living as if they were except for that marriage certificate.

Because of the location of the house, in the heart of London, fans became an even bigger problem for Jane than they had been previously. The property was protected like a fortress, but that didn't stop eager young girls from trying to catch a glimpse of Paul. Their home was totally encased by a high brick wall and a huge front gate covered in thick iron sheeting. The gate could only be opened mechanically, from the inside, after the visitor had been cleared to enter by Paul or Jane. The problem with having an intercom was that the fans would not leave it alone. They rang it almost constantly, day and night. It drove Jane to distraction, but once again, Paul was eating it up. He would often drop whatever he was doing to go outside and hang out with the girls, signing autographs and posing for pictures. McCartney still insisted that it was a good boost for his image.

In the summer of 1966 McCartney bought High Park Farm, a 183 acre property in Scotland. The couple decided to live a minimalist existence there. They even made their own furniture out of old wooden packing crates that they had found piled in the barn. It was a great place to escape the responsibilities of their otherwise hectic lives. At first, they took their baths in a stainless steel trough on a concrete slab, but Paul did eventually install a bathtub in the house.

While all this was taking place, work began on the quintessential album of the psychedelic era as well as a major breakthrough, the Beatles album *Sgt. Pepper's Lonely Hearts Club Band*. It took four months to record the entire album of twelve songs at a cost of $100,000. The idea behind this LP was revolutionary. The Beatles were to be portrayed, not as themselves, but as a completely separate band. It was a breakthrough concept album. For the sake of keeping up the premise of this separate identity for the group, *Sgt. Pepper*, announces "Billy

Shears", whom everyone had known for years. Shears was Ringo's character on the album, who sang "With A Little Help From My Friends."

The cover for this album was an accomplishment in itself. Once again, no one had ever seen anything like it. Peter Blake, the covers designer, put together a sort of mystical collage of personalities, sixty-two in all. Epstein hit the roof when he saw it and started to realize all the legal ramifications of getting permission to use the images of all those pictured. He begged the Beatles to simply use a brown paper bag as the cover, but they were determined to pull off another first. They even saw to it that EMI was provided with $40 million in insurance to cover any possible lawsuits by the people pictured.

Brian offered Robert Frazer, a well known gallery owner, to EMI as co-coordinator of the jacket artwork, while Frazer suggested that Peter Blake design the actual cover.

Originally, "The Fool" (*please see the beginning of Chapter 3 for more information about The Fool*) they eventually did paint the design on the side of the Apple building) was supposed to do the center, but their design ended up being badly out of scale. This led to the Beatles being photographed for the center of the cover.

Frazer had thought that it would be really cool to have the cover art done by a well known artist. The challenges an artist would have to contend with included the fact that the Beatles wished to be portrayed as a totally separate group. Frazer wanted them portrayed as a sort of marching band that one might see in a park. Peter Blake came up with the idea that if they set up the shot a certain way, the people in the crowd could be literally anyone. They started out by making a life-sized collage, and gradually adding all the other elements.

The original cover had a photograph of Gandhi, but EMI balked at that because they had a virtual monopoly on recording and film in India. Too much money was on the line and they didn't want to offend that nation. So Gandhi was removed from the cover. EMI finally agreed to a modified cover with Epstein's assurance that each person pictured on it (or their executors) would give their permission and indemnify EMI against a lawsuit.

At first Mae West would not agree to be on it, asking: "What would I be doing in a lonely hearts club?" However, each of the Beatles wrote her a personal letter about how much it would mean to them if she would appear on it and she agreed.

The only person that they had originally wanted who was not included, besides Gandhi, was Leo Gorcey of the Bowery Boys. It seems that he wanted a fee and EMI did not wish to open up a precedent for the others.

In the end, nobody sued, even though executives of the company were eventually told that about half of the people were never contacted to give their official permission for the use of their image. Fortunately, we were a much less litigious society in those days.

One thing that a number of readers have asked me about is exactly who are all those people on the cover of the *Sgt. Peppers* album? Below, you will see a list of names that can be matched up with the actual picture on the album cover:

1. Sri Yukteswar
2. Aleister Crowley
3. Mae West
4. Lenny Bruce
5. Karlheinz Stockhausen
6. W.C. Fields
7. Carl Jung
8. Edgar Allen Poe
9. Fred Astaire
10. Merkin
11. A Pretty Girl
12. Leo Gorcey (taken out)
13. Huntz Hall
14. Simon Rodia
15. Bob Dylan
16. Aubrey Beardsley
17. Sir Robert Peel
18. Aldous Huxley
19. Dylan Thomas
20. Terry Southern
21. Dion Di Mucci
22. Tony Curtis
23. Wallace Berman
24. Tommy Handley
25. Marilyn Monroe
26. William S. Burroughs
27. Sri Mahauatara Babaji
28. Stan Laurel
29. Richard Lindner
30. Oliver Hardy
31. Karl Marx
32. H.G. Wells
33. Sri Paramahansa Yoyananda
34. Figure of a Girl
35. Stuart Sutcliffe
36. Wax Figure of a Girl
37. Max Miller
38. A Vargas Girl
39. Marlon Brando
40. Tom Mix
41. Oscar Wilde
42. Tyrone Power
43. Larry Bell
44. Dr. David Livingstone
45. Johnny Weissmuller
46. Stephen Crane
47. Issy Bonn
48. George Bernard Shaw
49. If you know who this is please reach us on our website.
50. Albert Stubbins
51. Sri Lahiri Mahasaya
52. Lewis Carroll
53. T.E. Lawrence
54. Sonny Liston
55. A Vargas Girl
56. George (in wax)
57. John (in wax)
58. Shirley Temple
59. Ringo (in wax)
60. Paul (in wax)
61. If you know who this is please reach us on our website.
62. John
63. Ringo
64. Paul
65. George
66. Bobby Breen
67. Marlene Dietrich
68. Mahatma Gandhi (removed for political reasons)
69. An American Legionaire
70. Diana Dors
71. Shirley Temple

The largest group of musicians ever heard on a Beatles recording were assembled to record "A Day In The Life." They recorded the sound for this song four times, then added the four separate recordings to one another at different intervals to get just the right sound quality. If you listen very closely, you can hear the difference. The final "bunched chords" were produced when each of the Beatles, along with George Martin, played three different pianos, in the studio. All of them hit the chords as hard as they could, simultaneously. While this was happening the engineer was pushing the volume input faders way down, on the moment of impact. Then, as the noise gradually diminished, the faders were pushed slowly back up to the top.

"A Day In The Life" was taped amongst a huge gathering of top music makers such as Mick Jagger and Marianne Faithful. A forty-two piece orchestra was used for the album. They played for the album decked out in full evening attire, combined with some funky carnival disguises that the Beatles passed out to them. A noted violinist played the violin while wearing a big, red clown nose, while another held his bow in a fake gorilla's paw from an old costume. George Martin had scored twenty-four bars of music that built in intensity to the very end. The music played by the forty-two instruments was double-tracked again and again until it came to an earth shattering grand finale of sound. The last note of the album, that can be heard by human ears, trails off for a full forty-five seconds and the microphone pots were turned so high to catch the last fading tones, that the air conditioning at Abbey Roads studio can be heard in the background. The very last note was recorded at a frequency of 20,000 hertz, a frequency which can only be heard by dogs. If you don't believe me then enlist the help of a canine friend and watch his reaction.

The original overall concept of the album was to record something unified and continuous, like a novel or film, about how the Beatles grew up in Liverpool. That is the idea that the songs "Penny Lane" and "Strawberry Fields Forever" were born out of. That idea was scrapped, however, when the two songs were released together as one of the best back to back singles of all time. Because of this, the rest of the songs on the album reflect things that the Fabs were doing at that time. For instance, John took some of his lyrics from the January 17, 1967 issue of the *Daily Mail*: Four thousand holes in Blackburn Lancashire, and the entire song "Being For The Benefit of Mr. Kite" came from a poster hanging on the wall of John Lennon's house. The song is, word for word, what was written on this old theater bill. He bought it during one of his adventures through the antique shops of London. George Martin thought that a sort of circus, hurdy gurdy sound would fit with the theme of the song nicely. He created this affect by taping steam organ sounds,

cutting the tapes into different lengths, and tossing them onto the floor. They were then gathered up and reassembled at random to produce the music that you hear behind "Henry the horse dances the waltz." This was to be the last album on which the Beatles joined together, in spirit, and the whole project went very smoothly.

The latest fad that was destined to become the latest in Fab fashion was the look of Victorian militia. In fact, it was that look that inspired the whole concept of *Sgt. Pepper* in the first place.

The finished album came with a sheet of cut-out novelties such as a *Sgt. Pepper* picture card, a paper mustache, two badges, and a set of NCO's stripes. If this sheet remains uncut and intact in your album, it will certainly add to its value.

An unfortunate trait that is present in our culture is that we tend to freeze moments in time in terms of tragedies. The most memorable moments tend to spring from things such as protests of the Vietnam war. Events tend to crystallize in people's minds based on the shock and horror of the moment. Some noted examples are the assassinations of both John F. Kennedy and John Lennon. Most people remember exactly where they were when they heard each of these awful pieces of news. But *Sgt. Pepper* managed to change the angle of that focus in a way that no other album had ever done. It captured the attention of millions of people, in the same moment, and focused them all on something positive. This album caused a positive repeat of the phenomenon I have just described. Most people remember exactly where they were and what they were doing when they first heard the *Sgt. Pepper* album. The music brings up powerful emotions of the time in which it was introduced. And, much like the first moon walk, people had to experience it over and over again before they could fully comprehend the magnitude of it.

Old Jewelry & Accessories

A brass compact made with a push in mechanism to pop the lid open. It has a mirror on the inside of the lid and powder with a puff inside the base (shown in the next photo). A black and white fan club pose decorates the exterior of the lid. Value for the complete compact: G: $225 E: $300 NM: $400.

The flasher rings and display card shown here were made by Saymore Co. The rings are plastic and have a flashing front that alternates between a Beatle face and his name. There is a row of rings of each of the Fab Four; a total of 24 rings could be held on each display card. Value per ring: G: $10 E: $12 NM: $15. Value for the empty display card: G: $250 E: $350 NM: $425.

This photo shows the compact's interior.

Brooches, Lockets & Bracelets

This large "B" shaped brooch was made by the Novelty Brooch Co. of the United Kingdom. This brooch is an unusual design. The four Mop Tops are placed with their instruments around the "B". The brooch measures about 1 1/2" tall and came in a brass or chrome finish. Value: G: $75 E: $85 NM: $100.

This beetle-shaped brooch/watch combination was made by Smiths of the United Kingdom. This watch would pin to a blouse or shirt. The beetle has two red jewels for eyes. Value: G: $175 E: $225 NM: $300.

Brooch, brass finish: "The Beatles" and a guitar with a drum adorn the pin attachment. Hanging below the pin attachment is a heart shaped brooch with a 1" black and white fan club pose button set in the middle of the heart. "Nems Ent. Ltd." is found on the back of the heart. Value: G: $60 E: $85 NM: $110.

The book shaped locket hangs from a chain on a brass bow. The outside cover has a fan club photo and "The Beatles" on it; the inside opens to reveal ten black and white fold out photos. Also shown is a brooch put out by Rand which has a brass finish with a pin attachment decorated with "The Beatles" and a guitar and drum motif. Hanging from the bottom of the pin attachment is a 1" fan club pose button set into a brass coupling. Value for the locket: G: $65 E: $85 NM: $110. Value for the brooch: G: $40 E: $60 NM: $85.

A leather locket/necklace features "The Beatles" pressed into the leather cover. The locket unbuttons from the back and, from the inside, out folds ten black and white photos. To the right is a brass finish locket featuring "The Beatles" elevated in brass on top, and a push in clasp to open. This locket opens to four black and white photos, one of each Beatle. This locket would be attached to a chain or a pin. Value for the leather locket/necklace: G: $30 E: $50 NM: $70. Value for the brass locket: G: $40 E: $60 NM: $80.

This photo shows the inside of the leather locket.

2" round flasher button/ necklace, black and white. The set in flasher changes from Paul to George or John to Ringo. It is attached to a chain. Value: G: $50 E: $75 NM: $100.

This brass finish necklace/brooch is made from a 2" button with a fan club pose. "The Beatles" is printed on the button in black and white, then the button is set in brass, and made into either a necklace or a brooch. Value for each are the same: G: $40 E: $55 NM: $75.

"Beatle Brooch" made by Invicta Plastics Ltd.: beetle bug shape with a one inch group photo inset. The brooch measures about 2" in length and would pin to a blouse or shirt. Value given is for beetle and original card: G: $40 E: $55 NM: $75.

Plastic guitar brooches, each with an inset photo: shown here with either a group black and white photo or an inset color picture of Paul. They measure 4" in length. These originally came with a light colored card backing that reads "The Fabulous Beatles" and bears copies of their signatures, and a registered design Nems, 1964. These were made in Great Britain. Value for the group photo guitar or for Paul without the original card: G: $15 E: $25 NM: $35 each.

Brooch, put out by Mastro: it measures about 5 1/2" in length, was made in the USA, and has "The Beatles" on its base. The brooch uses two rubber bands for strings and is decorated with face shots and the first names only underneath. "Beatles" is printed on the head of the guitar. The brooch has an attachment on the back to slide onto a shirt pocket. These are not real easy to find intact. Value: G: $125 E: $175 NM: $175.

A brass finished bracelet put out by Kendall. It has a 1" fan club pose button set in the brass. "The Beatles, Official" is printed along with song titles on the bottom half of the original backing card. A framed in color fan club style pose with a yellow background graces the top of the original backing card. This card is 40% of the value given: G: $60 E: $90 NM: $125.

Bracelet: brass finished, put out by Kendall. This bracelet has four 1" buttons set in brass scattered around a chain as charms. (The card is same as the card for the Kendall bracelet.) Value with backing card: G: $95 E: $135 NM: $195.

Keyrings, Pens, Tie Tacks & Clips

Key ring: yellow plastic with a brass ring and a black and white group photo. Value: G: $3 E: $5 NM: $8. Record shaped plastic with metal key ring: commemorates the Shea Stadium concert. Value: G: $15 E: $17 NM: $20.

Adjustable brass finished ring, marked "© Nems Ent. Ltd." The ring features a fan club pose button set in brass. Value for the ring: G: $50 E: $65 NM: $85.

Writing pen, made by Press-Initial Corp.: brass finished, the pen has faces cast in brass attached to the clip. This pen also has an off-white plastic lower section with copies of the signatures and "The Beatles" drum head. This brass tipped pen came in a number of different colors. Value: G: $50 E: $65 NM: $85.

Lariat tie put out by Press-Initial Corp. This tie features a brass finished 1" medallion with "The Beatles" and their faces. There are brass tips on the tie ends. Original card (shown) is 40% of the value given: G: $75 E: $100 NM: $125.

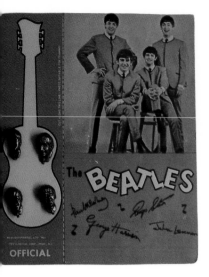

Tie tacks put out by Press-Initial Corp.: pewter finished faces, set of four. The original card (shown) is 40% of value given: G: $10 E: $15 NM: $20.

"Official Tie Tack Pin" put out by Press-Initial Corp. Each pin has a brass finished face. Original cards (shown) comprise 40% of the value given: G: $15 E: $25 NM: $30.

Ringo and George "Official Tie Tack Pins."

"Official Tie Tack Pin" by Press-Initial Corp. Each brass or metal finished guitar has four faces and "Beatles" between the faces. The value given is with the original card; the card is 40% of the value given: G: $15 E: $25 NM: $30.

Brass finished tie clip put out by Press-Initial Corp. The 1" medallion features the four Beatle faces around the top and "The Beatles" in the center of the medallion. The original card contributes 40% to the value given: G: $50 E: $65 NM: $75.

Black finished metal cuff links put out by Press-Initial Corp. These 1" medallion links, with Beatle faces around top and "The Beatles" in the center of the medallion, shown here on the original card. The card is 40% of the given value: G: $65 E: $90 NM: $120.

Belt buckle, brass finished: this buckle has a plastic cover over an early black & white photo. Value: G: $50 E: $75 NM: $90.

New Memorabilia: Watches

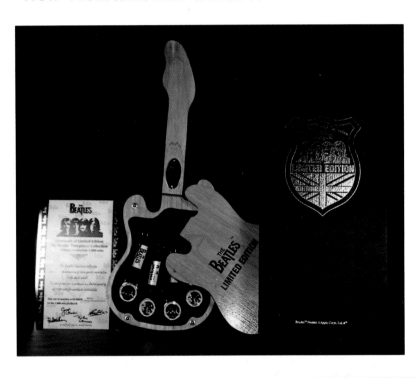

Watch set, limited edition: "Beatles Product © Apple Corps. Ltd." is written in gold lettering on the front cover of the black box. The wooden clear stained guitar shaped box contains a certificate with a limited edition number and four different faced watches with leather bands. A "The Beatles" tag wraps around each band. Value for full package: E: $300 NM: $385.

Watches, "Beatles Product © Apple Corps. Ltd.": the wooden clear stained guitar shaped box, adorned with "The Beatles" and Beatles silhouettes in black. A number of these, with different watch faces, were put out. Value per watch with guitar shaped wooden case. E: $80 NM: $95.

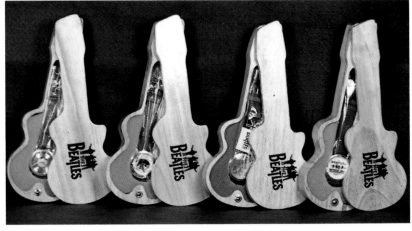

A variation on the Beatles watches with different boxes and watch face art. The values are the same.

Watch by Fossil: silver finished, black face, with black leather band. Limited Edition to number 10,000. Value is for the complete set as shown: E: $75 NM: $100.

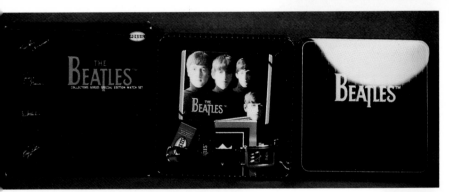

Rectangular gold finished watch by Fossil: the watch face has the Fab Fours' faces on top. "The Beatles" is written on the bottom of the watch face. The watch comes with a black leather band. Limited Edition to number 10,000. Value is for the complete set as shown: E: $250 NM: $300.

Watches, © 1989 Apple Corps. Limited, 1989 HBL Ltd. The Beatles watch line features three different styles (pictured); they have black and white fan club poses on the face. Value given is per watch with original package: E: $35 NM: $50.

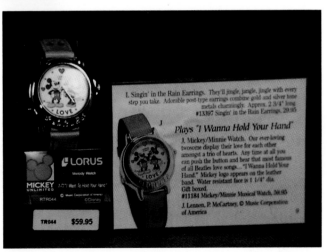

A melody watch by Lorus: gold finished with a brown leather band. Mickey and Minnie Mouse hold hands and the watch plays "I Wanna Hold Your Hand." This is a dual collectible for Disney and Beatles collectors. Value given is for the complete set: E: $65 NM: $100.

Lighters

A Zippo lighter with a key chain: boxed in a tin, this is a special edition product. "Let It Be" appears on the lighter and the tin. Value given is for the complete set: E: $30 NM: $35.

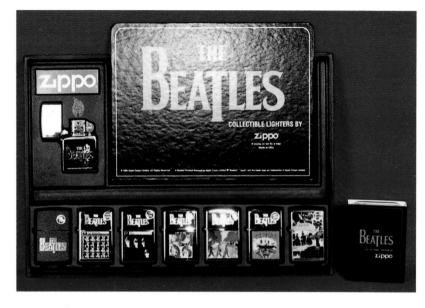

Zippo lighter set, "1996 Apple Corps. Ltd.": eight different covers comes in a display box. Value given is for the complete set: E: $225 NM: $275.

Medallions/Coins

Set of four silver medallions by Enviromint. One bust pose of each Beatle with plastic protector covers. Each medallion is one troy ounce silver and measures 1 3/8" in diameter. Value given is with the case: E: $125 NM: $150.

Following twelve photos: These limited edition silver medallions (the following 12 photos) each feature a unique medallion in an album cover that matches the medallion. Each medallion is one troy ounce silver, measuring 1 3/8" in diameter. Value given for each medallion with cover: E: $35 NM: $40.

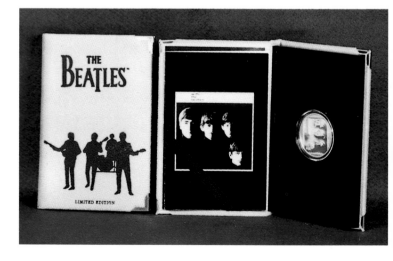

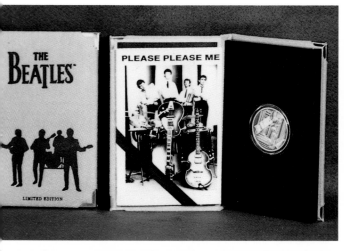

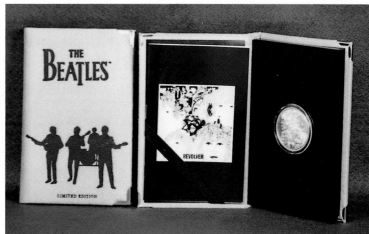

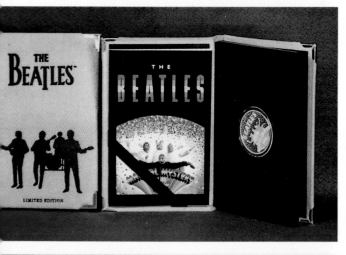

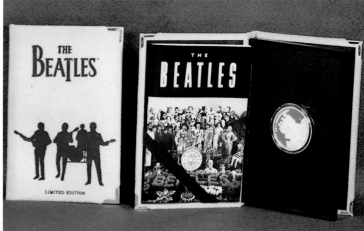

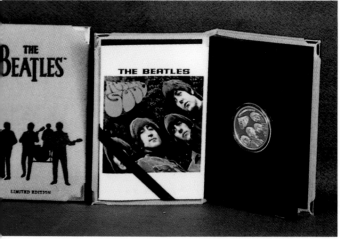

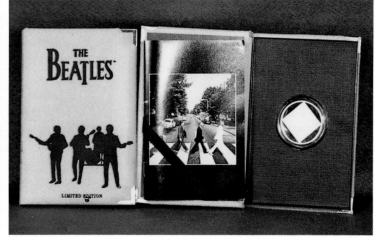

Miscellaneous New Memorabilia

From left to right: all four of these items were put out in a gold or silver finish, and all were made by "William Leigh Legends." (1) Charm bracelet, total of seven charms—four of faces, two album cover charms, and one guitar charm in center. Value for the charm bracelet on the original card: Silver: E: $55 NM: $60, Gold: E: $65 NM: $75. (2) Tie pin, says "The Beatles" on front. Value for the tie pin on the original card: Silver: E: $23 NM: $25, Gold: E: $25 NM: $30. (3) Badge, red ribbon. "The Beatles" at top of the badge. In the middle of the badge is the group in their Sgt. Pepper regalia and under the group is the word "forever." Value for the badge on the original card: Silver: E: $25 NM: $30, Gold: E: $30 NM: $35. (4) Logo pin, Fab Four full pose, set on a musical grid. A musical note appears on the left side; "The Beatles" is stamped across bottom right. Value given is for the logo pin on the original card: Silver: E: $32 NM: $35, Gold: E: $37 NM: $42.

Two different spoons. Left: the silver plated spoon has a black button-sized handle adorned with four Beatles faces, three on top and one below with "The Beatles" in the center. Value with the original package: E: $15 NM: $20. On the right: the spoon has a brass finish and a cast fan club pose on the handle. Value with the original package: E: $15 NM: $20.

Cloisonne pins, five different sets of four, each with four individual Beatle poses per set. Each set has its own box. Value per set: E: $18 NM: $20.

Belt buckle, brass finished: the buckle has a black inset with "Beatles" across the center. "Come Together" is printed under the Beatles. All of the text is written in a metal-flake design. Back is marked CPI © 77. Value: E: $12 NM: $15.

Key rings by Avedon Photos, images sealed in plastic with metal key rings attached. Value given is for the set of four: E: $20 NM: $25.

Brass finished ring with a cluster of Fab Four heads on top. These adjustable rings are marked "© Nems Ent. Ltd." Value for the ring only: E: $7 NM: $9.

Chapter Three
All You Need Is Love

The Beatles participated in yet another ground-breaking venture on June 25, 1967 when they appeared on TV just after the Arab-Israeli Six Day War. The purpose of this appearance was to express their thoughts on international peace and brotherhood. The song that they sang for this show was *All You Need Is Love*, and two hundred million viewers watched that night as the Beatles made a plea for peace and love around the world.

Simon Posthuma and Marijke Koger became involved in the project shortly after their arrival from Holland, where they claimed to have formed the "Trend Boutique," an avant-garde clothing store for the "bizarrely" dressed. They had designed all of the clothing for the boutique themselves and named each outfit after one of earth's elements such as "Wind" or "Rain." The pair had moved to London hoping to find work as stage designers. They made it into the Beatles inner circle through two young theatrical publicists, who happened to have Brian Epstein as one of their clients. Brian owned the Savile Theater at the time, and might have had some use for Posthuma and Koger's design talents. Their set designs, like their clothing, were bizarre and psychedelic. They decided to call their little design crew "The Fool" and they were hired to make all of the costumes for the "All You Need Is Love" production. The Beatles were intrigued by their far-out ideas and hired them to do some private work as well. They painted a piano and a gypsy caravan on John's property as well as a fireplace at George's Escher estate. As Simon explained to the *Sunday Times*, "The Fool" was a name with connotations beyond the obvious: "It represents Truth, Spiritual Meaning, and the circle, which expresses the universal circumference in which gravitate all things."

In September of 1967 the Beatles commissioned about $200,000 to "The Fool" so that they could design a clothing boutique for the Beatles that was to be stocked with "The Fool's" original designs. Paul announced that the boutique was opening by saying that they were creating, "...a beautiful place where you can buy beautiful things." McCartney got his inspiration for the name of the boutique from a Magritte painting that he had bought. They called the business Apple.

It was at this point in the Beatles' history that a young, blond Greek gentleman named Alexis Mardas (Magic Alex) entered the picture. His father held a high post in the Papadopoulos dictatorship. Alex had come to Britain only knowing two people: the Duke of Edinburgh and Mick Jagger (a strange combination).

Mardas' claim to fame was that he supposedly invented all manner of strange electronic gadgets. The first item that he invented was the "nothing box," which really peaked Lennon's interest. He would sit and stare at it for hours at a time, trying to guess which of the series of red lights would flash on next.

Alex had many other strange and wonderful ideas which he claimed he could make a reality "with a little capital." The Beatles certainly provided plenty of that. John was especially fascinated by this con man and actually believed that he had some sort of magical powers. In fact, he was so taken with the man's ideas that he insisted on taking Mardas with them everywhere. All he had to do to get John's undivided attention was to produce another mystical creation from his pocket. Some of the ideas that fascinated John the most were things like a telephone programmed to dial numbers to the command of a human voice, which was actually realized, but not by Alex and not until decades later. He also invented a force field designed to go up around a house and keep intruders at bay with a wall of colored air.

Both Cynthia Lennon and George Martin viewed the little man with extreme suspicion. Mardas became one of the few people who was allowed to visit Abbey Road studios while the Beatles were recording. He even had the audacity to lean over and whisper in John's ear about how outdated the equipment there was, claiming that he could provide the group with a seventy-two-track recording machine as opposed to EMI's eight-track one. He also claimed that he could make Ringo more visible by getting rid of the acoustic screens that surrounded him and replacing them with invisible and impenetrable sonic beams.

While all this was going on, The Fool was turning a respectable row house, in the business district of London, into the outrageous Apple Boutique. They hired art students to help them cover the side wall along Paddington Street with mystical psychedelic patterns, which evolved around the face of a huge Red Indian (not exactly politically correct for this day and age, but perfectly fine in the sixties). Of course Magic Alex showed up to create floodlights of his own design which were supposed to consist of a giant artificial sun suspended on invisible laser beams above Baker Street. You have to hand it to the man, he had one hell of an imagination.

When the boutique opened Patti Harrison's sister, Jenny, was hired to work in the shop. Pete Shotton was hired to oversee the oriental fabrics and exotic jewelry that The Fool had ordered.

The official opening date was December 7, 1967 and the Beatles held a lavish party and fashion show to kick it off. John and George were the only members of the group who were actually there for the festivities.

It was around this same period of time that Apple Corporation Ltd. was started. Magic Alex ran the electronics division and was hired by the Beatles to design a private recording studio for them. Alex's division of Apple, not surprisingly, became notorious for its unfulfilled promises. Despite all his "work" in the laboratory, not a single apple shaped radio, nothing box, or domestic force field ever rolled off the line. Alex was always "on the edge of a breakthrough" and always needing just a little more money in order to bring his projects to the public. Things went along smoothly for Mardas until the Beatles decided to move their recording efforts to the studio that he had been building in the basement of the Apple building.

George Martin had already visited the studio to inspect Magic Alex's technological marvels and not only was there no seventy-two-track recording console, there was no console at all. He hadn't even put in an intercom between the studio and the control room.

The Beatles had to actually bring in the sound equipment from Abbey Road. Magic Alex eventually got the ax when John, George, and Ringo hired Allen Klein as their new manager. He went on what he called an "economy drive" at Apple in order to dismiss the pampered, unproductive hangers on.

Shortly after *Magical Mystery Tour*, the Apple Boutique was sliding into chaos. The local business people petitioned to have the mural removed, claiming that it was a distraction and simply wasn't appropriate for that part of London. The Fool apparently had no clue about how to run a retail business. Their merchandise was either ludicrously expensive or cheap and shoddy. Shoplifting was rampant, especially among the employees. The new head of Apple, John Lyndon, sent out strong memos to The Fool, warning them not to take any more merchandise from the premises and forbidding any further spending without authorization. By the end of July the finances had become such a nightmare that they decided to close the shop. On July 30th the Beatles opened the store to the public and gave away their entire stock.

In 1968 the Beatles got into spiritualism in the Himalayas with guru Maharishi Mahesh Yogi. Though Paul and Jane stayed longer than Ringo and Maureen, they still returned before the Lennon's and the Harrison's. The only comment that Paul had about the "long, strange trip" upon his return to England was that, at first, the Beatles had believed that the Maharishi was somehow superhuman. Unfortunately, they were to come to the realization that he was just as fallible as anyone else, and fell prey to the same earthly delights. Jane, being a very spiritual person, was deeply disappointed by the fact that the Maharishi had made a pass at Mia Farrow.

The Beatles all still believed in love, however, and they each found it in their own way. The first member of the group to find his lady love was John Lennon.

John first met Cynthia Powell while he was in art school. They had a class in Lettering together, which John hated. He sat directly behind Miss Powell in class and rarely spoke to her in the beginning, except to borrow supplies from her, which he never returned. At first Cynthia was actually afraid of the James Dean mannerisms that John exhibited, but she was fascinated too. He had that dark and brooding side to his personality that young girls find totally irresistible. She loved the way he played the guitar. John would sit on the stage in the cafeteria and play his guitar and sing for the other students. A huge crowd would gather around to hear him play, and Cynthia found herself drawn to him like a magnet. At the time she was nineteen and he was eighteen. Older women became a pattern in his John's, as you will see.

Cynthia Powell was a good girl. She and her two older brothers were brought up in Hoylake, across the Mersey River from Liverpool. They were considered higher status by the average scouse (street term for Liverpool resident) and had a more upper crust accent. Cynthia spent most of her adult life trying to pick up on the scouse dialect so she would fit in with John and his crowd. When she first met John she was dressing in matching skirt and sweater outfits. Before that she had even dated the same boy every weekend for the past three years. All that was about to change. Her father died when she was seventeen and she started going to the Liverpool art school the very next year.

One Thursday in their Lettering class, the students had to pair off and give each other an optical test. As luck would have it, John and Cynthia were partners and they discovered that they were each almost blind without their glasses. Finally they had something in common and by the end of the class they had become close enough to nod to one another in the hallway. It was progress. They both showed up at the end-of-term Christmas party and John actually asked Cynthia to dance with him for the first time. He even asked her to go to a party with him after the dance, but the shy Cynthia told him that she was engaged to a boy in Hoylake, which wasn't true. She couldn't believe that she had told him that and she wasn't even sure why. "I didn't ask you to marry me!" he snapped and walked away. He did ask her out again though, to a pub where he and his friends hung out. It was near the art college and it was called Ye Cracke. This time she accepted. By the end of the evening Cynthia knew that she would love him for the rest of her life, but she would learn that John Lennon was not an easy man to love. Even though he was insanely jealous of any man that Cynthia even looked at, he didn't think twice about flirting with another woman right in front of her. She also found out very quickly what a violent temper he had, but she said that she could see past that to the helpless little boy underneath who had lost both of his parents at a young age. She made a promise to herself that she would never desert him the way that they had, and she didn't. In the end it was he who deserted her.

It wasn't long before Cynthia would have her first run in with the Beatles many female groupies. They were constantly following the boys about and she began to feel very insecure about it. She had already been a witness to what that could do to a relationship when Paul sent away his girlfriend and her roommate, Dot Rhone. He simply didn't want to be tied to one girl with all those other girls chasing him.

The summer of 1962 was an especially difficult time for Cynthia. Her mother was away in Canada and John was working and touring constantly. She was so broke that year that she had to apply for public assistance. Then, in August, she found out that she was pregnant with John's child. She told him about it the very next night. To her amazement John asked her to marry him.

They were married on August 23, 1963 in a civil ceremony. Brian Epstein strongly advised them to keep the whole thing a secret. Shortly after they were wed, Cynthia and their new son, Julian, moved in with Aunt Mimi at Mendips, John's boyhood home. This was the beginning of another difficult period in Cynthia's life. Now, she and Mimi not only fought over what they thought was best for John, they fought over what they each thought was best for Julian as well. To make matters worse, the baby cried day and night and Cynthia couldn't seem to find anything that would soothe him.

Eventually, Lillian Powell, Cynthia's mother, decided to move back to Liverpool with her daughter and grandson. This was a welcome reprieve for Cynthia and a graceful way for her to bow out of the situation with Mimi. Mother and son moved out of Aunt Mimi's house and into a small flat with Cynthia's mother.

The couple soon became inseparable. They spent every moment they could together. They started hanging out at the Jacaranda Club, which was the in spot for beat groups. The Jac was basically a room with benches lining the walls and narrow tables, where one could linger over a single cup of coffee for hours without anyone asking you to leave. Most people can remember a hangout like that from their college days. A place where you could talk to your friends or study between classes while listening to a hot new local band. The Jac was located in the bohemian district and, consequently, drew an interesting mix of people. The club was owned by a man named Allan Williams. He had converted his basement into a small club with a brick dance floor. Members of the local beat groups would hang out there, even when they weren't playing, to drink coffee spiked with their own liquor and listen to the West Indian steel band until dawn.

John's best friend at the time was another art student named Stuart Sutcliffe, who was widely known as one of the most talented students at the school. All the girls thought that he looked exactly like James Dean, as opposed to John who only acted like him. He lived in a cramped, paint-spattered studio apartment, in a house near the art school. Stu was so poor that during the winter months he had to burn his furniture to keep warm. John moved in with him for awhile and helped with expenses. The two roommates were very close. John not only admired Stu for his talent and creativity, but for the passion that he obviously held for his art.

The friend of John's that Cynthia liked the least at that time was George Harrison. He was only fifteen and he idolized John. In fact, he followed the couple everywhere. If they went to the movies together it wasn't unusual for George to turn up in the middle of their date, which Cynthia found most annoying.

To Cynthia's amazement, John asked her to accompany him, as his wife, on the Beatles 1964 American tour. At Heathrow airport they were even photographed together by the media. John's marriage was now a matter of public record. This caused a mad rush by the fans when they returned to England. Cynthia was quite relieved when they moved out of the city and bought a nice quiet house in the stockbroker belt of Weybridge. Things went very well for them there for quite awhile. They led a fairly normal family life and Cynthia was given an almost unlimited budget for decorating. Unfortunately, it wasn't meant to last.

Soon after the Beatles stopped touring, John and Cynthia's marriage started to stagnate. She cooked dinner for him every night and brought it to him in the sunroom, where they watched TV as they ate, hardly speaking to one another. John was at a loss as to what to do with himself. Offers were pouring in for him to write books, exhibit drawings, even design greeting cards, but he wasn't sure where to go from here. He finally accepted a role in a Richard Lester picture called *How I Won the War*. Once again, he took Cynthia with him on location during the

filming. The first thing that happened to the startled Beatle was that he got a crew cut and oval wire framed spectacles to help him get into character as Musketeer Gripweed. The specs were destined to become his trademark and started a fad; people all over the world began wearing granny glasses.

The marriage finally fell apart completely after their disastrous trip to see the Maharishi. It was on their way back to England, on the plane, that John broke the terrible news to her. He admitted that throughout their marriage he had never really been faithful to her.

By the time their plane landed, Cynthia was in a panic. She became very insecure about her life, and almost had a nervous breakdown in the weeks that followed. She had never suspected that John had been with as many women as he had, but she felt that something terrible must be about to happen or he wouldn't be telling her about it. He didn't take her to New York with him when he went for the opening of Apple.

A few weeks later John suggested that she go on a trip to Greece with Jenny Boyd and Magic Alex. Little did she know, that was to be the end of her marriage. When Cynthia left, John called his old friend, Pete Shotton, to come and keep him company. During that visit he asked Pete if he felt like having a woman around again. He told him excitedly: "I've met this woman called Yoko. She's Japanese." Then he called her and she came over. After awhile Shotton went to bed. When he got up the next morning John told him what his plans were. He was sitting in the kitchen, calmly eating eggs and toast when he told Pete that he hadn't even been to bed yet. Something had happened to him during the night and he was very excited about it. "Will you do us a favor?" Lennon asked. "Could you get us a house? This is it." And it was the end of his first marriage.

When Cynthia returned from her trip to Greece, in May of 1968, she found John and Yoko having breakfast together in her house. They were in their bathrobes, or rather, John was in his bathrobe, Yoko was actually wearing one of Cynthia's. She was stunned beyond belief.

When she walked into the kitchen John was standing there with a cup of hot tea. Yoko was sitting at the kitchen table with her back to Cynthia, but she recognized the hair right away. Then Yoko turned around to face John's wife with no hint of guilt on her face. Cynthia just stared at her, unable to comprehend what she was seeing. This woman seemed to her to be such an unlikely rival for John's affection. To begin with she was eight years older than John and more than a little out of shape. Not only that, but she was married herself and had a six-year-old daughter. "Oh, hi." Ono said.

Cynthia tried to act as if nothing out of the ordinary was happening. She said shakily, "We were all thinking of going out for dinner." Jenny and Magic Alex were still there, but they weren't saying a word. "We had breakfast in Greece and lunch in Rome, and we thought it would be lovely to have dinner in London. Are you coming?"

"No thanks." John replied.

Cynthia turned and ran out of the kitchen in tears. She started running from room to room gathering up her things. Jenny tried to help her while Magic Alex just watched in dumbfounded amazement. When she had gathered up enough of her possessions to get by on, she left the house with them again. Her mind was racing. She started thinking back on all the events that had led up to this moment. Why hadn't she seen it coming? She just couldn't understand why Yoko was the woman who finally helped to end her marriage. For as long as she could remember there was always some woman or other after John. But somehow he had never been tempted to leave her for them, until Yoko. She had something that the others didn't have, dogged perseverance that bordered on obsession. Ever since she had met John at her art exhibit at the Indica gallery she had been unshakable. In retrospect, she could see how John financing her schemes had only served to encourage her. The security guards at Abbey Road used to joke that Ono was part of the fence. Once, she actually threatened to chain herself to the front gates in an attempt to get in and see John. Yoko, in a word, was intense.

When these tactics didn't work, Yoko started her assault on his home life. She hit their house with such a barrage of phone calls that John was forced to have the number changed four times, but that still didn't stop her. When she couldn't reach him by phone she started sending dozens of letters. The letters first insisted, then demanded more money for her art projects. She even started threatening to kill herself if John didn't pay attention to her. Cynthia kept some of these letters to protect John in case she actually followed through with it.

Soon after that, Yoko took to showing up at their house in person. She would stand out in the driveway waiting for John to come out. She stood there from early in the morning until late at night, no matter what the weather, wearing the same scruffy black sweater and beat up old shoes. One day Cynthia's mother took pity on her and let her in to get a drink of water. She used the opportunity to leave her ring behind so that she could come back for it the next day. But it didn't stop there.

One night Yoko even showed up at a transcendental meditation lecture that the couple attended in London. When it was over, not only did she follow them out of the building, she even climbed into John's psychedelic Rolls between them. John and Cynthia exchanged embarrassed smiles over her head until the chauffeur dropped her off at Park Row, where she was still living with her husband and daughter. It was that night that Cynthia had asked John if he fancied Yoko. John just laughed it off.

Cynthia stood in the driveway staring back at the house in silence. Now this strange little woman had managed to take John away from her. As she loaded her suitcase into the trunk of the taxi with the luggage from her trip she wondered again: "Why?" Jenny and Alex offered to let her stay with them at their flat until she could get everything sorted out in her mind. As Cynthia gazed out the window watching the London streets flash by she realized that there had been some grain of truth in her suspicions after all...

Shortly after that, Asher traveled to America on an extended tour with the Bristol Old Vic theater company. Regrettably, the press was more interested in her relationship with the young McCartney than in her acting ability.

Before Asher returned to England after her tour, Paul surprised her by meeting her in Denver, Colorado, to celebrate her twenty-first birthday. He put together a lavish party in honor of the occasion. It was during the flight back to England that the idea for *Magical Mystery Tour* first occurred to him.

On Christmas Day in 1967 Beatle Paul finally asked Jane to marry him. He presented her with a diamond and emerald engagement ring, and, of course, she said yes.

In early 1968 Asher went away again on another theater tour. During her absence, Paul's roving eye got the best of him and he cheated on her with an over-zealous fan. In fact, he even moved her into their home while Jane was gone. When she returned unexpectedly in July, she found the two in bed together. It broke her heart. She turned and ran back down the stairs and out the front door never to return. Later that same month she appeared on a BBC television show and announced that their engagement was off.. Ironically, Paul had visited a psychic in Brighton just prior to the end of his relationship with Jane. She had told him that he would end up marrying a blonde and having four children. But that comes later in the story.

Last but not least, there is Ringo's relationship with the woman who was to become his first wife, Maureen Cox. Maureen left school at the age of fifteen to begin a career as a junior hairdressing assistant. She first met Ringo when she spotted him on the way to one of her hair-styling lessons. He was getting out of his Ford Zodiac when she asked him for his autograph. At that time Ringo was still with Rory Storm and the Hurricanes and Maureen was dating a guitarist from the group. Because she was the girlfriend of one of his mates he didn't actually start to date her himself until about three weeks after he had joined with the Beatles. She was standing in a crowd of girls in front of the Cavern Club. He smiled shyly at her as he went inside and asked her if she was going to be at the show the following night. She said she was. Ringo asked her if she wanted to go out with him after the show, but she couldn't because the show didn't get over until late and she had to be home before midnight. By this time she had turned sixteen and her parents enforced a strict curfew. Working under these restrictions, Ringo and Maureen's first real date ended up starting in the afternoon. Ringo picked her up at the beauty parlor that day, but when he first arrived she wasn't there. The other girls who worked there had sent her out to do some shopping; Maureen had been so nervous that she couldn't keep her mind on her work. Ringo waited for her in the reception area while all of the ladies in the shop made a big fuss over him.

Ringo and Maureen's first date together went very well. They went to the park, then to hear Frank Ifield sing. Afterwards, Ringo took her to a double-feature at the movies. After that, they went to the Pink Parrot bar for drinks and then to Allan William's Blue Angel club for a last dance. Even after all of this, Ringo still got Maureen home at ten minutes to midnight.

At first the couple tried to keep their relationship a secret. Ringo even denied that he knew a Maureen Cox to the papers. It just wasn't fashionable in those days for sex symbols like the Beatles to admit to having girlfriends. When the girls of Liverpool did find out about the affair Maureen was forced to quit her job at the salon because she was constantly being threatened.

When Maureen was eighteen, Ringo asked her father for her hand in marriage. They were married on February 11, 1965. The ceremony was held at Caxton Hall, the registry office closest to Montague Square. Ringo became a father in September of the same year and they decided to begin looking for a bigger house.

By the end of 1966, the couple moved to St. George's Hill, near the Lennon's. They called the house Sunny Heights. It was on this property that Ringo built the go-cart track that is featured in some of the Beatles publicity photos. He also started a custom mural in his game room, but he lost interest in it halfway through the project. He let his guests add to it over the years and it became quite a conversation piece. The couple's white Tudor house had twenty-six rooms, to which Ringo added a sauna, swimming pool, and numerous stained glass windows. He even built his own recording studio, calling it Starling Studio on the premises. Ringo wanted to make so many changes to his new home that he formed his own construction company. That way he could take out walls and add on rooms as he pleased. He built a whole new wing, with an extra living room, a third guest room, a workroom for his audio and video equipment, a private screening room, and a billiard room with a pool table flown in from the United States especially for the master of the house. He liked to tell this story whenever he played on it, which was quite often, as pool soon became a passion with him.

Price was no object at all when it came to decorating the house. Ringo actually had a piece of carpet for the living room custom woven so it would all be in one piece, because he detested the way that the seams looked when the carpet had to be cut. The couple also had six television sets, intra-room stereo systems, and more than twenty telephones (two per room, including a hotline to Brian's office). Ringo also made sure that he bought every imaginable kind of electronic gadget on the market at the time.

The Starkey's, along with Paul and Jane, joined the Lennon's and Harrison's at the Vasrmas Yoga Ashram in the Himalayas in early 1968. They showed up more to be part of the group than out of any spiritual connection with the place. When they arrived the staff showed them around a compound of stone cottages; each with five rooms and a four-poster bed, a swimming pool, laundry, open air amphitheater, post office, and dining hall. Needless to say, it was much less primitive than they had expected.

John and Paul wrote a lot of songs while they were on retreat in India. John wrote "Dear Prudence" as a dedication to Mia Farrow's reclusive sister. They seemed to be really enjoying their time at the Ashram. Ringo, on the other hand, was becoming pretty miserable. His stomach had always been delicate and the strange food in this land wasn't helping it any. Besides, he and Maureen missed their children and they wanted to get back to England. They were the first couple to leave the Maharishi behind.

Ringo met the woman that he was destined to have an affair with, Nancy Andrews, in California. Besides being an American she was eight years younger than Ringo. They ended up being together for a total of six years, but Ringo never did marry her. They did get featured in the papers together and she got her photo on some of his album sleeves. They even wrote a song together called "Las Brisas," which made it onto the album *Ringo Rotogravure*.

While all this was going on Maureen was still hoping that their love would weather this storm. She really didn't want to divorce Ringo. She finally started to realize the depth of his feelings for Nancy when Ringo began spending months at a time overseas. Ringo admitted the affair and suggested that they get a divorce. He even recommended a good lawyer for her. Maureen was absolutely heartbroken. The divorce hearing took place on July 17, 1975. Just before the hearing Nancy once again appeared in public with Ringo, when they went on a tour of Europe together, and pictures of them together were splashed all over the papers. Maureen showed up for the hearing noticeably upset over the publicity. She got custody of the children and they went to live in the house he had bought them in Little Venice. Even after the divorce Ringo took very good care of his ex-wife and children as well as her parents, but Maureen never really got over him.

Soon after the divorce, Ringo bought Tittenhurst Park from John and Yoko and turned it into a rental property and recording studio. Then, mainly for tax purposes, he signed the $1.7 million dollar property over to his children. He also gave up his British residency for tax reasons and bought a condo on the side of a cliff in Monte Carlo, where he then took up residency.

Ringo had always been attracted to life in the fast lane and he loved beautiful young women. That is what had initially attracted him to Miss Andrews. At first they were happy together in Monte Carlo, but then Ringo began to gamble heavily and they traveled from country to country almost constantly. It seemed as if he was always looking for the next big party.

Nancy eventually tired of their perpetual life in the fast lane. She left Ringo and went back to L.A., slapping him with a seven million dollar palimony suit into the bargain. Life in the fast lane caught up with Ringo in 1979 when he was rushed to a Monte Carlo hospital in critical condition. All of his drinking and carousing had finally caught up with his sensitive stomach and doctors actually had to remove part of his intestines. But as soon as he recovered from the surgery he returned to his old lifestyle.

While Maureen and Ringo were still living in Weybridge, Ringo had rented out their old flat to Jimi Hendrix, who painted the entire place black, including the furniture and silk wallpaper. Candles were burned on every table, scorching them with hot wax. Ringo sued Hendrix for destroying the place and the case was settled out of court.

Buttons, Old and New

"Flip-Buttons," also known as flasher buttons, came in blue and red. When the button is tilted back and forth, it flashes from the picture to the logo. These rings measure 2 1/2" in diameter. Value per button: G: $15 E: $20 NM: $25. Display card for Vari-Vue flip buttons would hold up to twelve flip-buttons. Value for empty display card: G: $100 E: $125 NM: $175.

Buttons put out by Green Duck Co.: a total of nine 1" metal buttons, including a cut gum dispenser label and a "Beatles 1964 Originals" display sheet. Value given is for all shown: G: $120 E: $150 NM: $175.

These four photos show some of the different faces and colors of the Vari-Vue buttons. The values are the same.

Another "Be A Beatle Booster!" button. This button has a red plastic 1/2" rim and measures 3" in diameter. Value: G: $10 E: $15 NM: $20.

Fan club buttons (left & right), put out by Green Duck, declare "Be A Beatle Booster!" Button (center) measures approximately 2 1/2" in diameter and is made of plastic. Fan club buttons measure approximately 3 1/2" and 2" in diameter. Value for the fan club buttons: Left: G: $5 E: $7 NM: $9. Right: G: $10 E: $15 NM: $20. Center: G: $10 E: $15 NM: $20.

Button, radio promotional: "The Beatles Sound Best on KRLA." This is a large button, approximately 3" in diameter, printed in red, white, and blue. Value: E: $8 NM: $10.

"Beatlemanie" button from Montreal: this large button, approximately 3" in diameter, has two red stars in the center on each side, "Yeah! Yeah! Yeah!" printed around the base of the yellow button, and the center of the button depicts a screaming fan. Value: E: $8 NM: $10.

New Buttons

Buttons, newer vintage: Yellow Sub cartoon characters of the group on two buttons. The button on the right has repeating faces. Value for each: E: $3 NM: $5.

Buttons, from, "Live at the BBC.":, pinback buttons with an attached 6" x 8" card. The buttons measure 1 1/4" in diameter each. Value given is for the set: E: $25 NM: $35.

Buttons, (enlarged to show detail) newer vintage: no markings. Value per button: E: $3 NM: $5.

As I mentioned in the previous chapter, Paul had come up with the idea for *Magical Mystery Tour* while on a flight from America back to England. He was just sitting there on the plane making some notes as to what their next project should be after *Sgt. Peppers Lonely Hearts Club Band*. He got the idea for this next venture from reading the writing of Ken Kesey about his adventures on a bus traveling cross-country with an unlikely group of hippies who called themselves the Merry Pranksters. Paul started to draw pictures of clowns, fat ladies and midgets in an attempt to put his idea in sharper focus.

Six days after the death of their manager, Brian Epstein, Paul arranged a meeting at his home to discuss the new project. McCartney wanted it to be an hour long TV special. By the time the group met Paul had already written part of the title song. He also planned for the production to be recorded, produced, scripted, directed, and edited by the Beatles, or more specifically, Paul himself.

A formal script was never written for the film. The Beatles worked entirely from an outline that seemed to change almost daily. John halfheartedly contributed a dream sequence that included the strange combination of fat ladies and spaghetti. The closest thing that they even had to a written synopsis of the production was a press release that read: "Away in the sky, beyond the clouds, live four or five musicians. By casting wonderful spells they turn the most Ordinary Coach Trip into a Magical Mystery Tour." The film was an unmitigated disaster. If Brian had still been alive he never would have allowed such a catastrophe.

On Monday September 11, a sixty-seat yellow and blue bus with signs on the sides that identified it as the Magical Mystery Tour, took off to Devon and Cornwall with a cast and crew of forty-three aboard. Carloads of Fleet Street reporters followed them along with ten to fifteen fans in their own cars. At Teigen the local constable escorted them out of town for disturbing the peace. Then they changed directions and headed for Brighton, where they filmed two disabled people sunning on the beach. When they stopped to eat, however, they discovered that they were thirty lunches short of being able to feed the cast and crew. Not only that, but the first night on the road the sleeping quarters had been underbooked and Paul and Neil Aspinall had to spend hours mediating arguments between fat ladies and dwarfs about who had to share a room with whom.

The next day they started out to the north. Wherever they went chaos seemed to follow. John finally got so fed up with it that he ordered the bus driver to stop. Then he stormed out the door and ripped the signs off the sides of the bus, tossing them into the dirt. Lennon was livid.

"They should have filmed that." Neil chortled, echoing the sentiments of everyone except Paul.

It was McCartney's plan to film the final scene of the movie at Shepperton Studios outside of London. Unfortunately, no one had thought to book any time on the sound stage. In desperation they leased an old airfield in West Mailing, Kent. A huge set was quickly erected. The scene for the grand finale employed over forty dwarfs, a dozen babies, and a military marching band in full regalia—a McCartney favorite.

When the production was finally finished Paul screened it for everyone at N.E.M.S. It was unanimously pronounced awful and most everyone wanted Paul to scrap it rather than air it and publicly embarrass the Beatles. McCartney's ego simply wouldn't let him do that. He was sure that he could still make the film a box office success. The rights to the show were sold to the BBC and it was shown on boxing day, December 26th. The critics called it, "blatant rubbish" then went on to say, "The bigger they are the harder they fall..." *L.A. Daily Variety* commented, "Critics and Viewers Boo: Beatles Produce First Flop With Yule Film."

The reviews were so bad that Paul ended up making a public apology on the front page of the *Evening Standard* for the fiasco. The film did manage to gross two million dollars from rentals to colleges. The soundtrack, however, proved to be a different story (the movie was so bad that it never even aired in America). The movie soundtrack grossed eight million dollars in its first ten days of release. It was released as an EP in England, where it hit the number one spot. This proved what United Artists had said when they endorsed *Hard Days' Night*. A Beatles film could end up being a complete flop and money could still be made on the soundtrack. But it did turn out to be a rather expensive lesson.

The next big Beatles project turned out to be an animated feature length film called *Yellow Submarine*. It was licensed by King Features and the Beatles hoped fervently that it would fulfill the stipulation in the Beatles United Artists contract for a third movie. While United Artists rejected *Yellow Sub* as the third movie in the deal, it later acted as a distributor for the piece, after it became an artistic triumph and a commercial success. The Beatles themselves had almost nothing to do with the making of this film, aside from composing the songs for it. Their voices were not even used and the voices that were used were very different from the actual quality and texture of the Beatles' own. The plot was written by Erich Segal, who later became a best-selling author of romance novels. The script was a psychedelic fantasy with political overtones. The Blue Meanies and Apple Bonkers were out to ruin fun as we know it. The Beatles set sail in the yellow submarine to Pepperland, so they could take the place of Sgt. Pepper's lonely hearts club band and save the day. Many strange things happen along the way. They pass through the sea of holes as well as having an adventure back and forth through time and growing both older and younger. They also meet Jeremy the Boob who is a nowhere man. In the end they do save the day and restore full color back to Pepperland.

The film opened in London on July 17, 1968. The initial reviews were not good at all, but that was probably due, in part, to the failure of *Magical Mystery Tour*. At first people were afraid to go and see another Beatles movie because of it, but as soon as it was viewed by the public it became very popular. It has reached the proportions of a cult classic with collectors, many of who collect only that specific genre of memorabilia. These are now some of the most rare and sought after collectibles on the market.

The last movie in the Beatles three picture deal was a bittersweet true life documentary of the groups disintegration. This film was originally Paul's idea and was supposed to be about the Beatles getting back to their roots and touring again. It would have been a great documentary, but none of the other boys wanted to go on the road again. In the end, all he could talk the others into was a documentary about the group making an album in the studio. However, they did end the documentary with a live performance. That is how the film *Get Back* became *Let It Be* and, in retrospect, a more fitting title could not have been chosen for this work.

The Beatles assembled on a sound stage at Twickenham Film Studios on January 2, 1970 to begin production on the project. An angry and tense atmosphere permeated the air from the start. Two sixteen millimeter cameras were running the whole time the album was being made and they captured some very volatile scenes. The Fabs fought almost constantly and they couldn't really get into the creative process. Paul tried to keep everyone motivated, but he came off as being rather pushy instead. He tried to tell the others how to play on each song, explaining every drum set, guitar line and

vocal, which became very annoying. John, George, and Ringo basically felt as if he were treating them like a backup group. They argued so much that after ten days of taping they really hadn't gotten anywhere. They decided to finish the album in their own Apple studio. Of course then all the problems that I discussed with Magic Alex's designs, or lack of designs, only made the situation more tense. When they finally did get the equipment they needed, Paul started trying to take over again. He tried to explain to George just exactly how he wanted him to play the guitar and George lost it, saying: "Look, I'll play whatever you want me to play, or I won't play at all! Whatever it is that'll please you, I'll do it!" Then when they took a lunch break he got into his car and left, vowing never to return. But after taking a few days to cool off, he showed up at the next business meeting and continued to work on the project. There were a number of these sort of episodes between the boys, but eventually they did manage to finish the album.

The final live concert on the roof of the Apple building is probably what saved the film. It takes a very grim story of a group falling apart and shows them pulling together one final time as the Beatles. Billy Preston played with them on that gig, making history in the process. It was bitter cold the day that they filmed this sequence, but they set up their equipment and started to play. The noise from the rooftop caused a crowd of people to gather in the street below. It didn't take the public long to realize what was happening. People were hanging out of windows and gathering on the adjoining rooftops to cheer the Beatles on. As the momentum of the event started to build the police arrived to try and stop it, but by then it was too late. The Beatles had already given their last public performance. Then John, in his Lennonesque style, bowed and said: "I would like to thank you on behalf of the group and myself and I hope we passed the audition." And the Beatles were no more ...

Clothing & Accessories

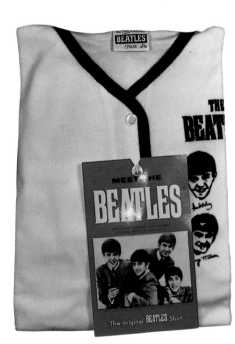

Dress, made in Holland: polka dot fabric with black and white faces of the Beatles in a vertical line down the front of the dress. On the right side of dress is a white guitar with both "The Beatles" printed on the upper section and copies of their signatures on the lower section of the guitar. G: $425 E: $575 NM: $700.

A shirt from 1964 with "The Only Authentic Beatles Shirt" tag sewn inside the collar. This shirt is white with black trim and has copies of the Beatles signatures beneath their faces, which are in the upper left corner of the garment. It originally came with the tag shown here, which adds 60% to the value given. Value: $65 E: $90 NM: $120.

Long-sleeved sweatshirt with fan club pose and "The Beatles" lettered above it. Value: G: $60 E: $75 NM: $95.

Jeans, with original insert and hang tags. The label reads: "Lybro SlimJeans." The style shown here is the "Ringo." Value is with everything mentioned: G: $375 E: $400 NM: $450.

This is a close-up of the insert that came with the jeans. As you can see, there are four different styles shown.

63

Shoes

Sneakers by Wing Dings, with the original box. The shoes are blue and are again decorated with the Beatles pictures, along with copies of their signatures. The sneakers are made of a canvas-type material with rubber soles. If the original box is not present, you must subtract 60% from the value given. Value: G: $450 E: $600 NM: $700.

Sneakers by Wing Dings, with the original box. The Fab Four is pictured on the box with copies of their signatures underneath. The sneakers are white, decorated with black printed faces and signatures. The shoes are made of a canvas-type material with rubber soles. If the original box is missing, you must subtract 60% from the value given. Value: G: $300 E: $ 400 NM: $475.

Sneakers by Wing Dings, with the original box. The Beatles are pictured along with copies of their signatures. The sneakers came with the original card you see here. If the card and box are not present subtract 75% from the value given. Value; G: $400 E: $550 NM: $625.

Nylons & Garter

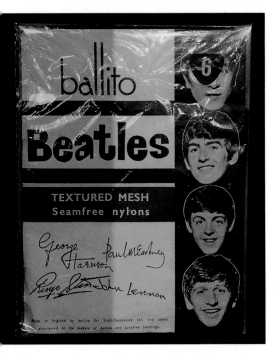

These nylons are manufactured by BRI Nylon, Scott Centenaire Ltd. These Carefree nylons are made in England and the value given includes the original packaging: G: $100 E: $125 NM: $150.

Nylons manufactured by Ballito, Scott Centenaire Ltd. This product is made in the U.K. The nylons are made of a textured mesh which is seamless. The Beatles faces can be seen on them as well as various guitars. You can also read their logo, "The Beatles," which appears along with each Fab's first name under his picture around the waistband of the hose. The value given is with the original packaging. Value: G: $100 E: $125 NM: $150.

Garter put out by Leonard Page and Company Ltd., United Kingdom. The garter itself is made of velvet and lace and came in assorted colors with a black and white fan club pose image. Value (sealed): G: $125 E: $155 NM: $185.

"Beatles Kinder Mini Pantyhose," with the original packaging. This item is previously undocumented to the best of my knowledge. The package contains a pair of nylons to fit a small child. Value with original package: G: $25 E: $35 NM: $40.

Purses and Bags

Black vinyl clutch purse with Beatles fan club pose and copies of the Fabs signatures in white. Their "The Beatles" logo can be found in the lower left corner. The bag measures 6" x 9 1/2" and comes in a variety of colors. Value: G: $140 E: $175 NM: $200.

White clutch purse with the Fabs and copies of their signatures in black. This purse has a leather strap attached to the zipper top. The bag is made of canvas, measuring 9 1/2" x 5 1/2", and comes with a card bearing a fan club pose. If the card is missing, subtract 10% from the value given: G: $200 E: $ 240 NM: $ 275.

Red vinyl clutch purse with Beatles fan club pose and copies of the group's signatures. Their logo "the Beatles" can be found in the lower left hand corner. The bag measures 6" x 9 1/2" and comes in assorted colors. Value: G: $140 E: $175 NM: $200.

White handbag featuring the Beatles' images and copies of their signatures. This bag has a brass handle and a built-in zipper pouch. The purse measures 10" x 10". Value: G: $325 E: $375 NM: $450.

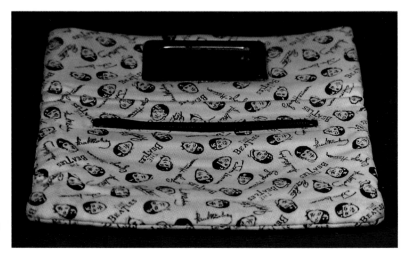

Black vinyl handbag with brass handles. "The Beatles" logo appears along with copies of their signatures in the lower left hand corner and along the base of the bag. The handbag measures 10" x 10" and came in assorted colors. Value: G: $250 E: $325 NM: $400.

White vinyl handbag with brass handles. "The Beatles" logo, along with copies of their signatures, appear in the lower left hand corner and near the bag's bottom. The item measures 10" x 10" and came in several different colors. Value: G: $250 E: $325 NM: $400.

Beige vinyl shoulder bag with black chord straps. The Beatles fan club pose along with copies of their signatures appears in black. The bag measures 9 1/2" x 10" and came in a number of different colors. Value: G: $250 E: $325 NM: $400.

Tan vinyl shoulder bag with a fan club pose and copies of the Fabs signatures appearing in black. This bag measures 9 1/2" x 10" and came in a variety of colors. Value: G: $250 E: $325 NM: $400.

White vinyl shoulder bag with a fan club pose and copies of the Beatles signatures. The bag measures 9 1/2" x 10" and has jute handles. Value: G: $250 E: $325 NM: $400.

White vinyl "Go Go" bag with vinyl handles on the top. This bag has a black and white fan club pose of the Beatles in the center. A sort of wreath of red lines surrounds the Fabs. The bag says "Go Go Beatles" across the top and still has the original hang tag. The back of the bag is made of blue vinyl. This item is made in Japan. If original hang tag is missing subtract 20% from value given. Value: G: $125 E: $175 NM: $225.

This photo shows the back of the "Go Go" bag , on opposite page bottom left, along with the original tag.

Caps & Hats

"The Ringo Cap" came in a variety of styles and colors (shown here). Value: G: $125 E: $150 NM: $165.

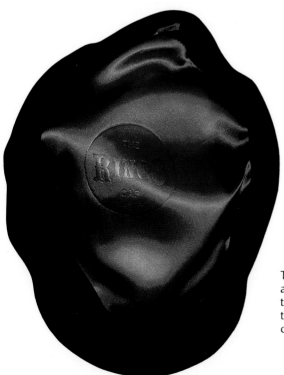 

This photo allows you to see the interior of the black Ringo cap.

The inside of the brown Ringo cap.

Black leather Lennon hat. Value: G: $125 E: $150 NM: $165.

Beach hat made by Lamron Co. It has a white front with a blue brim. "The Beatles" is printed on each side, while on the front you can find the Fabs faces along with copies of their signatures. Value: G: $80 E: $100 NM: $125.

Beach hat made by Lamron Co. It has a white front with a red brim. "The Beatles" is printed on each side, while on the front you can find the Fab's faces along with copies of their signatures. Value: G: $80 E: $100 NM: $125.

Hangers

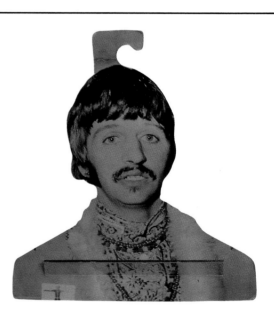

Die cut cardboard hangar with Ringo on either side. The hangers were put out by Saunders Ent., United Kingdom. Value: G: $80 E: $110 NM: $135.

Hanger made of die cut cardboard with a black and white photo of a Beatle on either side of each one. This picture is of George and the item is put out by Saunders Ent. of the United Kingdom. There is one hanger for each Fab. Value: G: $80 E: $110 NM: $135.

Halloween Costumes

The John Lennon Halloween costume put out by Ben Cooper. You can see the original packaging in the picture. The costume includes a plastic mask with brown hair and a shirt. A patch on the front reads, "Yeah! Yeah! Yeah!" If the original box is missing, you must subtract half of the value given. Value: G: $550 E: $675 NM: $775.

Paul McCartney Halloween costume, also put out by Ben Cooper. The costume includes a plastic mask with brown hair and a shirt. A patch on the front says, "Yeah! Yeah! Yeah!" If the original box is missing, you must subtract half of the value given. Paul and Ringo are the two most commonly found costumes in the set. This makes the value of this costume somewhat lower. Value: G: $475 E: $525 NM: $600.

George Harrison Halloween costume put out by Ben Cooper. The costume includes a plastic mask with brown hair and a shirt. A patch on the front says, "Yeah! Yeah! Yeah!" If the original box is missing, you must subtract half of the value given. Value: G: $550 E: $675 NM: $775.

Ringo Starr Halloween costume by Ben Cooper. The costume includes a plastic mask with brown hair and a shirt. A patch on the front says, "Yeah! Yeah! Yeah!" If the original box is missing, you must subtract half of the value given. Value: G: $475 E: $525 NM: $600.

Scarves

Red triangular scarf.: has vinyl strips along the top side to be used as ties under the chin. The scarf features a fan club pose and copies of the Beatles signatures. These scarves come in an assortment of colors. Value: G: $70 E: $85 NM: $100.

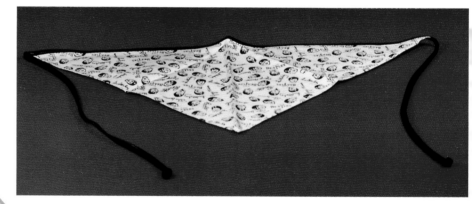

White triangular scarf: has black vinyl strips along the top side to be used as ties under the chin. The scarf features a fan club pose and copies of the Fabs' signatures. Comes in a variety of colors. Value; G: $70 E: $85 NM: $100.

Yellow handkerchief with red lettering. It has the Fabs' faces centered on the top in black. "The Beatles" appears in red underneath the group's faces. There are also song titles, guitars, drums, stars and, at the base of the hankie, you can see a big heart along with copies of the Beatles signatures. Value: G: $30 E: $40 NM: $50.

Blue scarf with beetle bugs and copies of the Fab Fours' signatures. The scarf is made by Scammonden Woolen Co. Ltd. of London. This scarf is shown with its original black and white hang tag, which is included in its value assessment. Subtract 20% from value given if missing hang tag. Value: G: $150 E: $175 NM: $225.

Green and white apron with black silhouettes of the mop tops. Features a repeating pattern and is previously undocumented. Value: G: $275 E: $325 NM: $375.

This Beatles blanket is put out by Whitney of the United Kingdom. There is a picture of each Beatle, with his first name beneath it, and "The Beatles" logo in the center. It measures 80" x 62". Value: G: $250 E: $300 NM: $350.

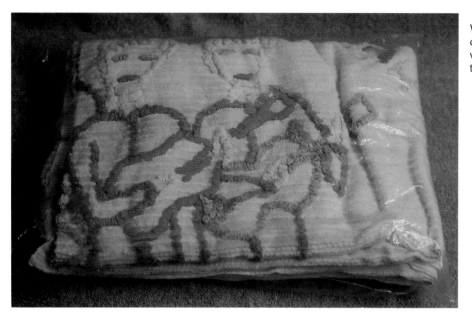

White chenille bedspread, in several different colors. The Beatles appear in the middle along with the saying "Yeah! Yeah! Yeah!" across the top. Value: G: $325 E: $375 NM: $450.

This is a wider overview of the bedspread.

Beach Towel, made by Towel Decorators, NEMS. It has "The Beatles" along with their first names and says "Yeah! Yeah! Yeah!" across the bottom. They are wearing swimsuits in the picture. It measures 65" x 35". Value: G: $125 E: $175 NM: $225.

New Clothing, Memorabilia and Accessories

This jacket was produced to commemorate the Beatles 1964 World Tour. It is made by Home Town Hero Limited Edition Jacket Co., San Francisco. This jacket comes with a CD jewel box as well as a numbered certificate. This particular item is number 1341 of 10,000. Value: E: $180 NM: $200.

Cavern Club T-shirt with Pete Best's autograph on the scene on the shirt's lower left. It is a white T-shirt with a scene of a band on stage. It was purchased at the new Cavern Club in Liverpool. Value: E: $100 NM: $125.

This T-shirt came from The Beatles Shop in Liverpool, England. The shirt reads, "It was a Hard Day's Night In Liverpool. The Birthplace of the Beatles." This T-shirt features clipped head shots of the Fab Four across the center front. Value given is with the original packaging: E: $35 NM: $40.

CD size book and T-shirt boxed set. The shirt is by Winterland Productions and the book was put out through Omnibus Press in 1996, A Division of Music Sales Corporation. Value; E: $35 NM: $40.

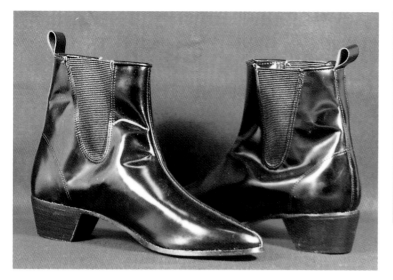

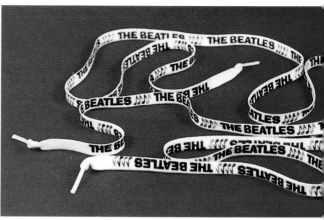

Beatles shoe strings in white with blue lettering and musical notes in various colors forming a repeating pattern. Value per pair: E: $5 NM: $7.

Beat Boots, 1996, no markings. These are black Beatles style boots with elastic for easy fit. Goes very nicely with Mr. Dailey's collection and makes it seem as though one of the Fabs just left the room for a moment. Value: E: $65 NM: $75.

Colorful Beatles character socks with each Fab's first name above his picture. Original tags should be present. Value: E: $7 NM: $10.

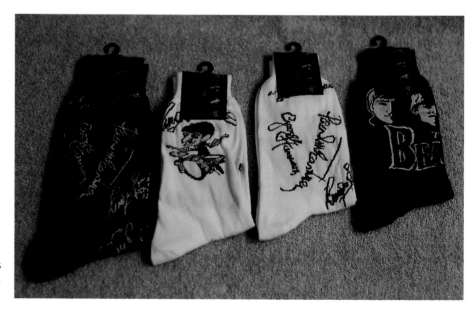

Another style of Beatles socks with original tags. Value: E: $7 NM: $10.

Black and white silk boxer shorts with a Beatles theme come in a number of different variations. Value: E: $25 NM: $30.

Neckties

Beatles neckties are made of a rich blend of silk and manmade fabrics, manufactured by Ralph Marlin. Several different styles are available. These ties vary in value. Value given is per tie: E: $15 NM: $30.

More Beatles ties.

Other varieties of the ties. The values are the same as those on the previous page.

Miscellaneous Items

Beatles theme suspenders also came in several different styles. They have brass fittings. Value: E: $15 NM: $20.

Other versions of the suspenders. Same values.

Reproduction of the 1964 dress pattern from the Netherlands. This is the fabric, not the actual dress. It was put out in 1995. Value: E: $20 NM: $25.

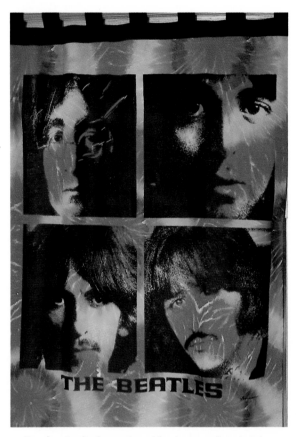

Beatles tie-died curtains with pictures of each Fab on them. Photos are from the White Album with John and Paul on top and George and Ringo on the bottom. They are made by Lifestyle Products Inc. Each panel of Fab fabric measures 45" x 40". This particular fabric has been made into curtains and the value given is for two curtain panels. Value: E: $30 NM: $40.

1988 beach towel by Apple Corp. Ltd. It is a rather colorful towel with "The Beatles" printed in yellow across the center bottom edge. The towel has a red border and features black silhouettes of the Fab Four in a Dezo Hoffman style pose. Value: E: $20 NM: $25.

Fanny pack, black with white lettering that says "The Beatles," from "The Bealtes Shop" in Liverpool, England. There is a zipper pouch in the top. Value: E: $18 NM: $22.

School bag from "The Beatles Shop" in Liverpool, England. The bag is black with white faces across the center. There are copies of the Fab's signatures in red underneath the faces. The bag has a handle as well as a shoulder strap. Value: E: $35 NM: $45.

This scarf is a souvenir of Liverpool. The red, white, and blue neckscarf has "The Beatles Liverpool" in black lettering and simply "The Beatles" on the head of the Ludwig drum. It is sealed in the original packaging. Value: E: $17 NM: $20.

Blue, white, and yellow cap with "The Beatles" printed in black on the front. There is a photo of the group receiving their MBE medals. This hat was a carnival giveaway. Value: E: $15 NM: $20.

Wristbands. Maker unknown. These garments are red and white with "The Beatles" on the white strip at the top and the bottom. Value for the pair: E: $5 NM: $8.

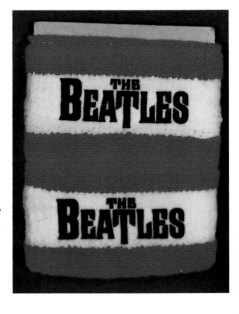

Each of the Beatles has made a legacy for himself in his own right, both with the group and on their own. I thought it would be interesting to look at them each, as individuals. George Harrison has received such labels as "the quiet one" and "the just a Beatle, Beatle" over the years. He is really a very fascinating and talented person. Much of Beatle lore tends to ignore both his contributions to the history of music and his own history as a human being. I think that it is high time somebody cleared that up.

George Harold Harrison was born to Louise and Harry Harrison at 12:10 a.m. on February 25, 1943. The first indication his mother had that he was interested in music came when he was thirteen years old. She was tidying up and picked up some of his notebooks from school. She couldn't help but notice that they were literally covered with sketches of guitars. As a surprise she bought him a very inexpensive acoustic guitar. At first George really showed little interest in it. In fact he kept it in an upstairs closet for the next three months. When he finally did pick it up, he found it very difficult to learn to play. He almost gave up several times, but something inside him just wouldn't let him give it up. Sometimes he would sit up all night practicing until his fingers bled. Through all of this his mother continued to encourage him.

With lots of practice, determination, and many long hours spent listening to other groups' records and trying to copy them, George began to be an excellent player. He soon outgrew his first guitar and was ready for something a little more advanced. Louise started saving up her household money until she had enough to spend thirty pounds on a good, solid wide-body acoustic guitar with white inlaid trim. George, being the independent young lad that he was, decided to earn the money to pay his mum back for the instrument. He never was the type of person who would accept what he considered to be charity from anyone. So he got a job with a local butcher and spent his Saturdays as a delivery boy.

George was destined to meet Paul McCartney while on the bus on his way to the Liverpool Institute. It was a long ride, about an hour each way, and it gave him plenty of time to daydream and horse around with the other boys. One of the boys, the son of a cotton salesman and an estate midwife from Allerton was really a lot of fun. His name was, you guessed it, Paul McCartney. Even though Paul was a year ahead of George in school, they quickly became friends. Paul was also very interested in music, and not only played the guitar, but owned his very own trumpet (his father was also a musician in his day).

Paul had been with John's band, the Quarrymen, for almost a year before he finally introduced George to the group. George recalls the very first time he met John Lennon: "I'd been invited to see them play several times by Paul, but for

some reason never got round to it before that. I remember being very impressed with John's big sideboards and trendy teddy boy clothes. He was terrible sarcastic from day one, but I never dared back down from him. Whenever he had a go at me, I just gave him a little bit of his own right back."

John was not terribly excited by the thought of having George in the group. It took some convincing before he would even give him a chance. Once it was all finally arranged, George tried out for the group by playing "Raunchy" for them in a basement club call The Morgue. He was formally brought in as a member on February 6, 1958, not long before his birthday. At least that is George's version of the story.

Paul tells a slightly different version of how George was accepted into the group. He claims that the audition took place on a bus that was on its way to Liverpool, but agrees that the try-out song was "Rauncy." Whichever story is true, George was now a Beatle.

The band got one of its first big breaks when they read in the paper that Britain's "Mr. Star Maker," Carroll Levis would be holding auditions at the Empire Theater in Liverpool for his *Carroll Levis Discoveries* TV show. It was scheduled to be filmed a few weeks later at the Manchester studio. An amazing variety of acts turned out for the occasion. John, Paul, and George called themselves the Moondogs for this audition. They actually were picked to be on the show. It was a beginning for the group.

Harrison met India's sitar virtuoso, Ravi Shankar, at a dinner party in the mid-sixties. He invited George and Patti to come to India so that George could study the instrument under him. It was the beginning of a long relationship as both associates and friends. These lessons enabled George to make Indian music a viable commercial commodity and part of the music mainstream.

The Harrisons did go to India in October of 1966 for a two month study vacation. They left London for Kashmir and spent their first night at Shankar's home in Bombay. Unfortunately the ever-present throng of Beatles fans gathered outside the house forcing them to leave because they could not concentrate on the lessons. Ravi took them to his Himalayan retreat where they spent the next seven weeks studying Indian mysticism and religion, and mastering the sitar, before returning to England.

On December 4, 1968, one of the more colorful events in the history of Apple occurred. The staff there received an alarming memo from Harrison explaining that several members of the Hell's Angels would be coming to visit the Beatles offices in London, sometime within the following week. He instructed the staff to show them around and be friendly with them ... without allowing them to take over the premises.

It seems that George had had a run in with Frisco Pete, the Hell's Angel who had approached him on the Haight-Ashbury street corner while he was in America the year before. Harrison had been checking out the scene in San Francisco. During their confrontation, George had invited him to come and visit him in London in an attempt to walk away from the situation unharmed. He never dreamed that Frisco Pete would actually take him up on his offer. Fortunately for everyone concerned only two Hell's Angels arrived at Heathrow airport. The others were refused visas because of pending criminal charges or due to the fact that they were still on parole or probation and consequently were not allowed to leave the country. Still, Frisco Pete showed up with his good friend Billy Tumbleweed and two motorcycles, which arrived collect ... Apple paid the shipping. The pair were followed to the Apple building by a band of smelly, stoned, long-haired California hippies wearing bells and love beads. The press office nicknamed them the California Pleasure Crew. The Apple crew was pretty shocked when the group first arrived, but recovered quickly and showed George's American "friends" around. Everyone was very civil to one another and no one got hurt, but that is the story of how the Hell's Angels invaded Apple.

I explained most of George and Patti's relationship earlier in the book, but I left off before I went into their buying Friar Park, a massive stone manor house in Henly on the Thames that actually once had been a convent. But I'm skipping ahead. Friar Park has been widely written about over the years because of its rather unusual construction. Sir Frank Crisp had the estate built and Sir Frank was an eccentric. Before George bought it there used to be guided tours of the property. The architecture is fascinating and I feel that the flavor of the house shed a great deal of light on the "quiet Beatle's" personality. If you didn't think that George was cool before you heard about his house and his lifestyle, you might want to re-think it now. I guess its those quiet ones who often have the most character.

Let me begin by explaining a little bit about why it is called Friar Park. The theme of the humble friar is evident almost everywhere you look on this vast estate. There are literally hundreds of stone statues of the whimsical little monks in the house as well as on the grounds. There is also a diverse mixture of Gargoyles along with interesting religious sayings over some of the doors and windows.

The friar free-for-all begins at the front gate with a dour looking fellow, carved in stone, standing there holding a battered old skillet. The sign beneath it reads, "Two holy friars." Now this gives you a sense of what you're in for right away. These fixtures really appealed to George's sense of humor. So much so that he took a picture of this piece and featured it on the inside bi-fold cover of his *Thirty-three and a Third* album. The best description of the estate, however, can be found in one of the old Friar Park guide books, if you can find one:

> Friars are met throughout the interior. Even the switches of the electric lights are the moveable noses of friars, which turn down and up as required. Friars also hold the electric lamps. The capitals of the pillars supporting the Hall show friars engaged in sleeping, dreaming, snoring, yawning and walking. In fact, friars in all profusion that any lover of friars could wish. (Giuliano 1989, 119)

As if this wasn't unusual enough, there are many more surprises to come. There are three beautiful manmade lakes on the estate. It seems that Sir Frank had one of the lakes equipped with stepping stones just below the surface of the water, so that one could give the appearance of walking across the surface of the lake. One can also find seven huge gardens, each with a different theme. One even includes a miniature replica of the Matterhorn which was built using 20,000 tons of gravel. The gardens were bursting at the seams with over 40,000 different varieties of flowers, plants, and trees. Sir Frank was, after all, a rather eccentric man who built the estate to suit his own tastes. It seems to suit George as well, as he is a very private person. He hasn't been too keen on visitors since John was murdered in 1980. Who can blame him? It is George's own private fantasyland, where he chooses to go to get away from the everyday world and be with his family.

There are still some wonderful and mysterious regions of the house left to be explored. Again, I referred to the Friar Park guide book, written back in the time of Sir Frank Crisp. The guide refers to the elaborate system of underground caves that were constructed beneath the home. After seeing pictures of, and reading about, George's Escher estate, this just seems to me to fit with his sort of personal taste. Sir Crisp had these underground caves flooded with water so that he and his guests could travel through them by boat. That way they could enjoy an after dinner cruise or a late night adventure, whatever struck their fancy. The caves were also lighted with soft pastel colored lights that added a truly mystical quality to the stalactite formations in the vast caverns. To make it more exciting, Crisp gave each of the separate caves a theme of its own. There was the skeleton cave which contained innumerable skeletal remains and distorting mirrors; the vine cave, with huge twisted knots of foliage hanging from the walls and ceiling and massive bunches of illuminated glass grapes, giving a sort of ethereal quality; and then there was the gnome cave, which was jam packed with the whimsical little fellows. Some of the statuary from this particular cave can be seen on the cover of George's *All Things Must Pass* album.

Each cave held its own special brand of romance and intrigue. Can you imagine the mind that came up with this fantasyland? Sir Frank was undoubtedly a very unusual person. He saw his hideaway as being more than a place to escape from the rat race; he saw it as a sort of doorway to a more spiritual realm. I think that it was on this level that it also appealed to George Harrison as he has always been a deeply spiritual person.

George purchased Friar Park in March of 1970 for $336,000. When he first bought it he really didn't know its full history. He had no idea that there was an elaborate cave system beneath the dwelling or even the extent of the estates original gardens. Between Sir Frank's ownership and that of George Harrison, the estate had become a convent and school for several years. The nuns covered over a lot of the original architecture, but George excavated the whole place after he found the original plans to Friar Park. It cost him hundreds of thousands of additional dollars to restore the eighty room manor house to its previous glory. The house was truly an elegant place with some rooms being as vast as ballrooms in a large hotel. Even the bathrooms were the size of an average flat in London.

During the excavation process, George discovered yet another interesting facet of the place. Besides the underground caves, there was a complete underground waterfall system. George added a few accouterments of his own to the place, including a swimming pool, heliport, tennis court, a rustic playhouse overlooking a beautiful clearing, an ornate fountain dedicated to Lord Shiva (from his religion), and of course, a state-of-the-art recording studio.

During this time George was very involved in the Krishna movement. He had always been a spiritual person and his home life started to incorporate his beliefs as well. He had his own personal guru, Bhaktivedanta Swami, the seventy-seven year old spiritual leader of the International Society for Krishna Consciousness. He invited this guru and several monks to come and live in one of the smaller houses on the grounds of his estate. Soon after that he began getting up with the sun to take a bath in cold water and study the Bhagarad-Gita (a book of the Krishna faith) before beginning his day.

Over the years Patti and George began to drift apart and their relationship became strained. Patti was lonely and miserable in the big house by herself. She was only twenty-six and had basically been relegated to staying at home for the rest of her life. George had forbidden her to have a career. She wouldn't have minded this so much if they had been able to have a family, but Patti was unable to get pregnant. This made her even more lonely and depressed. Patti was willing to pursue an adoption, but George was not. They had many arguments over this and Patti took to escaping to London for overnight shopping trips. Once, after a particularly heated discussion, Patti climbed up onto the roof of the manor house at Friar Park as far as the uppermost cupola, removed the OM symbol that always flew there, and replaced it with a pirate's skull and crossbones. You have to hand it to the Beatles couples, when they fought they really went all out.

By this time Ringo had purchased Tittenhurst Park from John and Yoko, who had moved to New York City. One night Ringo and Maureen invited George and Patti to dinner at their new place. After the meal they all sat around the table talking and George pulled out his guitar. He started to play it and sing love songs. Everyone was enjoying themselves when suddenly he put the instrument down and announced that he was in love with Ringo's wife. Maureen turned bright red and sort of shrunk into herself. Ringo stomped out of the room and Patti locked herself in the bathroom.

A few weeks later, when Patti returned from one of her shopping trips in London, she found George and Maureen in bed together. Neither Patti nor Maureen have either officially confirmed or denied this story, but shortly after this alleged incident both of the marriages ended.

Patti was very hurt by this incident. In a sort of combination of retaliation and self defense, she started to lead a more independent life again. She started to pursue her modeling career again, against George's wishes, and even made an appearance in an Ozzie Clark fashion show. It wasn't long before she found someone who caught her eye. Her first affair was with Ron Wood (now of the Rolling Stones).

Patti's most effective weapon against George eventually became his best friend, Eric Clapton. It had been rather obvious for quite some time to anyone who saw Patti and Eric together, including George, that Eric was in love with her. Still, that didn't stop the three of them from getting together, which often led to some very tense moments. One of the worst of these occurred at a party at Clapton's house. She and George had both been invited to the party, but George was still working on *All Things Must Pass*, so Patti decided to attend on her own. When George finished his session at the studio, at about 2:30

in the morning, he drove over to Eric's to pick her up. He looked all over for her and asked other guests if they had seen her, but nobody seemed to know where she was. Finally, he got back in his car and started off down the driveway when he spotted Patti and Eric walking together, hand in hand. George was furious. He slammed on the brakes, leaped out of the car, and started yelling at them so loudly that some of the other guests came out of the house to see what was going on. George was screaming that he never wanted them to see each other again. Then he grabbed Patti, dragged her into the car with him and sped off.

Eric was so upset by the whole incident that he hid himself away in his home, Hurtwood Edge, and tried really hard to start a new relationship with a woman by the name of Alice Ormby-Gore. He stayed away from Patti for months, but he could not forget her. While he was hibernating in his house he read the great Persian love poem, Nazimi's "Layla and Majnum," about the obsessive love between a lovesick man and a married woman. After that Patti became his Layla, in one of the most beautiful and heartfelt love songs that Clapton ever wrote.

During the summer of 1971, George received worldwide acclaim for his concert for Bangladesh. It took place in Madison Square Garden in New York City. The concert was organized to raise money for the starving minions of war-torn Pakistan. The plan was to raise money for aid, not only through ticket sales, but through the release of a live album and a documentary movie. A number of other rock superstars appeared with him for this event including Ringo Starr, Leon Russell, Ravi Shankar and Bob Dylan. Eric Clapton even showed up to perform. He and George have managed to remain friends until this day.

George also invited the other ex-Beatles to participate, but Paul flatly refused because he didn't want to stir up more rumors of a big Beatles reunion. John did accept George's invitation and flew to New York, where he and Yoko checked into the Park Lane hotel. The very morning of the concert John and Yoko had a terrible row. Yoko had discovered that she was not invited to appear with John and she was furious. John got in touch with George to try and remedy the situation, but George told him that he would rather Yoko didn't appear in this particular show. He felt that it would be insulting to some of the other performers to ask them to share the stage with John Lennon's wife. This caused such a rift between the two old friends that John did not appear in the show. In fact, he checked out of the hotel within fifteen minutes of talking to Harrison and took the next flight to London. He was so irate that he actually left Yoko behind and she finally caught up with him about two days later. One has to wonder what was running through John's mind at that time. In any event, the two never spoke to each other again before Lennon's murder in 1980.

All this time George and Patti's marriage had continued to go downhill. They didn't really see much of each other anymore and when they did see each other they didn't get along very well. They finally ended their marriage in 1974. That same year, Eric Clapton had decided to come out of hibernation and go on tour. Patti met up with him on the road, after her divorce was final, and they have been together ever since. They ended up getting married on March 27, 1979.

By Fall of 1974, George's career started to take off again. Perhaps the breakup had given some closure to his and Patti's relationship. Whatever it was, he was fully able to concentrate on his music once again. He made a multi-million dollar deal with A & M Records to distribute his Dark Horse label and plans were in the works for a new album. George went on a twenty-seven city tour of the United States to promote the *Dark Horse* album, making him the first Beatle to tour North America since the breakup of the group. The original deal that George made with the company was to put out a solo album by July of 1977 and help the A & M to sign several new artists. His contract with Apple expired just prior to this new commitment.

In 1976 Bright Tunes filed a plagiarism suit against George because they claimed that the tune to "My Sweet Lord" was the same as that of the Chiffon's hit of the early sixties, "She's So Fine." Harrison brought his guitar to court so that he could demonstrate for the judge exactly how he had gone about composing the number. The judge found him guilty of "unconscious plagiarism" and he had to pay $587,000 in damages to Bright Tunes. Ironically, by the time the case was settled, Allen Klein (the manager the Beatles chose to represent them after the death of Brian Epstein) had bought the Bright Tunes catalog, so the money ended up going into his company.

It was at A & M Records that George met a twenty-seven year old secretary named Olivia Trinidad Arias. He claims that Olivia is the first real true love in his life. Before he met her, he had only known infatuation. The couple moved in together in a rented house in Beverly Hills. She gave birth to their son Dhani after they had been together a little over four years. Dhani was born at the Princess Christian Nursing Home in Windsor. George was so excited by the birth of his first child that he rushed down to his friend Rodney Turner's car dealership in Henly to pick up a brand new baby blue Rolls in honor of the occasion. He had ordered the custom car when he found out that Olivia was pregnant. Dhani was born on August 1, 1978. George married Olivia one month later in a small ceremony near Friar Park, where they continue to live to this day.

Not much is known about Olivia because George is very protective of his family. He keeps her out of his performance life and only introduces her to their closest friends. George spends a lot of time with his family at Friar Park and even does much of his own gardening. He likes to feel a connection to the earth and prefers to work with the foliage on the estate himself rather than totally depending on a staff of gardeners.

George doesn't do as much recording as he used to these days. He has driven race cars in several charity events, however. I guess once you have lived life in the fast lane it is hard to stop completely. He has also started to invest money in the motion picture industry in recent years. Some of the productions he has invested in include *Time Bandits*, *The Long Good Friday*, and Monty Python's *The Life of Brian*. If anyone has earned the right to a quiet life it would be the ex-Beatles. It is good to know that George has finally found some peace.

China, Dishes & Glassware Items

Candy Dishes made by Washington Pottery of the United Kingdom. Each has a picture of one of the Fabs along with their first names. The dishes have gold rims with scalloped edges. The candy dish with Ringo on it also has "The Beatles" in black across the bottom. Value for the set of four: G: $325 E: $400 NM: $450.

Snack plates and a Biscuit plate, made by Washington Pottery of the United Kingdom. The plates on the left and right hand side show the band with "The Beatles" printed in black underneath. The snack plates are 7" in diameter; so is the biscuit plate, but it has a thumb hold that sticks out from one edge. Value per snack plate: G: $75 E: $85 NM: $100. Value for the biscuit plate: G: $85 E: $95 NM: $110.

This cup and bowl is also made by Washington Pottery of the United Kingdom. This photo provides an excellent example of the thickness of this pottery. In order to tell the difference between the original pottery and reproductions, hold the piece up to the light. If the light shines through it, it is a reproduction. The older pieces were made much thicker. The cup is 4" tall and has a group picture with the Beatles first names under each image. The bowl measures 6" in diameter. Value of the cup: G: $75 E: $85 NM: $100. Value of the bowl: G: $75 E: $85 NM: $100.

Newer Vintage China

Coal Port bone china set. This particular set was produced in England in the 1980s. This is an unauthorized set, but it is of excellent quality and has therefore become worth quite a lot of money anyway. The set includes a coffee urn, creamer and sugar, four dessert plates, and four cups with saucers. Value of set: G: $550 E: $675 NM: $725.

Mayfair fine bone china set, which was also produced in the 1980s. This was an unauthorized set too, but of slightly less quality than the set before—although it is a very fine set. This set includes a sugar and creamer and four plates. Value of set: G: $200 E: $250 NM: $300.

This teapot, put out in the 1990s, was purchased at "The Beatles Shop" in Liverpool, England. A three dimensional rendering of the group in pottery comes out from the top and "The Beatles" is printed on the front over a diagram of musical notes. A guitar extends from the top of the handle to the inside top rim. This piece is quite unusual because of its three dimensional aspect. Value: G: $75 E: $85 NM: $100.

Coffee Mugs

Paul McCartney Royal Doulton mug. It is 5 1/2" tall. Value: G: $150 E: $200 NM: $250.

John Lennon Royal Doulton mug. This is a company that is well known for its china and this set is truly exceptional. It was put out from 1984-1991 and features four mugs, one of each Beatle in full Sgt. Pepper's regalia. It is 5 1/2 " tall. Value: G: $150 E: $200 NM: $250.

George Harrison Royal Doulton mug measuring 5 1/2" tall. Value: G: $150 E: $200 NM: $250.

This plastic coffee mug, with its original cardboard insert, was manufactured by NEMS Enterprises. Each Beatle's picture can be seen on an orange background with their first names underneath in gold letters. Be on the lookout! While there are still some original inserts out there, the coffee mugs themselves are being reproduced to fit these inserts. Be sure you know exactly what it is you are getting when buying this piece. The mug in this photo is one of the reproductions, while the insert is original. The value is for the item in this state: G: $15 E: $20 NM: $25. Value for original mug, with insert (not shown): G: $70 E: $90 NM: $110.

Ringo Starr, Royal Doulton mug, 5 1/2" tall. Value: G: $150 E: $200 NM: $250.

Drinking Glasses

These drinking glasses are made by J & L Co. Ltd. of the United Kingdom. There is a color pose of each Beatle on the set of four. They have gold rims and are 4" tall. Value per glass: G: $75 E: $100 NM: $150.

These glasses were made in Holland. The glasses have color photos of the Fabs on each of the four glasses. They have gold rims and are 5 1/2" tall. Value per glass: G: $75 E: $100 NM: $150.

Set of four glasses manufactured by NEMS Ent. Ltd., London. There is a Beatle on each glass along with the appropriate first name. Each one also has musical notes, guitars, and records and measures 4 3/4" tall. Value per glass: G: $50 E: $100 NM: $125.

This glass was made in Holland and has a color group photo on it. "The Beatles" is printed on a red, white, and blue banner above the photo. The glass is 5 1/2" tall. Value: G: $100 E: $150 NM: $175.

This glass has a color group photo along with the words "The Beatles" printed on the drum head that appears on the front of the glass. This is a full length shot of the Fabs and the glass is 5" tall. Value: G: $75 E: $100 NM: $150.

This was a glass that Dairy Queen gave away as a promotional gift in Canada. There are black and white head shots of the Beatles with their first names underneath. "The Beatles" also appears in white print at the top of the glass, which is 4 1/2" tall. Value: G: $90 E: $105 NM: $125.

Ceramic Tiles

This tile was put out by Carter Tiles in the United Kingdom. It is a white tile decorated with full body caricatures of the Fabs and copies of their signatures. It is 6" square. Value: G: $175 E: $225 NM: $250.

"Picture Plaque," black and white ceramic tile with a red metal frame. It has head shots of the Beatles with collarless suits and ties along with "The Beatles" in black lettering. The tile measures 4 1/4" square and is "A Sixties Souvenir Product by Ole' Home Products." Value given is with the frame: G: $35 E: $45 NM: $50.

This tile was also made by Carter Tiles in the United Kingdom. The tile is white with a head shot of John Lennon and a copy of his signature. It has a light blue background and measures 6" square. Value: G: $100 E: $150 NM: $175.

New Memorabilia: Plates

Plates purchased at "The Beatles Shop" in Liverpool. Manufactured by Weatherby of the United Kingdom, the plates measure 5" in diameter and have gold trim. The Beatles faces can be seen in black and white against a picture of the Liverpool skyline on the left-hand plate. Below this are some Beatle vital statistics such as names, birth dates, and birthplaces. The plate on the right features a black and white group photo in its center. Value per each plate: E: $10 NM: $15.

This is a white tile manufactured by Carter Tiles in the United Kingdom. It has a head shot of Paul McCartney, along with a copy of his signature, on a light blue background. The tile is 6" square. Value: G: $100 E: $150 NM: $175.

This "Happy Christmas" plate features a piece of John Lennon's artwork called "Christmas Tree Scene". The plate measures 3 1/2" in diameter and was manufactured by Gartlan in 1997. Value: E: $10 NM: $15.

This tile is manufactured by Carter Tiles in the United Kingdom. It is white with a head shot of George Harrison, along with a copy of his signature, on a light blue background. It is 6" square. Value: G: $100 E: $150 NM: $175.

This tile is manufactured by Carter Tiles in the United Kingdom. It is white with a head shot of Ringo Starr, along with a copy of his signature, on a light blue background. It is 6" square. Value: G: $100 E: $150 NM: $175.

This "Happy Christmas" plate also features a piece of John Lennon's artwork called "Christmas Tree Scene". This version, however, is part of a limited edition of 10,000. It is also quite a bit larger, measuring 8 1/2" in diameter. It too is manufactured by Gartlan. Value: E: $30 NM: $35.

Coffee Mugs

These pictures show a nice mug collection that was picked up by super collector Dennis Dailey over the years. He has traveled all over the world, including a Liverpool pilgrimage, picking up new additions for his incredible collection. The mugs have various makers, but I can give you a pretty good idea of their average worth. Value for each: E: $10 NM: $12.

Miscellaneous Items

Salt and pepper shaker set. Maker unknown. Pink salt shaker is shaped like a TV while the base (in black) is the pepper shaker. The group is appearing on-stage on the screen of the TV. The shakers are ceramic. Value for the set: E: $12 NM: $15.

Shown here is a portion of a set of four unlicensed placemats with coasters. The placemats are made of white vinyl with color caricatures of the Beatles with instruments, while the coasters have a group pose from *Help!* on them. Value given is for the complete set: E: $12 NM: $15.

This plastic tray is made by Melamaster of Great Britain. It is black and white with "The Beatles" printed across the top and "Liverpool" across the bottom. There is also a picture of the Liverpool skyline in the background. Value: E: $7 NM: $10.

Chapter Six
Ringo The Fourth

Richard Starkey Jr. was born to Elsie and Richard Starkey Sr. on July 7, 1940. His mother gave birth to him in her home at #9 Madryn Street. Despite the legend to the contrary, Ringo was really the only Beatle who rose up out of the Dingle (a Liverpool slum). Ringo was an only child and he was very sickly when he was small. He had really horrible problems with his digestive tract and at the age of six he was in a coma for two months. It must have been very difficult for Ringo and his parents of meager circumstances to deal with a plethora of health problems. His father and mother were divorced in 1943, when he was only three years old.

The young Starkey developed an interest in music early on. Even as a small child he used to bang on empty cans and boxes. He didn't let his many illnesses hold him back either. He first started his drumming career playing in bands that he and other patients formed while he was in the hospital.

Ringo's mother got re-married in 1955, to a man named Harry Graves, who was a house painter. Ringo became very ill again on a trip with his mother and his new step-father. Richard had been so sickly all of his life that he had fallen way behind in his studies. He soon discovered that there was no way he was ever going to be able to catch up and graduate with his peers. In 1955 he got a certificate from the headmaster of the Dingle Vale school stating that he was leaving school. Without such a certificate he would never have been able to get a job. So far Richard's young life didn't seem very promising. What kind of a future could he expect to have? Finally, he took a job as a delivery boy for the British rail, but he was unable to hang onto it because of his ongoing health problems. His next job was as a waiter on a passenger steamer.

It was Ringo's stepfather who bought him his first drum kit. Harry got it for him in London and brought it all the way back to Liverpool on the train. His practicing didn't work out very well at first. Because of the complaints that they received from the neighbors, Ringo's mother would only allow him to practice for thirty minutes a day and it had to be in the afternoon.

Richard's grandfather eventually gave him the money for a down payment on a more sophisticated drum kit that enabled him to advance in his musical career. He started off playing with the Eddie Clayten Skiffle Group. They played the same basic venue as the Quarrymen.

The next group he belonged to was called the "Raving Texans," which is interesting because Ringo always had a sort of fascination with the state of Texas. In fact, he once looked into moving to Houston. After that he got together with Rory Storm and the Hurricanes. It was shortly after he joined the group that Richard Starkey became Ringo Starr. The name Ringo was derived from all the rings that he wore. The Starr part was added on so that his drum solo could be announced as "Starr Time."

Young Ringo was very shy when it came to the ladies, even after he reached the pinnacle of fame. He found it intimidating when young women started to throw themselves at his feet. He was a one woman man for quite awhile during his early days with the Hurricanes. He spent several years with a young woman who is historically remembered only as Geraldine. At one point he even gave her an engagement ring and asked her to marry him. The story goes that she returned it and the engagement was called off. One can't help but wonder what she thinks of her decision today.

The Beatles knew Ringo very well. They first met him during their Hamburg days, when he was still playing with Rory Storm. They watched him play with the group for several months before finally approaching him. He was fun loving, uncomplicated, and got along well with everyone in the group much better than Pete Best had. By that time Rory Storm's popularity had fallen off and the Hurricanes were stuck playing a brutal summer schedule at Butlin's Holiday Camp. It was while Ringo was playing this gig that George reached him to see if he would be interested in playing with the Beatles. They offered to start him out on a small salary for the duration of a probationary period. If things worked out to everyone's satisfaction during this time, Ringo would then become a full-fledged Beatle. He was totally into the idea from the start, going immediately to cut his hair in a Beatle cut. Although he was not a full Beatle yet, Ringo seemed to have ousted Pete Best. Ringo's mother and stepfather started to help him answer the piles of fan mail that he was receiving.

The Beatles first had the idea of replacing Pete Best with Ringo while he played drums with them—while the Beatles were performing as part of a back-up group known as the Beat Brothers—in a record booth at the Hamburg railway station.

The *Mersey Beat* newspaper was quick to break the news that Pete was out and Ringo was in. The article also informed people that George Martin was ready to have the Beatles come to London and record their first single for Parlophone.

This was the beginning of a difficult time in the group's history. Pete Best's fans rallied around him with a vengeance. Petitions signed by hundreds of girls, begging for his reinstatement in the band, poured into the office at the *Mersey Beat*. But it didn't end there. Some very ugly scenes followed for the boys. The first time they played the Cavern club with Ringo on the drums the crowd went wild. Girls were screaming, "Pete Best forever-Ringo never!" It must have been a very frightening experience for the group and for Ringo in particular, but it was about to get much worse. The following Monday night fist fights broke out, outside the club, while the Beatles were playing. Somehow George even turned up with a black eye the next day for defending the new member. Things did eventually settle down and Ringo was slowly accepted as the new drummer.

Pete Best, on the other hand, got a job as the deputy manager at the Garston Job Center; however, Best does still appear at various Beatles conventions around the world. He also speaks at many other related events about what it was like to almost be a Beatle. On the brighter side, he is now happily married and has two beautiful daughters whom he cherishes.

On September 12, 1962, the Beatles brought Ringo to the studio with them for the first time. It was a bit of a shock to George Martin who had already hired a drummer, Andy White, for the session. Martin told Ringo that under the circumstances he would let him audition for the job. After hearing him play, Martin decided to go ahead and use White on the drums. Ringo played tambourine at the beginning of that first recording session with the Beatles. He looked so miserable toward the end of it that Martin relented and allowed him to play drums on the last few tracks.

Ringo's parents were the last of the Beatles parents to move into a nice house purchased for them by their famous son. They chose a house that was tucked away in a cul-de-sac, on Gateway Park. They were quite happy there until Elsie came down with pneumonia in 1972. Despite her illness, she continued to help Ringo with his fan mail. He still came to stay with them at their home in Liverpool for Christmas and his mother loved to fuss over him the entire time he was there.

An incredible thing happened to the Beatles in 1965. Queen Elizabeth bestowed an MBE award (Members of the British Empire) upon each of the Fab Four. They accepted the awards at Buckingham Palace on October 26th. Ringo did accept the medal at the time, because his parents were so very proud of him, but he never did wear it. He kept it in a box with many of his other treasures so that he could take it out and look at it periodically.

The full and frightening impact of Beatlemania first became really evident to Ringo when he had to have his tonsils out. Fans gathered at the University College Hospital to wish him well. The scary part was that he had hundreds of requests from fans to let them have his tonsils after they had been removed. No one knows for sure what actually happened to them, but one has to assume that the surgeon properly disposed of them.

In 1966 Ringo and Maureen joined the Beatles in the Welsh seaside town of Bangor, where they were to learn about meditation from the Maharishi Mahesh Yogi. The guru's philosophy was basically, as he stated it to them, "The regenerative result of meditation is that all human vices and ego are eradicated bit by bit until a pure state of bliss is achieved.

Shortly after the Beatles arrival at the ashram, their manager, Brian Epstein, overdosed on his prescription medication and died. The guru advised them not to let Brian's death get them down. They should spread happiness, as Brian Epstein would feel that in his spiritual state and be happy too. The guru further explained that to become depressed about the death would be a form of self pity and that would be selfish. Still, all of the Beatles did attend the funeral.

Ringo and Maureen named their first born son Zak, because Ringo had always fancied that name. He was born on September 13, 1965. After his first child was born Ringo took

to looking around his property and thinking back to his own childhood in the Dingle. He remembered walking with his mum as she pushed a handcart with all their worldly possessions on it. He had certainly come a long way since then and his children would never know that kind of poverty. For this he is very grateful, but he finds himself thinking back on those days then looking at his current surroundings and saying to himself: "What's a scruff like me doing with all this lot?"

Ringo was in his first non-Beatle related film in 1968. It was called *Candy*. In it, Ringo played Emmanuel, a Mexican gardener with holy aspirations who had trouble controlling his inner stirrings. The other actors of note who appeared in this film were Richard Burton, Marlon Brando, and James Coburn.

His next movie venture was *The Magic Christian* with Peter Sellers, Raquel Welch and Yul Brynner. He also made a brief appearance on the comedy show *Laugh In*. When Joanne Worley asked him what it was like to be chased by all those girls he replied sadly, "Sometimes they don't catch me."

Ringo did a pretty amazing thing for Paul during the breakup of the group. *Let It Be* was due to be released in April of 1970, through Apple. Paul wanted to release his album before their group effort came out. Allen Klein explained to him that it was out of the question. *Let It Be,* the album, was due to be released in time to back up *Let It Be* the documentary. Because United Artists held the rights to the film and EMI held the rights to the album, it was almost impossible to shift the dates around so that they would coincide. Ringo too, had recorded a solo album called *Sentimental Journey*. It was due to be released just after *Let It Be*. Everything had already been set up and they told McCartney he would just have to take his turn with his album. Paul was so angry over this that he called the new owner of EMI, Sir Joseph Lockwood, to complain. Sir Joe told him that the ultimate decision rested with the Beatles, which upset Paul even more.

Not long after this incident, Ringo went to see McCartney to discuss the matter and try to reach some sort of compromise. He tried to discuss the situation with Paul calmly, but after he had only been there a few minutes Paul flew off the handle. He actually threw Ringo out of his house screaming, "I'll finish you all!" Instead of being angry at Paul, Ringo tried very hard to empathize with him. After all, he was in a tough position; he had Lee Eastman for a manager while the other Beatles had Allen Klein. This put him at a distinct disadvantage when trying to bargain with the others. In fact, the whole scene upset Ringo so much that he went back and told the others that if it meant that much to Paul to have his solo album released in April, then perhaps they should let him do it, to show their continuing friendship. Meanwhile, the release of Ringo's own solo album was pushed back, while the release of *Let it Be* was moved up. In the end, all three of the albums hit the market within a month of each other, which turned out to be a total marketing nightmare.

Ringo's first solo efforts were not as successful as he had hoped, which prompted the other three ex-Beatles to help him with an album. This turned out to be the closest thing to a reunion that the Beatles would ever have while they were all still living. They all collaborated on tape, but they were not in the same place at the same time while doing so. Each of them contributed at least one song to the project, which resulted in the *Ringo* album. It became one of the most popular albums of the year. In fact, two of the singles, "Photograph" and "You're

Sixteen," hit number one. He was greatly encouraged by this and started producing an album a year.

In 1974, Ringo decided to branch out and he invested in a furniture design company called Ringo or Robin Limited. The items created by this design company were quite unique. They carried such items as a table made from a Rolls Royce grill or a chrome-plated circular fireplace. This venture proved very interesting to Ringo while it lasted.

By 1976 Ringo was released from his contract at Apple and signed a deal with Polydor in England. His first album under that label was *Rotogravure*, followed closely by *Ringo The Fourth* and *Bad Boy*.

Ringo did a number of solo albums after the breakup of the Beatles. They were doing pretty well until he made *Goodnight Vienna* and his single "Only You" slipped down the charts in Britain. That was the last big hit he was ever to have in England. By this time he had moved to the United States, which didn't help to keep interest up in Britain. He made a home for himself in Santa Monica, California. He was happy to discover that the tax laws in the United States were much kinder to his pocketbook than those in Great Britain.

Ringo continued his acting career by making the movie *Blindman*, a spaghetti western. In this picture he played Candy, the psychotic brother of a Mexican bandit, who kidnaps the brides-to-be of fifty Texas miners, from a wagon train. The wagon train is being guided by "the Good Guy," who also happens to be blind.

Starr first appeared on a TV commercial in a Japanese clothing advertisement. Then he spent five days in the Bahamas making a Sun Country wine cooler ad. He even played the father in an Oldsmobile commercial. In that ad, he is running from frantic, screaming female fans, jumps out a twelve story window, and lands in a Cutlass driven by his daughter Lee. They speed off making good their escape and then you hear, "It's not your father's Oldsmobile."

Ringo was not without political motivation. He became very concerned with certain causes, much like his old mate, John Lennon. In 1979 Ringo participated in a Labor Day telethon to aid medical research. Ringo and Zak made a stand together against racism by taping their own contribution to *Live Aid* called "Sun City," a recording project that would aid anti-apartheid movements in South Africa and the Americas. Ringo also participated in ARMS (Action for Multiple Sclerosis) by spending a day with two terminally ill children for the "Dreams Come True" foundation.

In 1980 Ringo participated in a production called *Caveman*, which would change his life forever. He went to Mexico to begin shooting a movie which was slated to be a spoof of other caveman pictures. Starr gave one of his best performances in this movie. He played a clown and the critics loved it. So did someone else ...

It was on the set of *Caveman* that Starr was destined to meet the woman who was to become his second wife, Barbara Bach. Ringo and his first wife Maureen divorced. Maureen would go on to remarry as well. Maureen's second husband was Isaac Tigrett, the founder of the Hard Rock Cafe chain.

Barbara Bach's best remembered role (before becoming Ringo's wife) was as a co-star in the James Bond film *The Spy Who Loved Me*. The couple started dating during the production of the film. Things were going so well between them that the following month he took Barbara to London to meet his children. We almost lost Ringo the same year as John when Ringo and Barbara's car went out of control, knocking over three lampposts before finally coming to a stop. The two were on their way to a party in Surrey at the time. They had gotten up to highway speed when Ringo had to swerve sharply to avoid another vehicle. The road was slick from the rain and they went into a skid from which Ringo could not recover control of the car. He injured his leg in the crash, but was able to pull Barbara out and help her to safety. Ringo was so relieved to have made it through this mishap that he had pieces of the shattered windshield set in little gold lockets for he and Barbara to wear. He also had the wrecked car crushed into a cube and displayed it as sculpture on his estate, much as John Lennon had done after his car accident with Yoko, Julian, and Yoko's daughter, Kyoko.

Lennon's murder was a very low point in Ringo's life. He and Barbara flew to New York immediately, to help comfort Yoko. While they were between planes in Miami a young fan callously commented, "At least the rumors that you're getting back together will stop now."

Ringo and Barbara did their best to comfort Lennon's widow before returning to England. The Sunday after John was shot, a ten minute, world-wide silent vigil was held in John's memory, at Yoko's request. Ringo stayed at home that night, preferring to be alone in his silence and his grief.

As you can well imagine, this horrible and senseless crime caused the other ex-Beatles to be afraid for their own lives. It prompted very tight security around the three remaining ex-Fabs. Just as no one could understand why some madman had cut Lennon down in his prime, they had no way of knowing whether or not some maniac would come after one or all of them.

The Starkeys hired several bodyguards and kept guard dogs around their home twenty-four hours a day. Ringo was very careful when it came to seeing visitors or being approached by anyone that he didn't know. He remembers that era with great sadness, "Suddenly I felt I could be a target for the next madman." It was an extremely frightening time.

On April 27, 1981, Ringo and Barbara were married. The wedding took place at the Marlyebone Registry Office in England, possibly because the couple felt that it was too dangerous to be married in the United States at the time for fear of more violence. All of the remaining Beatles were there for the event, which stirred up more rumors of a reunion in the press, despite Lennon's death. This was the first time that Paul, George and Ringo had been seen together since John's murder. Ringo had dearly hoped to have everyone together again for this happy occasion, but Mark David Chapman had put an end to that dream in a split second.

Barbara's wedding dress was designed by David and Elizabeth Emanuel, who had previously made gowns for people like Princess Diana. Barbara's dress was beautiful and old fashioned, while Ringo was dressed in a much more contemporary style. He was dressed all in black, with dark sunglasses. Fans crowded around the "Fab Three" as they were leaving the ceremony.

At the reception instruments of all sorts were set up on a stage for those present who wanted to play. "Strawberry Fields Forever" was sung as a sort of dirge for the fallen Lennon.

Each of the wedding guests was given a five-pointed silver star to remember the occasion by. Their wedding cake was also shaped like a star in Ringo's honor. The couple moved to England and Tittenhurst Park, after that, in order to get back to Ringo's homeland and away from the gun toting public of the United States. When an attempt was made on President Reagan's life the following year, Ringo was certain that his deciding to return to England had been the right choice.

To follow up, regrettably, Ringo's ex-wife Maureen passed away on December 30, 1995, at the age of forty-seven. The cause of death was listed as complications from a bone marrow transplant that had been necessary while Maureen fough a battle against leukemia. She died at the Fred Hutchinson Cancer Research Center in Seattle with both Ringo and Isaac by her side. She was survived by her four children and her eighty-two year old mother.

The illness had started the year before, when Maureen fainted at the opening of one of Isaac's restaurants in L.A. She was diagnosed with leukemia two weeks later.

Ringo and Maureen's oldest son, Zak, has the same blood type as his mother and donated bone marrow, blood platelets and white blood cells to try and help the doctors to save her life.

Yellow Submarine Memorabilia

Yellow Sub alarm clock, manufactured by Sheffield. This item is getting really hard to find, especially with the box, as it is a highly sought after piece. Because of that, there have been some reproductions showing up on the market. The original casing of the clock is psychedelic, while some of the reproductions have a silver metal casing. The Yellow Sub logo can be found on the face of the original. The clock itself is made of metal and has yellow alarm bells on top. If the original box is missing, you must subtract half of the value given. Value with box: G: $2,400 E: $3,600 NM: $4,500.

Diecast Yellow Submarine manufactured by Corgi Toys. There are two versions of this piece (as seen in the picture). These two pieces are shown in their original boxes, which greatly adds to their value. The sub on the left has yellow and white hatches, which are rare finds because there were less of those manufactured than the subs with the red hatches. This makes the first sub much more valuable. The original boxes came with a blue plastic packing insert that the sub fits into snugly. Values given are for the subs with their original packaging. Value: Sub with rare yellow and white hatches: G: $750 E: $1,000 NM: $1,200. Value: Sub with red hatches: G: $675 E: $750 NM: $800.

Blue Meanie Halloween Costume manufactured by Collegeville Costumes. This costume came with a plastic Blue Meanie mask. "Beatles The Yellow Submarine" was emblazoned on the front of the costume. Subtract half of the stated value if the box is not present. Value: G: $625 E: $700 NM: $800.

Character Clothes Hangers

Paul McCartney, Yellow Sub hanger by Henderson-Haggard Inc. Value per hanger: G: $90 E: $125 NM: $150.

John Lennon, Yellow Sub hanger by Henderson-Haggard Inc. The picture was in full color and the hanger was double-sided with a plastic hook. It measures 16" tall and had "John" printed on it in white. Value per hanger: G: $90 E: $125 NM: $150.

Ringo Starr, Yellow Sub hanger by Henderson-Haggard Inc. Value per hanger: G: $90 E: $125 NM: $150.

George Harrison, Yellow Sub hanger by Henderson-Haggard Inc. Value per hanger: G: $90 E: $125 NM: $150.

Banks

Yellow Sub character banks. John and Paul are shown here. They were made of papier-mâché and were manufactured by Pride Creations. The banks are 8" tall and have original stickers on the bottom reading, "King Features & Pride Creations." They also originally had black, rubber plugs. Value per bank: G: $300 E: $425 NM: $500.

Yellow Sub character banks: George and Ringo. Same value & description as the John and Paul banks.

Set of four Yellow Sub character figurines. These figures are of very fine quality and are made by Goebel of West Germany, a company that is well known for its fine quality porcelain. They stand 8 1/2" tall and have a blue Goebel mark on the bottom. These are very special items and quite hard to come by. For more information, please write to: "Gobel Collector's Club, 105 White Plains Road, Tarrytown, New York 10591." The value given is for the set of four: G: $7,000 E: $10,000 NM: $12,000.

Desk Accessories

This Yellow Sub pencil holder has colorful movie characters around the outside, one of each Beatle. Their names are printed in gold letters underneath each figure. The pencil holder is made of cardboard and is 3" in diameter and 4" tall. Value: G: $550 E: $625 NM: $700.

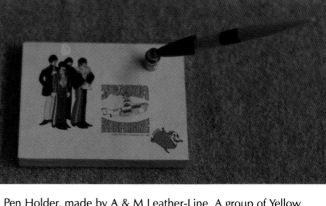

Pen Holder, made by A & M Leather-Line. A group of Yellow Sub characters appears on the left side of base. The words, "The Yellow Submarine", in orange letters, surrounds a picture of a small Yellow Sub with Jeremy the Boob on the lower right-hand corner. The base measures 5 1/4" x 4" and is 1" thick plastic. Value for set: G: $625 E: $700 NM: $750.

Yellow Sub Letter Holder, also made by A & M Leather-Line. This letter holder is made of sturdy cardboard. Value: G: $625 E: $700 NM: $750.

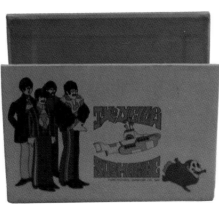

"The Beatles Yellow Submarine" Poster Put-Ons by Craft Master. Shown in the original box, these Put-Ons came with a 15" x 21" pre-numbered poster and a sheet with more than 60 stickers that could be placed on the poster. If the box is missing, the value given must be cut in half. Value: G: $175 E: $250 NM: $325.

This mobile was put out by Sunshine Art Studios. The one shown here was never assembled and came with string to connect it together and hang. It was made of cardboard and measures 9 3/4" x 14 1/4". If the mobile has been assembled, half of the value given is lost. Value: G: $150 E: $200 NM: $250.

Yellow Sub Stick-Ons, marked DAL MFG. Corp. The sealed package has one sheet of Yellow Sub stickers. A Popstickles Decal stick-on ad is facing the camera on the back of the package. There is a sheet of cardboard in the center to separate the items. Value is for a factory sealed in the shrink wrap item: G: $20 E: $30 NM: $35.

These watercolor sets are put out by Craft Master. The box on the left includes six 8" x 10" pictures with two different colors of paint, a pallet, and a brush. Value for the boxed set on the left: G: $100 E: $130 NM: $165. Value for the boxed set on the right: G: $75 E: $100 NM: $120.

Wall Plaques, Bulletin Boards, Bookmarks & Coasters

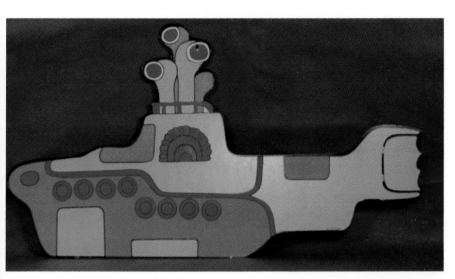

Yellow Sub wall plaque was made by K. Cennar Ent. It is 21" x 12" and is made of sturdy cardboard. There is a small hole at the top for hanging. Value: G: $50 E: $70 NM: $85.

Yellow Sub wall plaque of Glove, also made by K. Cennar Ent. Measures 21" x 9" and is made of cardboard with hole at the top. Value: G: $50 E: $70 NM: $85.

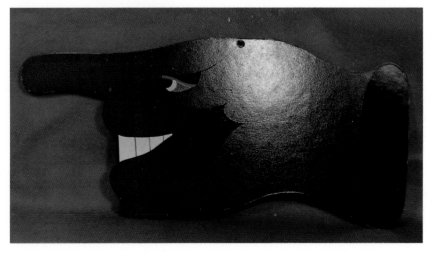

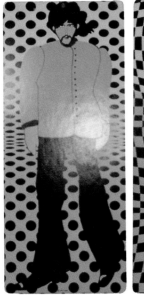 

Yellow Sub Bookmarks (John, Paul, George, Ringo, Old Fred, and an Apple Bonker). Made by Unicorn Creations Inc., each bookmark measures 3" x 9". Value for each: G: $12 E: $15 NM: $20.

Yellow Sub wall plaques of George and Ringo, made by K. Cennar Ent. They measure 21" x 9", were made of cardboard, and drilled at the top for hanging. All four of the Yellow Sub characters were put out with a variety of backgrounds. Value per each: G: $50 E: $60 NM: $75.

Two Yellow Sub bulletin boards. One (on the left) has the Head Meanie on it and the other (on the right) has Max. Same value and description as the other two boards offered by Unicorn Creations Inc.

Two Yellow Sub bulletin boards: the board on the left features a group drawing of the Beatles while the model on the right features the Snapping Turk. These bulletin boards came with a black sticker with a Yellow Sub on the front; they also came factory sealed in shrink wrap. Put out by Unicorn Creations Inc., each was made of sturdy cardboard measuring 23" x 7 1/2". If still factory sealed, add $40 to the value given. Value for each: G: $20 E: $30 NM: $40.

Set of 12 Yellow Submarine Party Coasters with assorted characters from the movie. Made by K. Cennar Ent., this set is shown in original packaging with the header card inserted between the two sets of six coasters. Coasters are 3 1/4" square. Value is for the entire set with its original packaging: G: $100 E: $115 NM: $125.

Back side of the Yellow Submarine
Party Coaster set.

Calendar, Gift Book, Greeting Cards & Key Rings

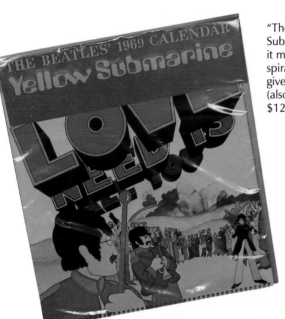

"The Beatles 1969 Calendar Yellow
Submarine." Made by Golden Press,
it measures 12" square and has a
spiral binding. Add 25% to the value
given if the original mailing envelope,
(also shown) is present. Value: G:
$125 E: $140 NM: $175.

Original mailing envelope for the 1969
Yellow Submarine calendar.

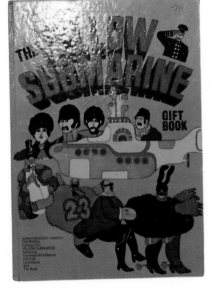

The Yellow Submarine Gift Book by
World Distributors of the U.K. This is a
hard cover, authorized edition based
on the feature length cartoon film.
Value: G: $50 E: $65 NM: $85.

Yellow Sub Character Key Rings made by Pride Creations. From left to right: John, Paul, George, and Ringo. They measure 6" x 2 1/2" with a chrome ring at the top. Value per key ring: G: $30 E: $40 NM: $45.

Greeting Cards put out by Sunshine Card Company, with original box. The lid is shown on the left and the box includes fourteen cards with envelopes. The box itself measures 4 1/2" x 9". Value given is for the cards with the original box: G: $90 E: $110 NM: $140.

Binder & Notebooks

Yellow Sub Three-Ring Binder, put out by Vernon Royal. A variety of Yellow Sub characters appear on both sides of the cover. It measures 10 1/4" x 11 1/2" Value: G: $115 E: $175 NM: $250.

Notebooks, one small, 5" x 7 1/2", and one standard size Yellow Sub spiral notebook, manufactured by Vernon Royal. Notebook paper should be present. Value small: G: $100 E: $130 NM: $155. Value standard: G: $130 E: $155 NM: $175.

Puzzles & Switchplate covers

Yellow Submarine 100 piece puzzle: "Sea of Monsters". Made by Jaymar. © King Features Syndicate, Suba Films Ltd. MCMLVIII (1968). Value: G: $30 E: $40 NM: $50.

Yellow Submarine puzzle: "In the Yellow Sub". Same description and value as "Sea of Monsters".

Yellow Submarine puzzle: "Meanies Invade Pepperland". Also by Jaymar, this puzzle has over 650 pieces and measures 19" x 19" when fully assembled. Value: G: $60 E: $80 NM: $90.

Cardboard Switch Plate Covers, made by DAL Manufacturing Corp. Sealed in original packages, from left to right: The Beatles, Snapping Turk, Glove, Head Meanie, and Max. They measure 6 1/4" x 11 3/4". Value per switch cover in original package: G: $35 E: $45 NM: $50.

103

New Memorabilia: Cartoon Cels, Christmas Ornaments

Yellow Submarine Cartoon Cell, purchased at an auction in Liverpool during the annual Beatle celebration. It is a limited edition print of the original cell and is #42 of 450. King Features 1968. Value: E: $200 NM: $250.

Yellow Submarine Cartoon Cell, also purchased at an auction in Liverpool. Same as the previous cel but smaller, it is #68 of 327. Value: E: $95 NM: $125.

Christmas Ornaments. Undocumented, they consist of glass bulbs with various scenes from the movie. Value for the set of four: E: $25 NM: $30.

Character Pillows

Yellow Sub soft sculpture hanging pillow. Maker unknown. Purchased at "The Beatles Shop" in Liverpool, England. Value: E: $10 NM: $12.

Glove soft sculpture pillow. Same description and value as the Yellow Submarine model.

Mugs, Postcard & Stationery

Back of the Yellow sub coffee mug.

Yellow Sub Coffee Mug. Value: E: $10 NM: $12.

Post card purchased in Liverpool with a picture of a structure built to look like the Yellow Sub. Value: E: $3 NM: $5.

Sheet of Blue Meanie stationery. Value per sheet: E: $1 NM: $2.

James Paul McCartney was born on January 18, 1942 at Walton General Hospital. The McCartney family started out living in a furnished room in Anfield, in a council house in Knowsley Estate, Wallasey. Then they moved to another council house in Speke. They lived there in exchange for Paul's mother, Mary's, skilled service as a midwife. Finally, they moved to #20 Forthlin Road in Allerton, about a mile from where John Lennon was living.

Paul's mother died of breast cancer when he was only fourteen. Paul was completely devastated. He and his mum had been very close. Mary had wanted to protect her sons from the terrible truth about her health, and so she never told them that she was ill. This made it an even greater shock for the boys when she died only two days after being admitted to the hospital. To try and keep his mind off of the terrible tragedy, Paul started to play the guitar with a passion. His father, Jim, bought his first one for him for about thirty dollars.

After his wife died, Jim McCartney stayed close to home and took the responsibility of raising his two boys, Paul and Mike, very seriously. It was only after they were grown up and making a success of their lives that he started to think about his own future once again. When Paul became famous he insisted that his father retire and he bought Jim a nice home to retire in. Then, in 1964, Jim got remarried to a woman by the name of Angela Williams, whom he had only known for three days at the time. During those early Beatle years, Paul made sure that his family had everything that they needed.

When the boys were younger, Jim McCartney had encouraged them musically by signing them up for piano lessons and such, but neither one seemed particularly interested and quit after only two or three lessons each. After that, Jim gave Paul an old trumpet and he learned to play a few tunes on it by ear. When he got tired of the trumpet, Paul took up the guitar. He started out with the cheap acoustic that I mentioned earlier and he was absolutely fascinated by it. The young McCartney started to become more and more interested in rock 'n' roll. In fact, he and his friend, Ian James, used to ride their bikes all around Liverpool with their instruments strapped to their backs, looking for a gig.

Soon after that the young McCartney began attending the Liverpool Institute, which just happened to be right next to the art college that John Lennon was attending. In fact, once the two got to know each other they started skipping school together to practice songs at Paul's house and teach each other chords. They went to Paul's house because everyone was at work or school and there was little chance of getting caught. Soon, they started writing songs together. They wrote one hundred songs that first year.

Paul was the first to compose a song on his own. It was called "I Lost My Little Girl." That is what started up the competitive force that was to drive the Beatles to stardom. After seeing what Paul had done, John too began to write songs. John was good at getting a song started, but then he would get stuck. However, Paul was very good at writing the middle eight, which was just the combination they needed to produce great songs. While they usually went to Paul's house because it was safe during the day, sometimes they went to see John's mother, Julia, at her house. Paul really found Julia to be a likable character.

Ironically, John's Aunt Mimi thought that Paul was a bad influence on him, while Jim McCartney thought that John was a bad influence on Paul. Many were the times that Mimi wouldn't even let young Paul in the house. But somehow they always managed to work around these little difficulties.

Paul was there for John when his mother was hit and killed by a drunken off-duty policeman in the summer of 1958. He remembered all too well, the pain he had felt when his own mother died of breast cancer, when he was only fourteen. The two Fabs became even closer as a result of this terrible tragedy.

Now it was George's turn to enter the picture. Paul had introduced him to John and John had finally agreed to give him a chance to audition. George played "Raunchy" and shortly afterward he was asked to join the group.

Paul's first real girlfriend was a girl named Dorothy Rhone, or Dot, as he preferred to call her. She was from a suburb of Woolton called Childwall, where she was a clerk at a pharmacy. When they met she still lived at home with her parents. Paul wrote the song "P.S. I Love You" for her. At the time Brigitte Bardot was all the rage. Paul liked her so much that he asked Dot to bleach her hair, which she did.

In 1961 Dot and Cynthia went to visit John and Paul during their gig in Hamburg. Cynthia stayed with Astrid, at her house, and Paul and Dot stayed together on an old river barge owned by the bathroom attendant at the Top Ten club.

Upon their return to Liverpool Cynthia and Dot became roommates at a boarding house. They had gotten to know each other pretty well by this time and were fast friends. It was while they were living in this boarding house that Cynthia first learned that she was pregnant with Julian and Paul broke up with Dot because so many women were chasing after him and he didn't want to be tied down.

Paul soon developed quite an eye for the ladies and it caused him more than a few problems. His problems in this area started while they were still in Hamburg. It seems that one of the waitresses who worked at one of the clubs in Hamburg turned up pregnant after being rather friendly to Paul. The woman's name was Erika Huber, and she filed a paternity suit against Paul, in Germany, after her little girl, Bettina, was born. Nothing happened to him as a result of that suit because the German authorities could not pursue the matter in Great Britain. Consequently, the family threatened to file a paternity suit against him in his home country and in 1966 he paid Erika $27,000 to keep the child's existence a secret without ever knowing for sure the true paternity. Of course DNA evidence wasn't what it is now, by any means.

Then, in Spring of 1964, another girl, this time in Liverpool, gave birth to a baby boy that she claimed was Paul's son. Her name was Alice Doyle and she and her mother consulted a local attorney named D.H. Green. In the beginning, all the girl wanted was enough money to buy the baby a carriage. The matter would have been settled very quickly if the girl's mother had not told her brother about the problem they were having. The uncle smelled money immediately, lots of it, and decided to go after it. Figuring that the child was potentially worth a fortune to him, he went to work on Paul, offering to keep the story out of the papers for $10,000.

Paul, not wanting the hassle of going to court and fighting it, offered them $6,000, which the uncle turned down. Then, later that summer at the premiere of A Hard Day's Night, handbills were passed out among this crowd of half a million people, who were waiting to see the show, alleging Paul's paternity in this matter. This man did not know when to stop. He also began sending out poems about Paul's alleged love child to all the newspapers. But his greed had ultimately fouled the deal for him. By this time so many rumors were circulating about all four of the Beatles that his claim was no longer taken seriously. It is a shame that some people try to ruin a person's life over money. This has happened to many other celebrities in recent memory. The celebrities often try to help out monetarily for the children and it ends up backfiring on them because the people in question just want more, and more, and more.

That still wasn't the end of Paul's troubles when it came to paternity suits. There was another woman in Liverpool, in 1964, named Anita Cochrane, who claimed that McCartney had gotten her pregnant. She gave birth to a baby boy named Phillip and Paul gave her three thousand pounds in settlement, with no admission of fatherhood. He was beginning to see the writing on the wall in these cases and had the presence of mind to put a clause in the settlement, prohibiting her from coming back and making any further claims against him in the case.

Despite this clause and the threats of Paul's attorneys to press charges against the Cochrane's for extortion, mysterious and cynical poems kept making their way into the local newspapers over the next three years. These poems concerned the alleged relationship that the two had supposedly had.

This particular child turned out to be a very responsible adult. When he was told about his father, in his late teens, he refused to make any public statement about it to the press. Instead, a family spokesperson told the media that Phillip was not interested in Paul's money and preferred to make his own way in life. What a refreshing change from some of the battles that Paul had to fight. And it wasn't over yet.

Just when Paul thought all this paternity business had been left far in the past, it came back to haunt him once more. In 1981 McCartney's love child from Germany began to turn up in the tabloids again. By this time, Paul McCartney was married and had children of his own; it was a very difficult and embar-

rassing situation for him. He was very upset about the fact that even though there was no proof whatsoever that he was the father, the press still represented him as such, and his children were deeply affected by it.

Then on February 22, 1983, in the district court in Berlin, the Huebers filed suit against Paul McCartney again for a monthly support payment. They also wanted Paul to announce publicly that he was Bettina's father. The worst part for the McCartney's was that under German law, if paternity could be proven, then she would someday inherit ten percent of Paul's estate. The one point in their favor was that this decision could only be enforced in Germany, and again, only if paternity was proven. That still would have cost Paul's family his German royalties, which could be frozen and used in partial payment in the event that the Huebers won the suit.

By this time Paul had really become frustrated with the entire situation. It had started to hurt his family and he is a very devout family man. In an effort to establish his innocence he even agreed to submit to blood and tissue tests later that month. He just wanted the whole thing to be over so that he and his family could have some peace. Unfortunately establishing his innocence wasn't enough to resolve the matter and make the Huebers leave him alone. Despite the fact that both tests showed a ninety percent rating, indicating that he was not the father, the case didn't end there. The court ordered him to pay monthly child support payments anyway. Paul, feeling that the decision was unfair, refused to honor the court's ruling. Who could blame him? What kind of justice is that?

Two months later, this woman claiming to be his daughter garnered international headlines once again by posing in the nude for High Society magazine. Bettina's mother attempted to defend her by saying: "She did the session because she is broke and Paul hasn't paid her any maintenance money yet (the child was twenty years old at the time). All Bettina wore in these photos was a pair of long leather gloves. She was also holding a small, plastic guitar in an obvious attempt to capitalize on the McCartney name. It did get the young woman a lot of public attention, but she never got the end result that she was after.

Justice in this case was very slow in coming, and it came in a roundabout way. Bettina took Paul to court two more times in an attempt to extort money from him, but each time she lost. In fact, she was then ordered to pay all of Paul's legal expenses for the whole ordeal. Ever the gentleman, Paul knew that she didn't have the money and paid the expenses himself, glad to have put the whole sordid affair behind him. But Bettina had not yet played her last hand. She had one final irony up her sleeve. Instead of being grateful to Paul for not holding her liable to pay him the money that she rightfully owed him, but did not have, she chose to turn his generosity around on him. She implied that there was something fishy in the fact that Paul had paid these legal bills, saying she was suspicious of his motives in doing so. She even had the audacity to threaten to take him back to court again, but she never did.

Paul was ecstatic when the Beatles were given the MBE award in 1965. John, on the other hand, was typically unimpressed. In fact, he tucked his invitation into a pile of papers in the bottom of a drawer. The Beatles were presented the award by Queen Elizabeth herself and John remembered it this way: "Brian put us in neat suits and shirts and Paul was right behind him. We had to do a lot of selling out then. Taking the MBE was a sellout for me. You know, before you get your MBE the Palace writes to ask if you're going to accept it, because you're not supposed to reject it publicly and they sound you out first. I chucked the letter in with all the fan mail until Brian asked me if I had it. He and a few other people persuaded me that it was in our interests to take it, but it was hypocritical of me to accept it."

Not long after this historic event the Beatles started to get very tired of life on the road. This prompted them to make their appearance at Candlestick Park, on August 29, 1966, their last concert appearance. They decided that from that time on they would make all their music in the studio.

One of the albums that the Beatles produced together in the studio was originally slated to be called *Everest*. However, in the end they decided to call it *Abbey Road*, after the studio itself, and pose for the cover on the crosswalk outside.

Although John is the Beatle who had a reputation for being the artistic member of the group, John Dunbar, the owner of the Indica gallery where John and Yoko first met, gave Paul a new perspective on art. Dunbar was the first person to introduce him to the avant-garde film work of Michelangelo Antonioni. McCartney also became an admirer of the Greek sculptor, Takis, and his bizarre collection of magnetic machine art. McCartney and Dunbar even went on to make some underground films of their own. They started going around London with two sixteen millimeter cameras, filming anything they saw that was the least bit out of the ordinary. Then they would take the footage to Paul's studio in his St. John's Wood home, where they would dub in the soundtrack.

It was the Beatles, and Paul in particular, who first thought up the idea of making music videos. He started out by making eight millimeter films and showing them to Antonioni. Then in 1968 a writer from Britain's *Punch* magazine wrote an article about Paul's films *The Defeat of the Dog* and *The Next Spring Then*. There were overexposures, double exposures, blinding orange lights, quick cuts from professional wrestling to a crowded parking lot to a close-up of a television weather map. There were long still shots of a gray cloudy sky and wet gray pavement, jumping Chinese ivory carvings and slow motion studies of Martha, his sheepdog, and his cat. He also made this into his own version of a music video by synchronizing it with the Modern Jazz Quartet and Bach.

By 1973, Paul had become involved in more than a few other film projects. One was called *The Bruce McMouse Show*. It was supposed to be a partially animated diary of the first Wings European tour from the point of view of a mouse. After having children of his own, McCartney had become interested in producing a film especially for kids. Anyway McMouse lived underneath the stage with his wife Yvonne and their children; Soily, Swooney and Swat. It was a nice idea, but it was so far removed from the type of work that the public was used to seeing from Paul that it never quite got produced. The only remnants of the project that has been seen since that time are some early animation roughs of the main characters, which were offered for sale by a Beatles memorabilia dealer in New York a few years later.

On April 16, 1973, Paul made his acting debut on American television with *James Paul McCartney*. The special was only an hour long, but it allowed Paul to demonstrate his diversity of talent. Wings did a short concert for the grand finale. The critics were not at all impressed by the show; *Melody Maker* called it

"overblown" and "silly." Still, it has withstood the test of time nicely and is still a favorite among collectors of McCartney memorabilia.

The next film venture that Paul embarked upon was *Give My Regards to Broadstreet*. The basic plot involved a world-famous rock star whose master tapes kept coming up missing. The rock star's assistant was an ex-con and so he fell under the umbrella of suspicion immediately. The remainder of the film was about the search for those tapes.

The film closed after only two weeks. It did not go over well at all with the critics. One of Paul's fondest dreams in life had been to make a movie himself. He was very disappointed in the reviews that his movie received and told Gene Siskel: "I'm too human for all this criticism. I don't like sitting around with someone telling me they don't like my picture. I'm just a real little person inside this box."

By the summer of 1970, the Beatles were no more. The group had come to a long slow end, over time, which is all too clear in the film *Let It Be*. Paul and his attorney did file a formal lawsuit on December 31, 1970, petitioning to order the Beatles partnership dissolved and demanding to see their records regarding assets and liabilities. The other Fabs tried to block this move by hiring their own attorney, but it finally happened anyway. McCartney could never reconcile himself to accepting Klein as a manager.

Things went rapidly downhill from there between Paul and the other Beatles. One day, on the way to court, John decided that he and the other Fabs would pay Paul a little visit at his home. John had the driver take them around to his house, where John got out and climbed over the wall that surrounded McCartney's estate. Then he opened the front gate and came back out to the car to get some bricks out of the trunk. At first, George and Ringo were unsure what to do, so they just stood there in the street watching. Then Lennon proceeded to throw a brick through one of McCartney's downstairs windows. At that point the three of them started laughing hysterically as they piled back into the car and prepared to leave. In the meantime, Paul had run out of the house to see what was going on. When he saw who had broken his window he just stood there, dumbfounded, looking at the three people who used to mean the most to him in the world. The whole breakup was extremely hard on Paul. In fact, he has said that the only other life event that caused him more pain than the Beatles breakup, was the death of his mother when he was fourteen.

After the breakup of the group in 1970, John and Paul's relationship was never the same again. The hard feeling between them never softened enough for them to overcome everything that happened during that time. One of the biggest bones of contention between them had to do with the money that was tied up in the whole Apple fiasco.

Something else happened between Paul and the other Beatles that didn't help their relationship any. It all started one day when John was reading the paper and he saw an article that said Dick James (the Beatles music publisher) was selling his percentage of stock in Northern Songs (the Lennon and McCartney Publishing Company) to Sir Lew Grade at ATV. Both John and Paul were shocked to think that Dick would sell them out like that without even giving them an opportunity to buy the stock themselves. But the time had come for him and Dick was ready to get out. He had put many years of his life into the company and he knew that once Lennon/McCartney stopped writing new songs together it was all over. They had already refused to sign an extension on their song-writing contract and Dick knew that it didn't bode well for the future of the company.

Allen Klein suggested that the Beatles make a counter bid for the stock. In order to raise the money for this John and Paul would have to put up their own shares in Northern Songs as collateral. Allen Klein even put up 145,000 shares of his MGM stock in order to try and help them with the counter bid. When it came Paul's turn to put up his stock, that is where everything began to go terribly wrong. He breached trust with the other Beatles in a irreversible way. Not only did he refuse to put up his own stock to help raise money for the counter bid, but under Eastman's advice he had secretly bought up stock in his name alone. By the time the other Beatles heard about it, Paul already had 751,000 shares to John's 644,000 shares. The lie was what cut John to the quick. He was furious and exploded at Paul: "You bastard! You've been buying up stock behind our backs!"

"Oops, sorry!" said Paul. That was the only explanation that the others got from him. Tactics were definitely becoming dirty in the aftermath of the breakup and it would end up costing them more than just their friendship.

Something unusual happened then. The brokers on the London market identified the holders of the outstanding shares of Northern Songs without telling the Beatles or ATV. They arranged a meeting between the three largest shareholders so that they could pool their shares and form a consortium which represented almost fourteen percent of the company. This was a large enough percentage for them to potentially take control. Then on May 3rd, ATV extended the date on their bid for Northern Songs' stock until May 15th. If they had not won control of the company by then, they intended to accept the Beatles partial bid of forty-two shillings, sixpence a share.

Two days before the deadline ATV announced to the press that they had failed in their takeover bid. A formal statement was printed in the *Financial Times* explaining that ATV had come within 150,000 shares of owning forty-seven percent of Northern Songs. The Beatles had won this round.

While all of this was going on, John, Yoko, and Paul were trying to come to terms with the consortium. Lennon got so upset that he refused to work for a company in which he had no say. This upset the consortium and caused them to side with ATV even though they had already admitted defeat in the papers. The consortium signed a deal with them shortly before the Beatles' own bid expired at 3:00 p.m. The Beatles had just lost their company. Then, to add insult to injury, ATV hired Dick James to sit on the board of directors.

Paul decided to make his final break with the Beatles by making his first solo album. He took his family to their farm in Scotland to make the album and get away from the whole mess. It was during Paul's absence that the "Paul is Dead Hoax" rumors got started (see my first book).

Paul's life was threatened during the first Wings tour. They were in a bar in Sweden when a man walked up to Paul and told him quietly that he was going to blow him away. Then the man walked calmly to the other side of the bar, never taking his eyes off of Paul. Just then Laine and McCullough came into the bar. Paul quickly told them about what had happened. They were shocked and quietly slipped across the bar and came up on either side of the dark stranger. "Got a problem lad?" asked McCullough.

"No, why?" the stranger asked nervously.

The two band members threw him down on the floor and held him down while they searched his pockets. It was a very tense moment. The threat turned out to be this man's idea of a joke. Some joke. The group left the club badly shaken.

The next really big shock for Paul came at the end of 1980 when John Lennon was shot down in cold blood in front of the Dakota apartment building. Paul was so devastated by this needless tragedy that he didn't go on tour again for several years.

Yoko was the one to call Paul and break the terrible news to him. Right after it happened reporters were crawling all over AIR studios trying to get a statement from the grieving McCartney. A special contingent of anti-terrorist bodyguards (a radical move back then) was hired to protect Paul. Later that day, he did make a statement to the press about his feelings for his late partner, saying that he had loved John like a brother and respected him immensely for the part he had taken in the peace movement.

Paul went on to dedicate an entire issue of his fan club publication, *Club Sandwich*, to John's memory. Linda had taken some very warm and personal photographs of him, which also appeared in that issue.

Another horrible tragedy almost occurred in the McCartney family in 1983 when a plot to kidnap Linda from their Sussex home was uncovered. A former British soldier named Allan Gallop and two accomplices had planned to grab her in a military style raid on the McCartney estate. Gallop had been watching the family for more than a week in order to become familiar with their routine. He was planning to hold Linda hostage at a remote farmhouse until a twelve and a half million dollar ransom was paid for her safe return. Fortunately for Linda, the kidnappers did so much bragging about their plan that the local police got wind of it before they had a chance to try and pull it off.

Paul and Alistair Taylor had not seen each other since Klein had let him go during the big lay off at Apple. It seems that one day when Taylor was clearing some old books from his library he came across Paul's original sketch design from the 1968 Apple want ad. Alistair had heard that Paul was heavily into collecting Beatles memorabilia and decided to call him up and see if he was interested in the piece. He and Paul had been fairly close in the old days and he was looking forward to talking with him again, but like so many other people who came in contact with the new McCartney, he was in for a big disappointment. He recounted the story at a Beatles convention in 1984:

> I was unemployed and I wrote and said: "Hey I found this old sketch you did. Do you remember being in my flat? We were drinking coffee until two in the morning. We must have thrown dozens of these things away..." It literally dropped out of a book after fourteen years. Then his manager rang to say that Paul wasn't interested. So I said, "Fine." The next thing I know Paul himself rang and just dived straight in by saying, "It's not yours to sell and you've no right, you know." I haven't spoken to the guy in fifteen years and we were once so close that I was taken aback. So anyway, I ended up by saying, "It is mine, it was in my house and I need the money, so I'm going to go ahead and put it into Sotheby's." So I put it into Sotheby's, and the next thing I know there was an injunction from McCartney's lawyers, so I had to settle out of court. I sold

it back to Paul at an agreed figure which was about one tenth of what it was worth. (Chicago Beatlefest 1984)

Paul was ripped off a lot in his early days as a Beatle—they all were—and perhaps he is trying to somehow make up for that, but Taylor had never been anything but nice to him. Some things are just difficult to understand. Obviously, he was left with some bitterness from the money that he lost in the old days.

Another rather interesting story regarding Beatles memorabilia—McCartney memorabilia in particular—concerning a gift that Paul wished to bestow on the Eastern Bloc. He wanted to give them a special listening treat and planned to release a collection of fifties oldies there in 1988. The original plan was to issue some recently recorded rock standards in England as if they had been smuggled in from Russia on the underground market. He initially had trouble selling the idea of bootlegging his own album to the executives at MPL (McCartney's company). Paul's business manager, Richard Ogden, went ahead and pressed a couple of dozen copies of the LP, packaged them in Russian-looking jackets and gave them to McCartney as a Christmas present.

McCartney got a second chance at bringing his idea to life when Mikhail Gorbechev's perestroika and glasnost warmed up relations with Russia. At that point MPL sent Ogden to Moscow to meet with officials from the state run Melodya record label. Melodya signed a licensing agreement which allowed them to produce 400,000 copies of the album which was called *Back in the U.S.S.R.*. Paul wanted this album to be released only in the Eastern Bloc countries, but as soon as it came out, it started turning up in England and America as a specialty collector's item. The price of the album in those countries was around two hundred dollars. Paul's "bootleg" album was being sold on the underground market in Western countries. McCartney found the whole thing very disturbing.

Meanwhile, back in Russia, fans from Georgia to Siberia were lining up to score a copy of this hot new release. In fact, it sold out within the first forty-eight hours. After that there wasn't a copy to be found anywhere in the Eastern Bloc. Due to the demand for and popularity of the album, Paul agreed to promote the LP by doing a live transcontinental satellite discussion with the Russian people through the BBC World Service, out of London. Paul talked to callers live for nearly an hour, both about the new album and his time with the Beatles.

McCartney was always an excellent PR man and he made some very wise investments over the years. He was recognized in the November 1983 issue of *People* as "The Richest Man in Show Business." Today he is a billionaire and makes more money in one year than most major airlines. In fact, MPL is the largest independent music publisher in the world. While following the advice of the Eastman clan, Paul has bought a vast array of copyrights on everything from "Happy Birthday" to "Ghostriders in the Sky".

MPL also had control over such mainstream musicals as *Mame*, *La Cage aux Falles*, *Peter Pan*, *A Chorus Line*, *Grease*, *Hello Dolly*, and *Guys and Dolls*. McCartney also held interests in the song-writing catalogs of composers like Scott Joplin and Ira Gershwin.

Paul and Linda both really enjoy investing in art. The couple has a multi-million dollar collection of classic works by Magritte, Picasso, Edward Paolozzi, and a personal friend, William de Kooning.

Paul made an attempt at working closely with another performer in 1983 when he teamed up with Michael Jackson during the making of the *Pipes of Peace* album. Paul remembers Michael coming to him and saying, "I wanna make some hits."

McCartney and Jackson sat around on the top floor of Paul's offices in London and wrote "Say Say Say" together. Despite the teaming up of two of the top rockers in the world, the *Pipes of Peace* LP was named *Billboard* magazine's most disappointing album of the year. It was also the only album that McCartney had ever played on that didn't make the Top Ten in America. Still, McCartney and Jackson decided to continue to work together and started calling themselves "Mac and Jac." The two famous rockers first met at a Wings party aboard the Queen Mary, and then again, at another Hollywood party. At the second party Paul told Michael that he had written a song that he thought would be perfect for Jackson. The song was called "Girlfriend" and Jackson remembered the song during a recording session with Quincy Jones on his first solo album. He called Paul up to ask him if he could use the song on his *Off the Wall* album.

After that, Michael wrote a song called "The Girl Is Mine" that he thought would be perfect for McCartney. In fact, it became a McCartney/Jackson duet. It was issued as a single in the U.S. and Great Britain and made it into the top five in both countries.

This was another great music team. Mac and Jac could have potentially done things as great as Lennon/McCartney. In Jackson, Paul had found someone to collaborate with that he felt was on the same level musically as he was. They could have gone on to be another great song-writing team if it wasn't for something that Michael did, that greatly upset Paul and ended their relationship.

Two years after their work together on *Pipes of Peace*, Jackson bought the rights to ATV Music, including the Northern Songs catalog of Beatles classics. His winning bid for the body of work was fifty million dollars. Paul was very upset about the whole thing. He felt tricked and betrayed by someone that he thought he could trust.

Paul had tried to buy the songs at the same time, but had been outbid by a secret bid left by an unknown person, who later turned out to be Michael Jackson. When the songs initially went up for sale, Paul and Yoko joined together for the first time to try and buy the rights to them.

Paul and Yoko discussed making a wide range of offers for the portfolio, but Yoko felt the songs could be had for much less than they actually ended up going for. CBS, Warner Communications, Paramount, EMI, and the Entertainment Company all wanted to be the victors in this bidding war. Pretty high stakes. Michael Jackson put in a secret bid behind everyone else's back and became the new owner of the songs in 1985.

Paul later found out about a little known provision in American copyright law, which stated that if a composer passes away during the first twenty-eight year phase of a copyright, his or her heir can claim an additional term of the same duration, regardless of any pre-existing publishing agreements. As a result, McCartney may well be right to feel that Yoko intentionally short-circuited his bid to control the songs, knowing that the copyrights would eventually revert back to the Lennon estate without her having to lay out a penny. While in America, publishing companies offer renewals, that is not true for England. In other words, after twenty-eight years the composer is given a chance to renew with the original publisher or not. John's renewals for the songs he composed with McCartney have been steadily coming up. This gives Yoko a chance to get the right to get back the rights to these songs. Paul can't because all of the Beatles signed away their rights while they are still alive.

To add insult to injury, the suggestion has even been made that Ono may have actually assisted Jackson in putting the deal together. If true, a very nasty trick to have played on her late husband's former partner.

In the end, Paul just had to grin and bear it, knowing that his one real chance at holding onto the Beatles' great song writing legacy was most likely gone forever.

This rug is made in Belgium and features the Fab Four's faces near the bottom right and a drum near the top left. Value: G: $300 E: $360 NM: $400.

Wall Hangings

Turkish Wall Hanging. Uncertain date of origin. Measures 40" x 54". Value: E: $40 NM: $50.

Irish Linen wall hanging by Ulster. Made in England. Value; G: $140 E: $160 NM: $185.

111

New Memorabilia

Beatles painting on black velvet. Made in Mexico. Value: E: $75 NM: $100.

North American Tours Lithograph. Design by Gary Grinshaw. *Photo courtesy of Ochs Archives.* Value: E: $90 NM: $100.

The following lithograph photos have the same description and value as the *With The Beatles* limited edition.

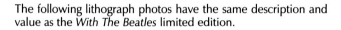

A Hard Day's Night limited edition litho.

With The Beatles limited edition ART Rock lithos, 1990 Apple Corps Ltd. Phillip Cushway Lithos, North American Tours. Value given is with frame and per image: E: $225 NM: $250.

Help! limited edition litho.

The White Album limited edition litho.

Beatles '65 limited edition litho.

The Beatles Yesterday and Today limited edition litho.

Revolver limited edition litho.

The Beatles, Please, Please Me limited edition litho.

Rubber Soul limited edition litho.

Sgt. Pepper's limited edition litho.

Beatles For Sale limited edition litho.

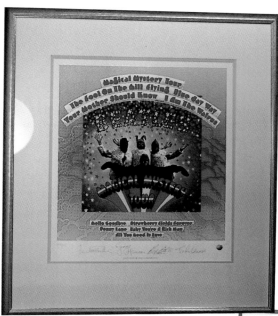

Magical Mystery Tour limited edition litho.

Abbey Road limited edition litho.

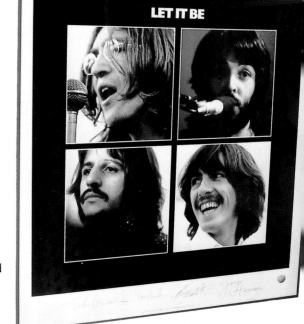

Let It Be limited edition litho.

Linda Louise Eastman was born in Scarsdale, New York, on September 24, 1941. Her father was a Harvard graduate who had officially changed his name from Epstein to Eastman. He was a well known New York attorney in the field of arts and entertainment. Linda had two sisters and a brother, but she was very close to her mother, Louise Linder. Louise was the daughter of the founder and CEO of the Linder department store chain. When Linda was only eighteen years old, her mother was killed in a plane crash. She was completely devastated by the loss. Linda graduated from Scarsdale High School, then went on to Sarah Lawrence. Shortly after that, she enrolled in college in Denver, Colorado, to try and get away and get some perspective on the tragedy of her mother's death. While attending school there she met a geology student by the name of Bob See. They eventually married and Linda gave birth to her first child, a baby girl named Heather, in 1962. The marriage became rocky after that and the couple ended up divorcing. Linda moved to Tucson for a year before returning to New York and becoming an assistant at *Town and Country* magazine.

While she was working for *Town and Country* magazine, an invitation to a Rolling Stones press party aboard a yacht arrived at the magazine and Linda decided to attend. She also decided to take her camera to the party and take a few pictures. That was the beginning of her career as a rock photographer. At the party she was introduced to Mick Jagger and they soon became friends.

Rock photography became a passion for Linda right way. She really got into it. Her portfolio was full to overflowing with pictures of rock stars. Not long after that first foray into photography Linda was named informal house photographer at the Fillmore East. It was the opportunity of a lifetime. Every big name group of the day that you can imagine played there and Linda was soon credited as being one of rock's hippest and prettiest photographers. During her stint there, she was connected romantically with Steve Winwood, Tim Buckley, Warren Beatty, Eric Burdon, Stephen Stills, Mike Bloomfield and Al Kooper. In fact, Linda was also gaining a reputation for being an ardent fan.

According to Ms. Eastman, she met her future husband, Paul McCartney, for the first time, backstage at Shea Stadium in 1966. The author of *Rock and Other Four-Letter Words* invited Linda to come to London and photograph some high level groups. In fact, she was one of the select few to receive an invitation to photograph the Traffic session. After the shoot she decided to hang out there in London for a few days and see what was going on. One night she went with the bassist from the Animals to a night club called the Bag O' Nails. It just so happened that Paul dropped in that night to catch the show and ended up

sitting at the table next to Linda and they were introduced to one another.

By the next afternoon she was calling NEMS. She talked to Peter Brown and asked him if she could come by the next day and show him her portfolio. What she was really hoping was that she could get one of the coveted passes to the *Sgt. Pepper* press party at Brian Jones's house. It was no secret that these press passes were worth their weight in gold. Brown agreed to take a look at her work and he really did like it. As she was leaving she presented him with a large blow-up of Brian Jones. He called after her, telling her to be sure to bring her camera with her to the bash at Brian's house.

When Linda arrived at the gathering she found Paul sitting in a chair by the fireplace nervously smoking a cigarette. Linda promptly whipped out her camera, got down on her knees in front of the chair and started snapping pictures of McCartney in quick succession. She wanted to get some time to talk to Paul, but it didn't happen on that occasion. Instead, she was escorted out with the other photographers.

Linda tried to contact him by phone the next day, only to discover that his number, as well as those of the other Beatles, were actually billed to Harry Pinkster for security reasons. Pinkster worked for the P.R. firm that helped them to buy houses and other property in safe areas. She discovered this when she called the number that she had gotten from Paul and asked for him. Pinkster started to explain the situation to Linda, but she didn't believe him. Determined to get through to McCartney, she kept calling back until Pinkster was finally forced to unplug the phone so he could get some sleep. She finally had to give up and return to New York.

She had just gotten back to the U.S. when one of her friends, who also happened to be a rock critic, sent her a picture of herself with Paul, that was taken by another photographer at the party. She liked the picture so much that she blew it up and hung it on the wall of her apartment. Now she was more determined than ever to meet Beatle Paul. She would soon get her chance. Paul traveled to New York in May to announce the opening of Apple. His itinerary included a press conference, a meeting of the board of directors at Apple, a photo layout in *Life* magazine, and an appearance on the *Tonight Show*.

At the press conference Linda slipped Paul her phone number. To her amazement, he called her later that same day and made plans for them to get together that night. At that time he was still engaged to Jane Asher, and he was afraid that if Linda showed up at his hotel, they might be photographed together. And he didn't want Jane to suspect anything. Instead, he arranged to meet her at an East Side apartment, where they ended up spending the next few days together. During this marathon "interview" Paul happened to mention to Linda how fond of children he was. She was delighted and arranged for him to meet her six year old daughter, Heather. In fact, Paul actually baby-sat for her while she went to do a shoot at the Fillmore. That was the beginning of what was to be a long-lasting relationship. When it was time for him to go back to London, Linda missed Paul McCartney terribly.

A few weeks later, McCartney was back in the United States to speak at a record convention for Capitol, in Los Angeles. After that he rented a bungalow at the Beverly Hills Hotel with three bedrooms. And, ever the rogue, he made good use of the entire space. In the first bedroom he had secreted a young Hollywood starlet, while in the second was a famous call girl. Finally, in the third was Ron Kass, a business associate. Things were going quite well for a very busy Paul until Sunday morning. The phone rang and it was Linda calling from the phone in the lobby. Paul didn't miss a beat. He told her to come on up. When Linda arrived, he let her in and asked her to have a seat on the sofa. Then he went in and instructed the other two girls to leave and joined Linda on the sofa while they gathered up their things. The Hollywood starlet left in tears. Linda spent the night that night and the next day Paul took her sailing with him on John Calley's yacht (the head of production at Warner Brothers). She even took the flight back with Paul and Ron as far as New York. Paul flew on alone to London.

After that encounter, Linda began calling Paul and writing to him on a regular basis. A bit later Paul talked her into coming to London for a visit (by this time he and Jane had broken up for good). He and Linda co-habitated together for awhile there, but they both started to miss Heather, so they decided to bring her to London to live with them. The trio moved into the house on Cavendish Avenue where Paul thoroughly enjoyed playing at being a husband and a father.

By late in the year, 1968, Linda finally took Paul home to meet her parents. They liked each other very much from the start and before long Paul asked Lee Eastman to help him straighten out the mess at Apple.

By February of 1969 Linda was pregnant. Paul was thrilled and asked her to marry him. In the beginning, she actually said no. She enjoyed her work and being on her own. She really was not ready to get married again. However, she did eventually agree to marry Paul.

As soon as the news of McCartney's upcoming nuptials hit the street, hundreds of young women started to show up on Cavendish Avenue. The night before the wedding was the worst for Linda. Young women stood outside wailing and crying about the loss of the last eligible Beatle. It was rather unnerving.

The next day, March 11, 1969, Paul and Linda were married at the Marlebone Registry Office. Hundreds of fans and reporters turned up for the ceremony, which took all of ten minutes. Then the happy couple had to fight their way through the crowd in order to get back to their car.

The big problems started for Linda when Paul not only wanted her to be a part of Wings, but wanted her to be his new song writing partner as well. It started with McCartney asking his wife to play keyboards, despite her inexperience. Just as Stu Sutcliffe had joined the Beatles to play the bass without any prior musical experience, so Linda became a member of Wings, with nothing to fall back on except her enormous desire to please her husband and her naturally competitive spirit.

The critics were brutal when it came to Linda. They criticized everything about her, saying that her ability to play the piano was minimal, her vocals were worse, her clothing was sloppy, and she didn't shave her legs. The initial reviews were hard for her to take.

The thing that caused the most problems, however, was Paul's collaboration with her in his song writing efforts. He simply enjoyed being with her and wanted to involve her in every aspect of the music business. This eventually started a big legal battle with Lew Grade and Northern Songs over Linda's musical ability, or lack of same. It all started with the release of a single called "Another Day." The problem arose from the fact that both Paul and Linda were listed as writers of that particular song. What this meant to Grade was that one half of the publishing rights (millions of dollars in all) would go directly to Linda without Northern Songs getting any part of her share. Lew felt that it was a scheme on Paul's part to cheat him out of part of his money. He made the argument that Linda was obviously not a musician of comparable composition ability to Paul. Grade insisted that one hundred percent of the song writing credit be given to Paul and he took the McCartneys to court over it.

The essence of Grade's lawsuit was that Linda had no musical ability whatsoever. Paul's lawyers argued that Linda's level of musical ability was not the issue. They argued that Paul had a right to compose with absolutely anyone that he chose to compose with regardless of their musical experience. Surprisingly, the McCartneys won the suit. Paul still didn't want any hard feelings between himself and Lew, so he agreed to star in a TV special that Grade produced called *James Paul McCartney*.

On the other hand, Paul and Linda went on to write seven of the eight tracks on their *Wild Life* album together. Their relationship still seems to be quite good even after more than twenty-five years of marriage. Although they have been known to have disagreements from time to time, the hard feelings never seem to linger for long.

In February of 1972, Paul and Wings went off in the English countryside in a van, very much as the Beatles had done in Neil Aspinall's van eleven years earlier. The group was trying to get back to Paul's roots, an itch that he got once in awhile, by spontaneously stopping at various places and offering to play. They first stopped at Nottingham University and asked if they could give a free concert for the students the following evening. Paul also asked that the administration not tell the students what was going on so that the press wouldn't show up. Can you imagine the looks on those student's faces when Paul McCartney came out on that stage?

Wings gave a free concert that night, for over seven hundred students. The group went on to spend the following summer and fall touring Europe in a double-decker bus with clouds and rainbows painted on it. I think this is the sort of thing that Paul had meant to portray when he made *Magical Mystery Tour*. A documentary of this trip could have been very effective.

I would like to wrap up this section on Linda Eastman McCartney by telling you a very touching story about the couple and their feelings for one another. The story revolves around one of Linda's photo exhibits at an art gallery in London. She did a one woman show in September of 1982 and it didn't go exactly as planned. In fact, thirty-seven of the pieces did not sell. Paul knew how disappointed Linda would be when she found out, so he bought them himself. It was a very sweet gesture, but unfortunately the media got wind of it and the *Sun* splashed the story across its front page. When Linda found out, she was so touched that he would go to all that trouble, just to keep her from being disappointed, that she actually cried.

It took awhile, but eventually the whole affair began to blow over. Paul and Linda's first child together, Mary McCartney, was born on August 29, 1969 at 1:30 a.m. She weighed six pounds, eight ounces and Paul couldn't have been more proud of her. He even put her on the cover of his *McCartney* album.

By this time all the pressure from the press and the mess at Apple—just everything in general—was catching up with Paul. He took his family on vacation in Scotland, which caused rumors of his death to begin circulating. In fact, the whole story got so out of hand that Paul agreed to a press conference with a handful of reporters at his farm in order to clear it up.

When Paul and Linda started to have children of their own they started to outgrow Waterfalls, their small circular home in Sussex. It was a very interesting dwelling, shaped like a gazebo, with all of the rooms sort of cut into wedges, like pieces of pie. The problem with this design was that you could hear everything that was going on in the next room. Nowhere in the house could a person find any real privacy. They bought the property next to them, East Gate Farm, in 1982. They razed the old farmhouse on the land and Paul designed a five bedroom house to take its place. It was a lovely estate, complete with stables and a paddock for their thoroughbred horses, a swimming pool, and a sixty-five foot watchtower. This was one of Paul's own ideas and he said that it was built so that the family could enjoy the lovely scenery surrounding the farm. After John's murder, a large fence was also built around the property.

Inside the grounds ducks, geese, and peacocks roam freely, along with the McCartney's sheep. Paul and Linda are each very fond of hearth and home and they have made a comfortable little nest for themselves. Their home is actually quite modest. There are no gold records on the wall, no awards or memorabilia. Even most of their art collection can be found in Paul's offices.

I am afraid that it is my unhappy duty to report the death of Linda McCartney. She died after this manuscript had already been sent to the publishing company, but my editor was kind enough to allow me to add a few words about her.

Let me begin by saying that Linda was a very caring and talented person, independent of her famous husband. She cared very deeply about animals, doing everything that she could to protect them, as well as being a devout vegetarian. Paul has asked us to remember her for those things as she would have wanted it that way. I would also like to say that she was one of the best rock photographers who ever lived, capturing the most famous rockers in very candid, and sometimes heartwarming, poses.

In 1989 Linda published a vegetarian cookbook called *Linda McCartney's Home Cooking*, which was filled with some of her best recipes. Then, in 1991, she came out with her McVege line of vegetarian cuisine. These efforts alone served to make her a millionaire, but she had many other talents as well.

In 1995 Linda was diagnosed with breast cancer at the Princess Grace hospital. It was then that doctors found a malignant tumor in her breast. She had it removed and underwent chemotherapy.

Linda passed away on April 17, 1998, at the McCartney home in Tucson, Arizona. She was fifty-six years old. The breast cancer that she had battled for over two years spread to her liver and ultimately took her life. The couple had been married for twenty-nine years and were still deeply in love.

I would like to take this opportunity to clear up some of the rumors that were circulated surrounding Linda's death. There were rumors in the beginning that Linda died in Santa Barbara, which is not true. In fact, some of the fringe elements of the press caused Paul and his family further grief over this simply because the family wanted some privacy during Linda's passing. When certain reporters started nosing around in Santa Barbara, it was discovered that no death certificate had been filed, and Linda's body had already been cremated. This started speculation of an assisted suicide. Anyone who knew Linda, knew that this was not even a possibility. She loved life and her family far too much for that. When an investigation was actually launched to look into the matter Paul was forced to reveal a long kept family secret, and give up another little piece of the family's privacy. Santa Barbara was a code that they used so that no one would know where they were actually going. Their real destination, when they said this, was their ranch just outside of Tucson. It was one of Linda's favorite places.

Paul and the children kept her death a secret for the first two days, so that they could grieve in peace. They had hoped to be able to fly back to England before word of Linda's death leaked out. That is why the initial statement to the press had been that she died in Santa Barbara.

At the time of this writing, the couple's daughter, Mary, was planning to marry in May of 1998 and Linda had very much wanted to attend. In fact, the wedding had already been moved up after she found out her illness was terminal, so that she wouldn't miss it. Her passing, at this time, was a bit of a shock. She had been feeling better over the past couple of weeks and her death was unexpected. Linda had been out horseback riding and doing other things that one does on vacation and there was nothing to indicate that this would happen.

Paul remains absolutely heartbroken. Linda was the love of his life. In fact, he loved her so much that the only nights that they ever spent apart were during his incarceration in Tokyo for possession of marijuana.

Paul scattered Linda's ashes over the grounds of their farm and long-time home in Sussex, England.

Linda will long be remembered for her fabulous rock photography, devout vegetarianism, and her work as an animal rights advocate.

Paul is planning a tribute album in memory of the love of his life. It will feature songs that the couple recorded together. Paul, though admittedly heartbroken, will somehow carry on...

Newspapers

An original *Mersey Beat* newspaper, Volume One, #13. Headline reads, "Beatles Top Poll." Dated January of 1962. This is one of three copies still known to exist. Paul McCartney's name is misspelled in the article. Value: G: $1,000 E: $1,500 NM: $2,000.

Another original *Mersey Beat* newspaper with a picture of Pete Best on the cover along with the headline, "Beatles Record". Volume One, #23. Dated 5-31 thru 6-14, 1962. Value with frame: G: $175 E: $250 NM: $300.

Tickets

A Hard Day's Night original movie ticket. Admission was 90 cents back then and this particular ticket came from the Aynor Theatre in Aynor, South Carolina. The theatre opened in 1964. Value: G: $15 E: $25 NM: $30.

A Hard Day's Night unused original Special Premiere ticket from the El Monte Theatre. Value: G: $15 E: $25 NM: $30.

Help! unused original movie ticket from the Port Theatre, Corona Del Mar. Value: G: $10 E: $20 NM: $25.

Concert Tickets

Candlestick Park, San Francisco, August 29, 1966. Value: G: $250 E: $350 NM: $425.

Suffolk Downs, August 18,1966. Value: G: $75 E: $100 NM: $125.

Lyrics & Music Books

The Beatles Greatest Hits, 1977, Creative Publishing Corp. Value: E: $12 NM: $15.

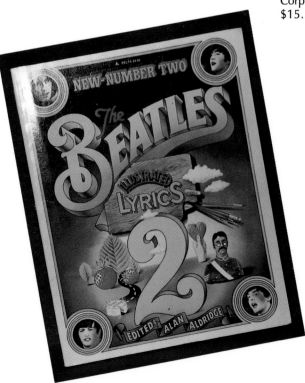

The Beatles Illustrated Lyrics 2. © 1971 by BPC Publishing Ltd., London. A Dell Special Publication, it is the second volume of a two volume set. Value: G: $15 E: $20 NM: $25.

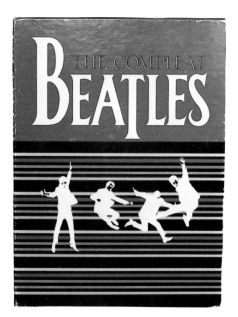

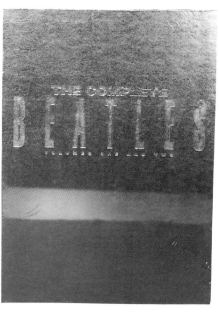

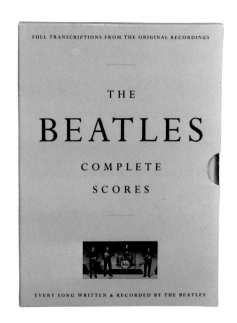

The Compleat Beatles music book with a slip-on cardboard cover. Delilah/ATV/Bantam. Value: G: $15 E: $20 NM: $25.

The Complete Beatles, Volume One and Two. Put out by the Hal Leonard Corp. Value: G: $15 E: $20 NM: $25.

The Beatles Complete Scores. This book includes a full transcript of every song ever written and recorded by the Beatles. Value: G: $15 E: $20 NM: $25.

Advertisments

"Vox: It's What's Happening". Vox registered warranty and an advertisement for amplifiers. Made by Thomas Organ Company 1965. Value: G: $25 E: $50 NM: $75.

Merseyside Decal from Liverpool. Value: E: $3 NM: $5.

Reproduction VeeJay record ad for amplifiers. Value: E: $5 NM: $8.

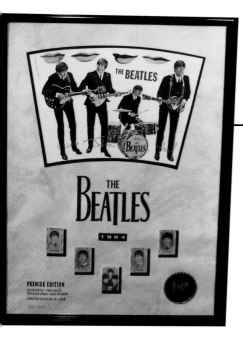

ART Rock premiere, 1964 edition issue with uncut cup insert. Also includes an ad promoting limited edition Hallmark stamps of 1964. Value: G: $50 E: $65 NM: $75.

Books

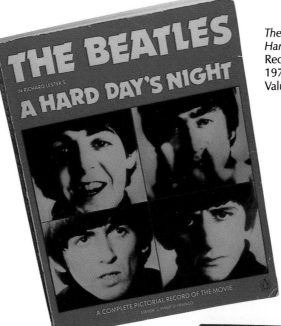

The Beatles in Richard Lester's "A Hard Day's Night", Pictoral Record. Penguin Books Ltd. © 1978 Chelsea House Publishers. Value: G: $20 E: $25 NM: $30.

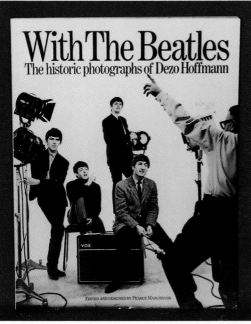

With The Beatles, The Historic Photographs of Dezo Hoffman. © 1982 Omnibus Press. Value: E: $20 NM: $25.

Beatles Poster Book with 24 posters. Value: E: $10 NM: $15.

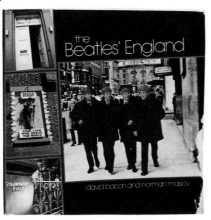

The Beatles' England by David Bacon and Norman Maslov. 1982, A 910 Press Book. Value: E: $10 NM: $15.

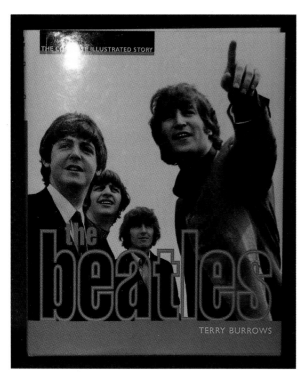

The Beatles, The Complete Illustrated Story by Terry Burrows, Carlton Books Ltd. 1996. Value: E: $10 NM: $15.

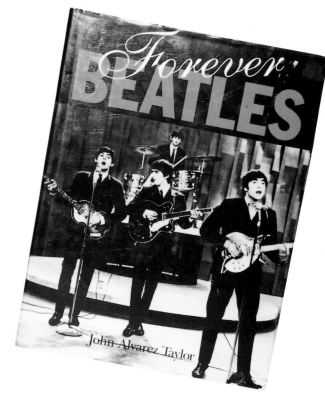

Forever Beatles by John Alvarez Taylor. © Brompton Book Corp. Value: E: $20 NM: $30.

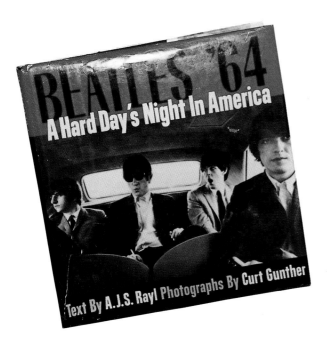

Beatles '64, A Hard Day's Night In America by A.J.S. Rayl, September 1989-first edition. Value: E: $20 NM: $25.

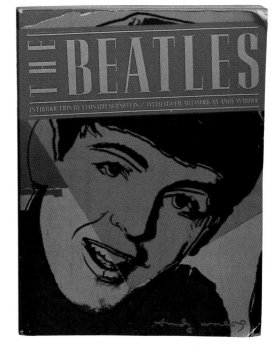

The Beatles with cover art by Andy Warhol. Text by Geoffrey Stokes, Times Books Rolling Stone. © 1980 by Rolling Stone Press. Value: E: $30 NM: $35.

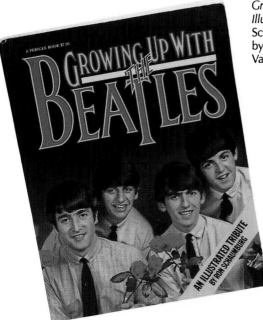

Growing Up With the Beatles, An Illustrated Tribute by Ron Schaumberg, Perigee Books, © 1976 by Delilah Communications Ltd. Value: E: $15 NM: $20.

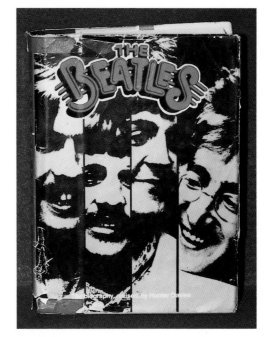

The Beatles is a hard cover edition of the Hunter Davies authorized Beatles history. Value: E: $35 NM: $45.

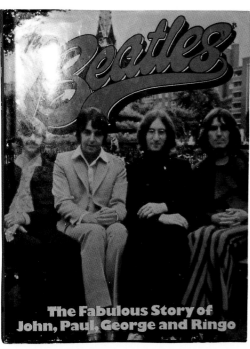

The Beatles, The Fabulous Story of John, Paul, George and Ringo Octopus Books Ltd., 1975. Value: E: $15 NM: $20.

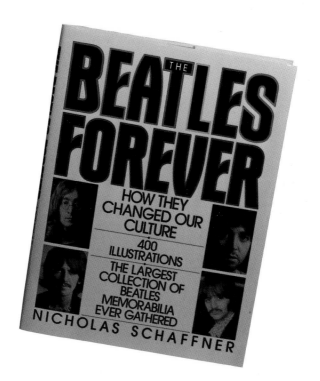

The Beatles Forever, How They Changed Our Culture by Nicholas Schaffner, Fine Communications, MJF Books. Value: E: $25 NM: $30.

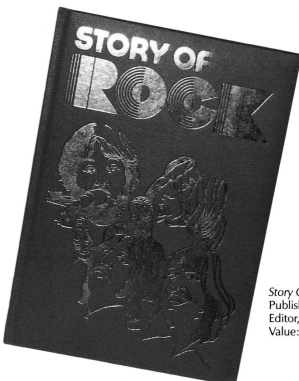

Story Of Rock BPC
Publishing Ltd. 1973/76,
Editor, Jeremy Pascall.
Value: E: $10 NM: $15.

The Beatles Companion, The Fab Four in Film,
Performance, Recording and Print by Ted
Greenwald, 1992. Michael Friedman Publishing
Group Inc. Value: E: $25 NM: $30.

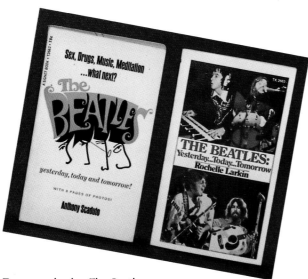

Two paperbacks: The Beatles
Yesterday...Today...Tomorrow by Rochelle Larkin,
1974, Scholastic Book Services and The Beatles
Yesterday, Today, and Tomorrow by Anthony Scaduto.
Value per book: E: $10 NM: $12

The Beatles Yesterday, Today and Tomorrow by
Anthony Scaduto, first edition 1968, Signet Books
and The Complete Beatles Quiz Book by Edwin
Goodgold and Dan Carlinsky, Warner Books. Value
for first edition book: E: $20 NM: $25. Value for
second book: E: $10 NM: $12.

Calendars

The Beatles 1989, 16-month calendar. Value: E: $12 NM: $15.

The Beatles 1995 calendar with a black and white photo of the group on the cover. Put out by Oliver Books. Value: E: $12 NM: $15.

The Beatles 1990 calendar. It came in two different sizes and was made by Cleo. Value large: E: $12 NM: $15. Value small: E: $7 NM: $9.

Let It Be 1997 desk top calendar. Put out by Day Dream Inc. Value: E: $7 NM: $9.

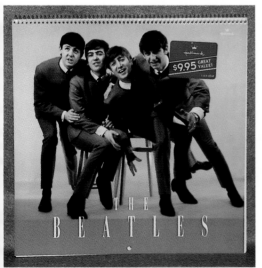

The Beatles Hallmark calendar, 1996. Value: E: $12 NM: $15.

Abbey Road 1996 desk top calendar. Put out by Day Dream Inc. Value: E: $7 NM: $9.

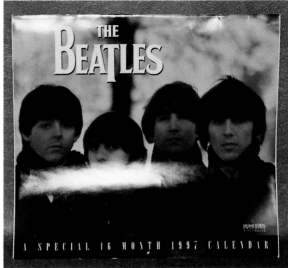

The Beatles Home Town calendar 1997. Value: E: $12 NM: $15.

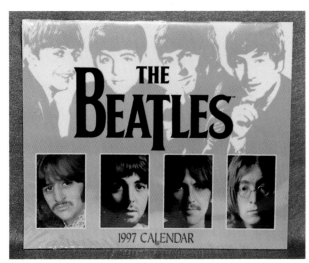

The Beatles 1997 calendar. Value: E: $12 NM: $15.

The Beatles Magical Mystery Tour official 1997 calendar. Put out by Danilo. Value: E: $12 NM: $15.

Comics

"The Beatles Experience" comic book series, with comic #1-#4. While these are unauthorized items, they are very well done, with wonderful art work and lots of Beatles history. Value for each: E: $10 NM: $15.

Another part of "The Beatles Experience" comic book series. Volumes #5 to #8.

126

Membership Cards-Post Cards

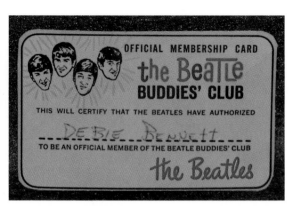

Official Membership Card from "The Beatle Buddies' Club". Uncertain of year. Value: E: $10 NM: $12.

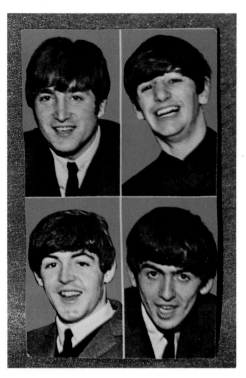

Dig Magazine Postcard. Blue with the Fab Fours' faces. Value: G: $15 E: $20 NM: $25.

"The Beatles" postcard, shows the group in their collarless Pierre Cardin style suits, 1964. Value: G: $15 E: $20 NM: $25.

Two 6" x 9" postcards. Value for each: G: $25 E: $30 NM: $35.

New Trading Cards and Chase Cards

Four Signature Cards from Sports Time Inc., 1996, Apple Corps Limited. A Beatles™ product. A copy of each Beatle's signature can be seen on the front in 24 kt gold. In order to get the Signature Series, you must buy packages of trading cards from Sports Time and look for the various chase cards. The corresponding Signature Series redemption card can be sent in to get each card in the series. Sports Time will stamp the redemption card and send it back to you upon request. Hang onto them. This set is beautiful and already collectible. Value for the set of four: E: $100 NM: $120.

Redemption card that was mentioned above. Value per each: E: $5 NM: $7.

Sports Time Promotional Card, marked P1 on the back upper right hand corner. It was put out to promote the quality of these cards. The initial trading card set for 1996, (not shown), contains one hundred numbered, full color cards. This includes a set of 5 checklist cards mixed in with the first one hundred. Once your set has been assembled it should contain the following chase cards: twelve gold record cards, five "Magical Mystery Tour" cards, and ten "Meet The Beatles" cards. Chase cards are slipped in randomly. The original set of one hundred does not contain any chase cards. Pictures of this set, not shown here, can be seen in Volume Three of this collector's series. Value for the initial set of one hundred (not shown): E: $35 NM: $40. Value for the promotional card only: E: $8 NM: $10.

Set of twelve Gold Record chase cards. On the back of each card all of the songs that were on the album are listed, along with who wrote them, and additional Sports Time information. Value for the set with frame: E: $45 NM: $48.

Set of five "Magical Mystery Tour" chase cards from the Sports Time set— has movie facts on the back. Value for set: E: $55 NM: $60

Set of ten "Meet The Beatles" chase cards. Value: E: $60 NM: $70.

The River Group chase cards. Half of the set of twelve is shown. These cards are double-sided. 1993 Apple Corps Ltd. Licensed by Determined Productions Inc. Printed in USA. There are twelve chase cards in this set, including ten #1 hits cards, and another "Very Limited Edition" set of two chase cards with one set of photos from the Beatles first concert and the other with a set of photos from their last concert. Value per card: E: $5 NM: $7.

Beatles "Abbey Road" 23 kt gold trading card, licensed by the Beatles in association with Apple Corps Ltd. They are hand sculpted and come with a plastic holder and a foil-stamped box. Each card is stamped with an individual serial number. Value: E: $35 NM: $40.

"Beatles For Sale": another 23 kt gold trading card with the same description and value.

Miscellaneous Items

"The Beatles Collection" Liverpool press kit, which is presented: "From Liverpool to the World." This picture shows you the box that the kit came in. Value for the entire kit: E: $60 NM: $75.

This shows the contents of the aforementioned press kit: "The Beatles 1958-64" early history. Also includes reproduction copies of a program, and a Quarrymen business card as well as a Beatles business card. An Allen Williams promotional sheet for the "Introducing The Beatles" album by Parlyphone comes with a 12" x 12" picture book. UFO Music Ltd., London. Value given with the entire press kit photo.

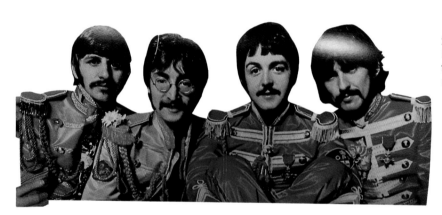

Sgt. Pepper's countertop display is a die-cut head shot photo of the Beatles in full military regalia. Value: E: $30 NM: $40.

This is United States currency with a Beatles photo inserted on the face of the bill. It was made by the U.S. Treasury Department and is legal tender. Value: E: $10 NM: $12.

Chapter Nine
"Hey Jude" (When Your Father Is A Beatle)

I think it must have been very hard to be the children of such famous celebrities as John, Paul, George, and Ringo. Yet each of the Beatles had children and I wondered what it was like for them growing up, so I decided to include them in the research for this book. What I found was that these children have each grown up to be remarkable people in their own right. I would like to begin with Julian Lennon, as he was the first child born to a member of the Fab Four.

John Charles Julian Lennon was born to John and Cynthia Lennon on April 8, 1963 at Sefton General Hospital in Liverpool. Although he was born with the umbilical cord wrapped around his neck, he grew up to be a healthy, happy young man.

When Julian was born the Beatles were on tour so John was not with Cynthia for the blessed event. He did arrive shortly thereafter wearing a disguise to try and keep the fact that a Beatle was married and had a child from the record buying public. The Beatles manager, Brian Epstein, went so far as to advise them to keep the news out of the papers, despite the fact that he was Julian's godfather.

When John did arrive at the hospital, quite a touching scene ensued. He rushed into Cynthia's room and began talking a mile a minute: " Oh Cyn, I love you. Where is he then? Was it awful? Who does he look like?"

When he had finally settled down a bit, John was able to cradle his son in his arms for the first time. He beamed down at the baby and then at Cynthia: "He's bloody marvelous, Cyn! Isn't he absolutely fantastic? Who's going to be a famous little rocker like his Dad then?"

These words were to haunt Julian for much of his life. In the beginning, he was afraid to try his hand at rock and roll. After all, how does one begin to follow an act like the Beatles? Julian didn't want to ride John's coat tails into the music business, he wanted to make it on his own merit. Music was something that he truly loved and was actually very talented at. When he first started out he was afraid he would never be able to produce the kind of quality music that his Fab father had. Then, as he got older and his own style matured, he feared that every song he wrote sounded too much like his father. He is one of the few musicians to ever be criticized for allowing the Beatles to influence him. Other musicians are proud that the Beatles influenced them, but for Julian it became a double edged sword. It has taken him many years to come to grips with the value of his own unique image, but he has managed to show the world that he is a talented individual in his own right.

Julian's induction into the circle of fame and fortune came at a very tender age. The Beatles and their entourage were continually followed by fans and members of the press. Privacy soon became a thing of the past, and a few stolen moments here and there became very valuable to the lot of them.

Cynthia would be pushing Julian along in his pram, out to do a bit of shopping or run a few errands, and the crowds would descend upon them. At first, she tried to deny that she knew John Lennon at all, but the secret wasn't destined to be kept. As soon as the media found out about the marriage and the fact that John had a child, the relatively peaceful life of mother and child was shattered. The phone began to ring at all hours of the day and night, waking them from their sleep. Whenever Cynthia left their apartment she was pursued and photographed, up close, and with telephoto lenses. A sort of madness ensued around anyone closely connected to the Fab Four. John soon found that photos of his wife and child were surfacing everywhere. The private life of this little family was no more.

John began to encourage Julian to pursue music early on. He bought him a drum kit when he was only five years old and gave him his first guitar when he was eleven. He also encouraged his son's artistic endeavors by putting some of his art work on the album *Christmas Time Is Here Again*. That same year, Julian played drums on John's *Walls and Bridges* album. Later, when he and John discussed the session he reflected wistfully: "If I'd known I was going to be on the album I would have played better."

Julian gave some very graphic examples of why it was hard to be the son of a Beatle, "There were times when being John Lennon's son was very difficult. Older boys wanted to beat my head in because I was a Beatle's son, and others would force me to play the guitar and then poke fun at me because it sounded awful."

Julian lost his father for the first time when he was only five years old. At that time Lennon married Yoko Ono. There is a strange sort of irony among the Lennon men when it comes to parents. John's own father, Alfred Lennon, had also left him when he was five years old. Later, when he was killed, John's son Sean was only five years old. It would appear that five is not a lucky number for the Lennon clan.

John suffered another loss at the age of seventeen. He was just getting to know his mother, Julia, again when she was struck and killed on her way to the bus stop. Tragically, Julian was to lose his father at the age of seventeen, when they too were just getting close to one another once again. Julian had always adored his father. He always looked at him as being somehow larger than life. To this day he says he finds himself referring to his dad in the present tense.

When Julian was eight years old, Lennon moved to New York City to be with, and eventually marry, Yoko Ono. Though he was shocked at the separation of his mom and dad, he eventually learned to accept her. When asked about his father's relationship with this woman he said, "I at last came to understand this weird relationship my dad and Yoko shared. It was so intense, like their complete sharing of everything, almost to the point of telepathy. It was weird ... Crazy, but wonderful."

Yoko gave birth to a son, Sean Ono Lennon, in 1975 and once again John and Julian began to drift apart. Determined to make up for past mistakes, John took over the care of Sean from the time of his birth. He told a reporter later that he had decided to raise Sean "in an attempt to atone for having missed Julian's childhood. There's a price to pay for inattention to children" Sadly, he missed a great deal of Sean's childhood also, when his life was taken so tragically in 1980.

Julian first played the piano when he was thirteen and visiting his father, Yoko and Sean in Montauk, Long Island, soon after Sean was born. The Lennon's next door neighbor had a piano and one day father and son decided to try it out. First, John played a couple of times and then Julian asked: "Can I have a go?"

It was during that visit that John's deep closeness and protectiveness of Sean first became evident. It was a difficult thing for Julian to come to grips with. He began to see that John fully intended to give of himself completely for this child. It was obvious that he was determined to be the kind of father to Sean that he had never been to Julian. Julian knew that his father had been very young when he was born, and that they had lived their lives in a virtual fish bowl of public opinion: "Still, I was a bit jealous." Julian confided, "but I never really said anything. I used to get shouted at a lot, and Dad would yell at me for laughing too much. Like, be quiet, Sean's sleeping." Despite a bit of jealousy in the beginning, Julian and Sean were to become very close in the end.

When asked, years later, how he felt about that period of his life and about his half brother Julian replied, "I love him and respect him and I'm really proud of him."

The young Lennon had no idea that his birthday of April 8, 1980, would be the last he was ever to spend in the company of his father. John threw a huge party for Julian on his boat in Palm Beach. He felt that he too was becoming really close to his dad at last. Seven months later, to the day, John Lennon was brutally assassinated outside his New York home in the Dakota apartment building. Julian was completely devastated by this tragedy. In many ways it mirrored the loss John had suffered, of his mother, many years earlier. They were both cut down in the prime of their life after finally becoming close to their children once again.

At this point Julian fell apart. He felt cheated out of his second chance with his dad at the hands of someone he didn't even know. He said, "When my dad first was killed I didn't feel anything but numbness, and I cried for a long time. The only thing that kept me going was a strange talk I'd had with Dad about a year before. He seemed convinced that the only way he'd miss out on old age was through a nuclear war. But he said if anything happened to him, he'd send a sign back to us that he was okay. He said he'd make a feather float down the room. Ever since his death, I've been waiting for that sign."

Depression soon got the better of Julian and he dropped out of school and moved to London. It was there that he had his own sort of lost weekend. In his grief, he drank and partied constantly to numb the pain. He even dyed his hair blonde for awhile, as if trying to come to grips with just who he was. He started telling everyone that he wanted to be a recording engineer, but he really wanted to be a musician. He began to make

cassettes of his songs, but was afraid to share them with anyone. Finally, one night, after he had had quite a lot to drink he played the tapes for his close friends. That was the beginning of a new career for Julian.

Julian's early performing life was quite difficult as well. Being the son of a Beatle and wanting to play music himself was not an easy task. John was a hard act to follow, even in his solo career and this held Julian back for many years. The young Lennon's band began its first stirring of life when Julian met Justin Clayton at school. In 1983 they started a band called Quasar, in which he played the drums and Justin played lead guitar. Unfortunately, they were unable to secure a contract from a record company. Charisma was the first label to sign the young Lennon.

It was at this point that Julian began to feel comfortable writing and recording his own songs. One of his greatest fears in doing this was that the public would think he was trying to cash in on his father's image. If you have ever heard his music, you know that this is not the case. *Valotte* was his first album and it went platinum. He has a distinct style all his own, although he definitely inherited some of his writing abilities from his father. His songs are honest and true to life.

Julian's very first concert was in San Antonio, Texas, in March of 1985. When the tickets went on sale, the concert was completely sold out in two hours. A critic was quoted as saying, "...A powerful concert debut that left little doubt that the son of the late John Lennon is his own man." Julian had come into his own at last. After that performance, his concerts continued to sell out wherever he went. MCA even made a film called *Stand By Me, A Portrait of Julian Lennon*, which shows scenes from his debut tour. That same year, he was nominated for a Grammy for best new artist. It was a very proud moment for the young Lennon. He felt he had finally proven himself as a musician. He didn't win that Grammy, but he did win an award from *Rolling Stone* for best new male pop singer.

His 2nd album, *The Secret Value of Daydreaming*, came out in May of 1986. He followed it with *Help Yourself*.

Julian is often asked if he thinks that John would approve of his career. He answers this question in the typical Lennonesque style, "I'm writing music and performing, why wouldn't he?"

After his father's murder, Julian was very concerned about his own safety while performing: "Originally I had my own plans for security and it was going to be heavy, heavy. But if somebody's going to do something to me, it's going to happen. I don't worry about it too much, cause I would just get, you know, depressed all the time."

Julian had difficulty coping with his mother's remarriage and his new stepfather, John Twist: "My stepfather was always trying to give the impression that he was more of a father than my dad was. I lived from birthdays to Christmas, just to be with him (his father)." And in the end it was Julian's stepfather who told him of his father's death, "This guy I hated said to me, 'I've got some serious bad news for you. I don't know how you're going to take it, so just be prepared.' and I knew already."

Shortly after hearing the news, Julian boarded a plane to join Sean and Yoko. The news of Lennon's murder was in all the papers and people all around him were reading them. Everywhere he looked, he saw his father's face. It was incredibly difficult for him.

When he arrived in New York, Yoko had still not told Sean that his father was dead. She waited for Julian to arrive and then asked him how he thought she should go about breaking the news to him. Julian told her, "You just have to tell the kid straight." He helped Yoko prepare what she would say to her son, but it took a long time because she kept falling apart in the middle of her speech. Finally, they sent for Sean and she broke the news to him: "I remember seeing the glint in Sean's eye when he actually understood what had happened. And then the tears started rolling."

Julian remained in New York for a few days mourning with his brother and stepmother and helping to console them. The people closest to Yoko then began advising him to leave because they felt that the resemblance between father and son was amazing and they feared that this might be a factor in her wanting him there.

"She did ask me to stay." said Julian. "She said, 'You can go to school here with us you know.' And I thought of the comfort that held for me." But Julian ended up leaving and going back to stay with his mother.

Julian spoke to his father for the last time just two weeks before his death when John had called him to play two cuts from his new album for him. It was a bittersweet memory. He still thinks of his father daily and believes that John is only gone for awhile in this life. In his heart, John is still near him, with him, a part of him...

John's other son, Sean Ono Lennon, was born to he and Yoko in 1975. Like his dad, Sean learned to fight for what he believed in early on. After his father's death, Albert Goldman's scathing book was released. The press leapt on the "information" that was "revealed" and Sean felt compelled to make the truth about his father known. He spoke to the *New York Post* about the book, saying, "At first I thought the book was very serious, but then I realized it was just a big joke. John was a great person as a father. I think he did enough fathering in the five years that I knew him. He was always around. Some fathers aren't as real as he was."

When asked how he lived through the trauma of his father being murdered he answered, "Subconsciously I knew that it was either flip out or take control of yourself and be normal. ... it's either not be a normal person or just try to deal with your life, and that's what I've done."

Sean also commented on memories of the time he had with his dad, "I'd always sit on his lap...just being together, because that was what it was like. We would always be together. It takes a lot of guts or feelings towards your child to just completely drop out of a career, you know, a pretty successful career, and just drop it and become a househusband. I just knew he was there, knew he was my father and knew that I loved him."

Sean too, is a musician, jamming to both his mother's songs and his own.

Ringo's firstborn son, Zak, arrived on September 13, 1965. He also decided on a career in music early in his life. When he was only four years old, one of his drawings was featured on the cover of the Christmas flexi-disc that was put out by the Beatles fan club in 1969.

In the beginning Ringo discouraged Zak from taking up the drums. His advice on his son's would-be musicianship was to listen to the records that he liked and learn to play the songs.

Ringo said of his son's wish to someday play the drums, "Like any kid, he wants to play with his own toys and mine as well."

Keith Moon (the drummer for the Who) just happened to be a good friend of Ringo's and Zak often hung out with them. He became a great fan of the Who and Keith Moon became his music mentor. He hung out with Keith and Ringo a lot and Moon encouraged him to have a go at being a drummer himself. Despite his Fab father's claim to fame, Zak has been known to tell friends that Moon is the best drummer that ever lived: "My old man's a good timekeeper, but I've never thought of him as a great drummer." Keith even bought Zak a seven thousand dollar drum set to help encourage him in his career.

Shortly after that, the young Starkey became a bit of a rebel. He always had an open invitation to crash at Keith's place for as long as he wanted and that was very tempting indeed: "Moonie was always there with me while my old man was far away in Monte Carlo or somewhere." Zak longed for recognition as a musician: "Being Ringo's son is a total pain. I'm always written about as Ringo's son, always classed with him in every single thing I try to do."

Zak was a big fan of punk rock and was soon destined to become the youngest member of the Next, who played at various parties in London and the surrounding area. They were also known to play such venues as South Hill Park Community Center and the Bridge House. These gigs were so close to Titenhurst Park, which was now owned by Ringo, that Zak was able to stay in a cottage on the property while playing them. When asked about his father's musical influence on him he replied: "I don't want any help from my dad. I want to prove that I can do it by myself. He hasn't done a thing to help me (to advance his career) and I don't want him to."

The next group that Zak became involved in was Monopacific. By this time Keith Moon had passed away, but the band still got the attention of the Who's John Entwistle, Roger Daltrey and Pete Townsend, which, I might add, was no small accomplishment. These three remaining members of the Who deemed Zak's impression of Moon's music to be the most accurate portrayal of his style. Zak was definitely coming up in the world of music.

The next band he was to play with was Nightfly which was composed of ex-members of such groups as Bad Company, Status Quo, and Whitesnake. As a result he was to play on such well known classics as Roger Daltrey's *Under A Raging Moon*.

Young Starkey's next gig was doing a musical version of *Wind in the Willows* with Steve Winwood.

Zak married Sarah Menikides on January 2, 1985. Shortly after that they made Ringo the first Beatle grandfather when Sarah gave birth to Tatia Jayne.

Ringo was blessed with two other children, a son Jason and a daughter Lee. Jason too, went on to become a drummer.

Being the doting father that he is, Paul has kept his children as sheltered as possible from public scrutiny. As a result, only the barest facts could be uncovered about them.

Heather, the oldest child, was born to Linda and Melvin See (her first husband) on December 31, 1963. She was followed by Paul and Linda's first child, Mary Louise (after his mother), born August 29, 1969. Next came Stella Nina McCartney on September 13, 1971 and, last but not least, the McCartney's only son, James Louis, who was born September 12, 1977.

Paul has tried very hard to bring his children up to be normal, compassionate people, despite the fact that they are surrounded by wealth and privilege. He had this to say on the subject of his children: "I don't want them to look down on ordinary people. I see that as the main danger when you get money, especially inherited wealth. You start to think, 'Well I'm better than him, anyway, I've got more than him', and you tend to look down on him..."

Paul added, "So my kids go to ordinary schools in order for them to learn how it is first. Then if you want be terrific and privileged afterwards, you can handle it. You've got some humanity and compassion with it. So I'm trying to bring them up to have values, to have heart, more than anything... I want them to actually care, you know, if someone gets hurt. And they do. They're very good kids like that."

These days Heather and Mary are all grown up and living together in a house in St. John's Wood. Heather is a potter by trade while Mary works as an assistant at MPL (Paul's company). The most recent research I could find tells me that Stella and James still reside at home with their parents.

The last of the Beatles children, Dhani, was born to George Harrison and his second wife Olivia on August 1, 1978. George was so pleased by the arrival that he rushed out to get a new baby blue Rolls Royce that he had ordered from a friend in Henly to celebrate the new arrival.

"My Bonnie" 45 rpm single, on a pink Decca label. Tony Sheridan and The Beat Brothers, record number 31382. This is one of the rarest 45s in the world. Value: G: $1,800 E: $2,200 NM: $2,500.

Flexi-discs

1963 trifold flexi-disc: *Sincere Good Wishes for Christmas and the New Year from John, Paul, George, and Ringo.* This is a fan club item and these items have been steadily climbing in price, especially since the recent Anthology Series. If the picture sleeve is missing, you must subtract one half of the value given: G: $225 E: $250 NM: $275.

1964 *Season's Greetings from The Beatles* fan club flexi-disc, which was mailed out to members at Christmas time. Made in USA. Value: G: $150 E: $175 NM: $200.

Official Beatles Fan Club: *The Beatles Third Christmas Record*, 1965. Made in the U.K. If the picture sleeve is missing, subtract half of the value given. Value: G: $90 E: $130 NM: $160.

Official Fan Club flexi-disc for the 1965 holiday season: *Another Beatles Christmas Record*. Value: G: $90 E: $130 NM: $160.

Fan Club, *Pantomime, Everywhere It's Christmas*, 1966. Made in the U.K. Value: G: $80 E: $105 NM: $125.

1967 seven inch fan club Christmas flexi-disc. The picture sleeve was designed by John and Julian Lennon and Ringo Starr. Value: G: $80 E: $95 NM: $110.

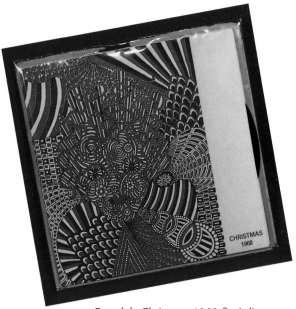

Fan club *Christmas 1968* flexi-disc.
Value: G: $80 E: $95 NM: $110.

1969 Fan Club Christmas flexi-disc. The cover was
designed by Richard and Zak Starkey. Value: G:
$70 E: $85 NM: $100.

Reel to Reels

Seven inch *Meet
The Beatles* in a
brown box. YIT-
2047. Value: RARE.

Meet The Beatles, in a brown box.
Capitol five inch. Z4-2047. Value:
RARE.

Seven inch *The Beatles' Second
Album* in a blue box. L-2080.
Value: RARE.

Seven inch *The Early Beatles* in a blue box. L-2309. Value: RARE.

Beatles VI in a blue box. 4-2358. Value: RARE.

Two complete albums: *Beatles VI* and *Something New* in a brown box. Y2T2382. Value: RARE.

Original Motion Picture Soundtrack from United Artists, *A Hard Day's Night*. JAX-6366. Value: RARE.

137

Beatles '65 in a blue box. L-2228.
Value: RARE.

Two complete albums: Beatles '65 and The Early
Beatles in a brown box. Y2T2385. Value: RARE.

The Beatles, Help! in a
blue box. L-2386.
Value: RARE.

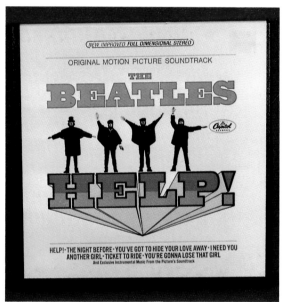

Two complete albums: Rubber Soul and
The Beatles Second Album in a brown box.
Y2T2467. Value: RARE.

Rubber Soul in a blue box. L-2442.
Value: RARE.

Revolver in brown box. Y1T-2576. Value: RARE.

Five inch *The Beatles Yesterday and Today* in a brown box. YT-2553. Value: RARE.

Seven inch, *The Beatles Yesterday and Today* in a blue box. L-2553. Value: RARE.

Sgt. Pepper's Lonely Hearts Club Band in a brown box. Y1T-2653. Value: RARE.

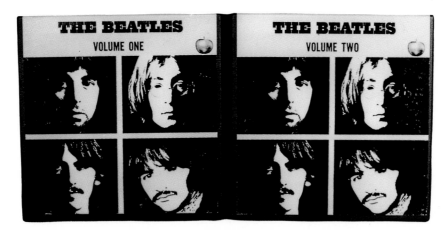

Seven inch, double reel set of *The White Album* in blue boxes. Volume One-L-101 and Two-L-2101. Value: RARE.

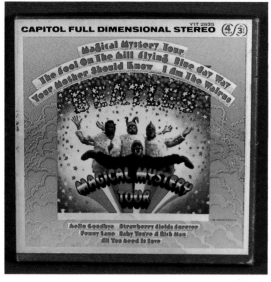

Magical Mystery Tour in a brown box. Y1T-2835. Value: RARE.

The Beatles, Yellow Submarine in a brown box. Y1W-153. Value: RARE.

Hey Jude in a blue box. Apple L-385. Value: RARE.

Abbey Road in a blue box. Apple L-383. Value: RARE.

Let It Be in a blue box. Apple L-3401. Value: RARE.

Records/Vinyl

The Beatles vs. The Four Seasons on VeeJay label. This is one of the three RAREST Beatles albums in the world. Mono DX-30. Value: RARE.

The Beatles vs. Frank Ifield on VeeJay label. Mono 1964. This is another of the three rarest Beatles albums in the world. Value: RARE.

The Beatles "Twist and Shout" on red vinyl. The following items are unlicensed wall plaques by "Now That's Music Celebrity Collectibles," now T.M. Inc. of Layana, California. Made from actual record covers. Value: E: $90 NM: $100.

The Beatles, "She Loves You" on red vinyl. Same description and value as "Twist and Shout."

The Beatles "Help!" on white vinyl. Value: E: $90 NM: $100.

This record box with the Apple label came with twenty-five Apple record sleeves. Value for box with sleeves: G: $25 E: $35 NM: $45.

Compact Discs/HMV's

The Beatles, Yellow Submarine HMV set. Value: G: $150 E: $200 NM: $225.

Help!, Rubber Soul, and Revolver HMV (The World's Best Music Stores) set. It includes a pin and a CD boxed set of the albums. Value: G: $150 E: $200 NM: $225.

The Beatles, White Album HMV set. Value: G: $150 E: $200 NM: $225.

The Beatles 1967-1970 HMV set. Value: G: $150 E: $200 NM: $225.

The Beatles, 1962-1966 HMV set. Value: G: $150 E: $200 NM: $225.

Miscellaneous Items

Boxed set of cassettes, fourteen in all, including two double albums. Value: E: $85 NM: $100.

Wedding Album boxed set on 8-track, factory sealed. Value: G: $45 E: $55 NM: $60.

"Real Love" single; came with picture sleeve and booklet. Vinyl Experience Ltd., U.K. Value: E: $10 NM: $12.

"Baby It's You" single; same description as "Real Love." Value: E: $10 NM: $12.

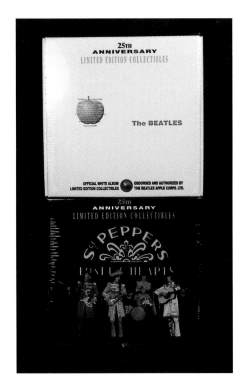

1994 Apple Corps Ltd., 25th anniversary, limited edition boxed set includes *The White Album/Sgt. Pepper's*. The set includes a T-shirt, hat, sticker, letter of authenticity and an Apple 25th anniversary pin. Value: E: $30 NM: $35.

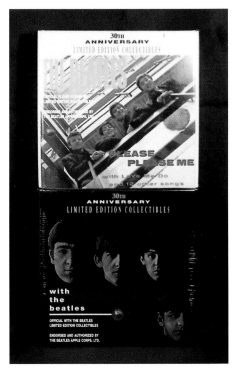

1994 Apple Corps Ltd., 30th anniversary boxed set: *Please, Please Me* and *With The Beatles*. Value: E: $30 NM: $35.

John Winston Lennon was born on October 9, 1940 at Oxford Street Maternity Hospital in Liverpool. His mother's name was Julia and his father's name was Alfred Lennon. His father was out to sea at the time of his birth. John didn't even get the opportunity to meet him until he was five years old. By the time he did return, Julia was ready for a divorce. Although he didn't want to get a divorce, he told Julia he would think about it if she would let him take John to Blackpool with him so that the two could get acquainted. At the time, he had no intention of ever bringing John back to her. In fact, he already had plans to immigrate to New Zealand with the child. Just as he and John were about to board a ship, Julia showed up demanding that Freddie return John to her immediately. Freddie insisted that he had just as much right to his son as she had and they got into a huge argument over who should have custody. Finally, they decided to let young John decide for himself who he wanted to be with.

It must have been a horribly wrenching experience for a five year old boy. After all, his father had just walked into his life and his mother was the only parent he had known. He didn't really want either one of them to leave again, but he was terribly afraid of losing his father before he ever really had him. Besides, he didn't think that his mother would actually leave him, so he chose his father.

To John's surprise, Julia kissed him good-bye and walked out the door. She was halfway down the street when the hysterical boy ran after her screaming: "Mummy! Mummy! I've changed my mind. Please, don't leave me!" He was in tears and badly shaken.

That proved to be the only time that John would see his father until after he had made it as a Beatle. To make matters worse for John, Julia did not keep him with her either, but sent him to live with his Aunt Mimi, the woman who actually raised him. Later, when John asked her about his parents, Mimi simply told him that they had fallen out of love and his father was too heartbroken to face coming back to see him. John soon forgot about Freddie, but Julia would continue to wander in and out of his life at random for years to come.

After John and Paul started playing together with the Quarrymen, they would sometimes practice at Julia's house. After awhile John even stated to leave his Teddy Boy clothes there so that Mimi wouldn't know about them, and so he could stop by there in the morning on his way to school. Julia became more of a friend than anything like a mother. John would even spend the night on her couch when he and Mimi had a fight. Mimi felt as if Julia was making her job more difficult by allowing John to hide out there, but it never came between their relationship as sisters and Julia visited Mimi's house (Mendips) often.

July 15, 1958 turned out to be a day that John would never forget. Julia stopped by Mendips for tea that afternoon and ended up staying until it started to get dark. John was not there at the time. In fact, he was over at Julia's house visiting with her new husband. When she realized how late it was getting, Julia headed for the bus stop. Suddenly, there was a screech of brakes and Julia was hit and killed by an off-duty policeman, which didn't exactly improve John's opinion of authority figures. Needless to say, John was completely devastated by his mother's death.

Mimi longed to help John find something to help take his mind off his mother. She ended up buying him his first guitar in the hopes that it would keep him occupied. She had no idea what she was starting. That guitar became John's world. He would play it until his fingers bled. In fact, he spent so many hours practicing that Mimi started to regret having bought it for him. She told him, "The guitar's all very well, John, but you'll never make a living at it."

When the Beatles first became famous John was probably the least comfortable with their new status. He had always been a rebel and a bit of an outcast. Now he was being singled out as a great intellectual. All of a sudden his sarcasm and dry humor, that had gotten him into so much trouble when he was younger, was now being interpreted as genius.

By March of 1964 Lennon had published his first book, *John Lennon, In His Own Write*. The book was filled with his drawings and his unique dialogue. It became a best-seller almost overnight and gathered wide critical acclaim. The *Times Literary Supplement* said it was, "Worth the attention of anyone who fears for the impoverishment of the English language." His work was even compared to that of James Joyce. After the book was released, John was honored at a Foyle's Literary Lunch on the occasion of Shakespeare's four hundredth birthday.

John and Cynthia began to outgrow their small quarters and moved to Kenwood, in Weybridge. It just so happened that John's long-lost father was working as a dishwasher in a hotel only a few miles from his new home. Freddie might never even have realized that his son was so close, or even that he had become famous, if it hadn't been for a washerwoman who worked with him at the hotel. She brought a newspaper into work with a story about John in it, saying that this Lennon had to be his son because they looked so much alike. Sure enough, she was right. Freddie was astonished by what he read. He showed up at John's Kenwood home the next day.

At first, John was polite and made friendly conversation with his father. But soon Freddie started to criticize everything about John, from his lifestyle to the way he had decorated his home. After that, Freddie still had the nerve to ask John for a loan. John promptly threw him out. A few days later Freddie returned once again and John slammed the door in his face. John felt that all his father was after was his money and this greatly disappointed him.

Still, Freddie found a way to capitalize on the fact that John was his son. He started telling the local papers the whole sordid story about being ejected from his son's home and they paid him for the story. He even sold the story of his life to a magazine called *Tit Bits* and recorded a single called "That's My Life." But, after he had basked in the light of his fifteen minutes of fame, he started to fade away again.

The Beatles continued to grow in popularity. In August of 1965 they got the chance of a lifetime. They would get to meet Elvis Presley at his home in Bel Air. It was quite a scene when the police understood that Elvis and the Beatles were all going to be in the same place at the same time. The police circled his house and waited tensely to see what would happen. Elvis answered the door himself. It was a very exciting moment, particularly for Lennon. As they walked into the house the group noticed that a jukebox was alternating between Beatles songs and Elvis's own material. Later in the evening they jammed together. It was a dream come true for the boys. Paul even felt comfortable enough to be rather cheeky. When Elvis played Paul's bass part on "I Feel Fine" Paul assured him, " Coming along quite promising on the bass Elvis."

Since I have already covered a lot of the material concerning John up to the point where he and Yoko met, I will begin with her and then bring them together.

Yoko Ono was born in Tokyo, Japan, on February 18, 1934. She was never very close to her father, who moved to San Francisco to be the head of a branch of the Yokohama Speci-Bank before she was born. She didn't really even get to know him until she and her mother joined him there in 1936. They lived in the United States for four years, until the attack on Pearl Harbor by the Japanese made it difficult for anyone of that nationality to remain in a high status position in the U.S.

Back in Japan, Yoko and her younger brother and sister were moved to a remote farmhouse that their mother had rented in the country so that they would be away from the war torn cities. It was a meager dwelling and their mother left them there with servants and went back to Tokyo. Shortly thereafter, the servants abandoned the children too. Yoko suddenly had to forage for food and clothing—after being used to a very comfortable lifestyle—until she was re-united with her parents.

In 1951 Yoko's father was named president of the New York branch of his bank and the family moved back to the United States. When she was twenty-three, Yoko eloped with a poor Japanese composer named Toschi Ichiyananagi. Her family was so upset by this that they cut off all money to her and refused to speak to her for years.

She and Toschi were married for seven years, during which time Yoko became an aspiring avant-garde artist. Their ideology was that the primary function of art lies in its power to shock and its ultimate success lies in the number of people who are, even accidentally, exposed to it. The first art that she ever had on exhibit was created to be burned or stomped on. In 1960 she had her first show at a gallery on Madison Avenue. The owner of the gallery was one of the inventors of a live event called "Flexus," which was the forerunner of happenings. Yoko soon became the queen of happenings and even wrote a book of instructional poems for participating in a happening called *Grapefruit*.

When Yoko was twenty-nine, she divorced Toschi to marry avant-garde artist and filmmaker, Tony Cox. They met in Japan and by August of 1963 they had a baby girl named Kyoko.

Yoko moved back to New York with Tony and they rented a loft in the Soho district. By 1966 she and Cox were invited to a symposium in London called "The Destruction of Art." As soon as they arrived, she called Dan Richter, an American friend from the art world, who got them a flat to stay in while they attended the symposium.

John and Yoko first met at the Indica gallery, which was run by Marianne Faithful's ex-husband, John Dunbar. Yoko had an exhibit there called "Unfinished Paintings and Objects by Yoko Ono" toward the end of 1966. John came in the night before the opening to take a look. He hung out for quite awhile examining her work, especially a painting that she had attached to the ceiling. There was a step ladder leading up to it and it had a spyglass attached to the top of it by means of a chain. If you climbed the ladder and looked at a circled spot on the ceiling you could read the word "Yes," printed in tiny letters. He also took an interest in an apple with a ticket price of two hundred pounds. When Dunbar saw what an interest John was taking in Yoko's work he sent her out to talk to him. She presented an interesting waif-like appearance. She was dressed entirely in black and had long, thick black hair down to the middle of her back. Instead of speaking to John, she handed him a card with a single word written on it, "Breathe."

John said, "You mean like this?" and started to pant heavily.

Then Dunbar, himself, took John down into the basement to see the live part of the exhibition. Several long-haired men and women were sitting around on the floor, darning the rips in a large canvas bag.

Yoko started to show John around the rest of the exhibition while Dunbar spoke for each of them, in turn. John was particularly taken with one piece that consisted of boards and nails with a sign that said, "Hammer a Nail In." When John asked if he could do so, Yoko at first told him no. Because the opening wasn't until the next day, she wanted him to wait until then to participate in this event. Because Lennon was a world famous rock star, who could potentially buy everything at the exhibit, Dunbar was embarrassed by Yoko's attitude. She saw it as merely looking after the integrity of her art. He told her softly: "Let him hammer a nail in. Who knows, he might buy it." After a brief consultation in the corner, Yoko agreed to allow John to hammer in a nail for five shillings.

At first John was angered by such a suggestion, but then he started to see the humor in the situation. The Lennonesque wit kicked in and he said, "Okay, I'll give you an imaginary five shillings and I'll hammer in an imaginary nail." This was exactly the sort of reaction that appealed to Yoko; a strong and lasting bond was created between them. John had always seen himself as being "more aware" than other people, able to see things from an angle that many could not, and he had felt like an outcast. Now here was a woman who shared his vision of not fencing oneself in with too many boundaries.

Shortly after their first meeting, Yoko asked John if he would care to help her next exhibition at the Lisson Gallery, in North London. This event was called the "Half Wind Show," because everything in it was only half an object. There was half a chair, half a table, half a bed, half a pillow, half a washbasin, and half a toothbrush. The whole concept appealed to John's sense of the absurd. He did end up giving her the money, but was horrified when Yoko suggested that his name should appear in the catalog. The only credit he would allow in the catalog was "Yoko Plus Me."

Shortly after the show, she sent him a copy of *Grapefruit*, which both puzzled and fascinated John. This was a book that she had published in a limited edition of 500. It was put out by the Wunternum Press, Tokyo, in 1964. It was a book of instructional poems with very interesting messages, such as, "Draw a map to get lost." At first John was annoyed by the book, but the more he looked at it, the more it interested him. It appealed to his sense of the absurd, and he finally agreed to speak with her again.

Later that year, she did a show at Brian's Saville Row theater, called "Cut Piece." The object of this show was for audience members to come up on the stage and cut off pieces of her clothing.

Yoko sent John more "inspirational poetry" while she was organizing a happening called "Dance Event." They contained such messages as "Watch the light until dawn" and "Dance." At this point she was a big joke to John and Cynthia, but that was about to change. After a meditation session in London, Yoko Ono climbed into the psychedelic Rolls, sat between them, and changed things.

John and Yoko ran into each other again at an art opening of soft sculpture in New York City. Lennon spotted her from across the room and they nodded to each other, but never spoke.

A few weeks later, Ono showed up at the Beatles office asking to see John. She wanted his financial sponsorship for one of her conceptual projects; namely, wrapping the lions in Trafalgar Square in canvas. The only person connected with the Beatles that she saw, that day, was Neil Aspinall.

John continued to see her at art exhibitions and she sparked a sense of respect in him that he usually reserved for men. She did things that Lennon himself didn't dare to do. In the beginning, the relationship between Ono and Lennon was purely intellectual. John had become her benefactor, and someone that she felt she could talk to about anything.

The other Beatles first came into contact with Yoko at Abbey Road studios. She hardly stayed in the background as had been the custom with Beatles women. Instead, she would sit beside John and watch him play. The other Beatles had never seen him act this way with any other woman. He seemed completely entranced by her, showing open affection for her during the sessions. They all figured that John would get tired of her eventually, as he usually had a fairly short attention span in these matters. In the beginning, they even referred to her behind her back as the "flavor of the month." But she didn't fade away. In fact, she left her husband and daughter to be with John, just as he left his wife and son to be with her.

Her very first night at Kenwood was the beginning of a partnership that would both confuse and deeply upset the other Beatles. No matter what, they had always hung out together. It was all for one, and one for all. Now, suddenly John had found a relationship that seemed to interest him more than the one he had with Paul, George and Ringo. It was a turning point in the way the group interacted together. John felt that he had found his life-mate and anyone who couldn't understand that be damned. He and Yoko were recording experimental tapes together from the beginning and he felt free, for the first time, to express himself in any way that he saw fit, and he did. It

must have felt like a wonderful new kind of freedom after the fishbowl sort of existence he had with the Beatles. He felt his creative juices flowing, not as Beatle John, but as John Lennon.

In June their first collaborative effort was presented to the public. It was a sculpture composed of two acorns, one labeled *John by Yoko Ono*, the other *Yoko by John Lennon*. The couple planned to bury the acorns as an event at the National Sculpture Exhibition, in May of 1968. The acorns were meant to symbolize peace and the simplicity of nature. John and Yoko dressed entirely in white and drove to Coventry in John's white Rolls. Outside the cathedral, on the grounds of which the acorns were to be buried, John and Yoko were met by a canon of the church, who told them that these objects could not be buried in consecrated ground. He also informed them that these to objects were acorns, not sculpture. Yoko became angry at this point and demanded that the British "sculptors" be called to vouch for her artistic integrity. A compromise was made and the acorns were buried in unhallowed ground. In the end it didn't really matter, because inside of a week they had been dug up and spirited away in the night by fans.

John and Yoko were developing a very intense sense of attachment to one another. They did everything together. They even participated in an art show at the Drury Lane Arts Lab. The show was made up of "wooden objects to be taken apart or added to." The people visiting the gallery took everything apart and kept the pieces as souvenirs.

When John and Yoko arrived for the debut of the stage adaptation of *In His Own Write*, the press openly confronted him with cries of, "Where's your wife?" It was a very tense and awkward situation.

In July John had his first art exhibition at the Robert Fraser Gallery in London. It was called "You Are Here" and was dedicated "To Yoko from John, with Love." They started the event by releasing 360 white balloons into the sky above Mayfair. Each balloon contained the message, "Please write to John Lennon in care of the Robert Fraser Gallery."

It was quite an elaborate set-up. In order to get to the exhibition, one had to first walk through a vast array of charity collection boxes in the shapes of pandas, puppets, and crippled children. The only other items were a circular piece of white canvas which said, "You Are Here" on it. John's hat lay on the floor in front of it, upside down with this inscription on the brim: "For the artist. Thank You." Later in the day, some art students brought in a rusty bicycle and John immediately added it to the show.

His public simply couldn't understand what he was trying to say these days. The critics were openly scornful of this art show. They even went so far as to say that if John were not a Beatle, he would not have dared to put such rubbish on display. Still, it was a very contemporary statement of the times. The 1960s was a time of freedom of speech, freedom of expression, and above all, the freedom to create without boundaries. You could let your imagination go where it would and John, being a big fan of Lewis Caroll, had quite an imagination. He was raised on books at Aunt Mimi's house and had developed a voracious hunger for knowledge. Contrary to what the public believed, he felt as though he were breaking free from the collective oneness of the Beatles; finally making some statements on his own. He would never have dared to try things like this when he was a Beatle. It just didn't fit with that particular image. Perhaps if he had found a way to balance out the two personas he could have had complete creative freedom and still been a Beatle when it struck his fancy. We will never know because many people just didn't give him room to do that.

In 1968, Yoko was pregnant with John's child. When Cynthia found out, she was heartbroken and petitioned for a divorce on the grounds of adultery. The divorce was granted to her.

The very day that the *White Album* was released, Yoko lost the baby. Now John was heartbroken. He had wanted this child so badly. While she was recovering from the miscarriage, John had another bed moved into Yoko's room so that he could be there with her, refusing to leave her for a second. It was quite touching in a very sad sort of way. Even when they needed the bed that he was using for a patient, John stayed, sleeping on the floor in a sleeping bag beside her bed.

Not long after this occurred, John and Yoko were secretly married on Gibraltar. John wore a white jacket and sneakers and Yoko wore a wide-brimmed hat, sunglasses and a miniskirt. The couple then posed for pictures and flew to Paris to let the press know about the wedding. Yoko described the ceremony this way: "We're going to schedule many happenings and events together. This marriage is one of them."

Following that train of thought, the next happening turned out to be their honeymoon, which they also turned into a bed-in to promote world peace. They spent a week in bed at the Amsterdam Hilton Hotel trying to explain to people that we could have world peace in our time if enough people really wanted it. They had hoped to get more media coverage than they did. To top things off the hotel only had rooms with twin beds, and they were cemented to the floor, three feet apart.

Two days later the couple took off for Toronto. From there they went to Montreal for a ten day bed-in at the Queen Elizabeth Hotel. The press was there on that occasion and John and Yoko were able to give over sixty interviews. The bed-in ended with a Saturday night sing-in. It was filmed by three different sources, who all managed to capture the first live performance of "Give Peace A Chance."

From there they went to Vienna for the TV debut of their film *Rape*, in which a young girl is being relentlessly pursued by the press. She feels frightened and alone, even in the midst of all these people. The act of rape was a metaphor for what they felt the press was doing to them by reporting on every aspect of their lives. Unfortunately, this sort of behavior hasn't gone away. Certain members of the "fringe" press made Princess Diana feel exactly the same way. It is all well and good to admire celebrities for what they do and what they stand for, but when we get into having to know every single aspect of their waking lives I think it ceases to be admiration and turns, instead, into a sort of voyeurism. Most reputable reporters know where to draw this line, but many of those in the news fringe do not.

John and Yoko's next happening took place in the Sacher hotel's Red Salon. There, the couple crouched on a table, inside a single bag. John explained that it was their way of demonstrating a new concept called "bagism" or "total communication." When communicating in this way, the speaker in no way distracted the listener by his personal appearance. You could get to know a person from the inside out, much the same way as you can in internet chat rooms today. John felt that this type of total communication could be used as a catalyst for world peace. The British *Mirror* said of the event, "A not inconsiderable talent, who seems to have gone completely off his rocker."

John was ahead of his time in many ways and some people simply could not bring themselves to look at the world through his eyes.

In the summer of 1969, John and Yoko planned a vacation with their children, Julian and Kyoko. They wanted the two to get to know each other; the hope being that they could someday be one big, happy family. They decided to visit one of Aunt Mimi's sisters in Scotland. Even though John had never driven a car before, he insisted on driving for the duration of the trip. A few days later, John drove, head first, into a ditch. Everyone in the car was hurt. John and Yoko both had some serious facial lacerations. John had to get seventeen stitches, Yoko got fourteen, and Kyoko got four. Julian was very lucky to be merely bruised and shaken.

The car was crushed into a cube, bloodstains and all, and shipped to Kenwood, where it was put on a platform in one of their gardens as a sculpture.

That same summer John and Yoko bought Tittenhurst Park, which was to be their new home. The house was just outside of Ascot, on seventy-four acres of wooded ground and gardens. It even had its own lake and over fifty varieties of vegetation.

Before they moved in they had the house completely renovated. They added a large, modern kitchen, as well as a soundproofed recording studio. All of the business areas of the house were repainted and re-carpeted in black, while the living areas were done all in white. They also had a small island built in the middle of the lake, so that they could row a boat over to it for a picnic.

It was at Tittenhurst that John and Yoko went into a sort of self-imposed exile. They took to staying in the master bedroom for months at a time and had their meals brought in to them on trays.

Paul was the one who finally got John to come out, by convincing him to help him work on the *Abbey Road* album. Yoko joined John in the studio. She was pregnant again, and they didn't want to be separated because of all the problems she had had in the past. They were both very fearful of another miscarriage.

Unfortunately, she did lose the baby, on John's birthday. Depressed and exhausted from another loss, the Lennon's decided to go on a vacation to Greece with Magic Alex. They started out by renting a yacht with no particular destination in mind. They just wanted to get away from everything for awhile. During what turned out to be a ten day cruise, John and Yoko decided to abstain from drugs and alcohol in an attempt to cleanse their bodies of toxins. This caused both of them to become very ill and brought out the worst in both of them.

When they got back to London, John and Yoko released *The Wedding Album* on Apple. This album consisted of recordings that they had made during their Amsterdam bed-in, including several minutes of John and Yoko simply repeating each other's names. It came with copies of newspaper clippings, a laminated picture of a piece of their wedding cake, and a copy of their marriage license. It has now become a valued collectible.

One day while John was reading the paper, he began thinking about what was going on in Vietnam and all the starving children in Biafra. It upset him so much that he decided to return his MBE award in protest over his government's involvement in these situations. He sent his driver to Aunt Mimi's to pick the award up for its return to the Queen. Mimi later said of the incident, "If I knew what John wanted it for, I never would have given it to him."

With the medal in hand, John dictated a letter to Queen Elizabeth on Bag Productions stationery, saying: "Your Majesty, I am returning this MBE in protest against Britain's involvement in the Nigeria-Biafra thing, against our support of America in Vietnam, and against "Cold Turkey" slipping down the charts. With love, John Lennon of Bag."

He added the bit about "Cold Turkey" as an afterthought and ended up regretting it. It was meant to sort of lighten the mood of returning the medal but, instead, he felt that it came off feeling more like a publicity stunt, which it was not. John and Yoko delivered the medal themselves to the tradesmen's entrance at Buckingham Palace. A spokesman for the Palace told the press that it was ironic: "that he should return the medal, as the first MBE's that were returned were from people protesting that Mr. Lennon...was given the award in the first place."

John Brower, a well-known concert promoter, called John in September to offer him free plane tickets as well as tickets to the Toronto Rock and Roll Festival, simply for attending. John agreed to come if he and Yoko could appear together. Of course, Brower agreed. This was the first time that any Beatle had appeared in a solo performance, or any performance for that matter, since their rooftop concert for *Let It Be*.

John's appearance was unexpected and when he took the stage a riot almost broke out, the crowd was so happy to see him. When the crowd had settled down a bit, John went to the microphone and told them, "We're just gonna do numbers that we know, y'know, because we've never played together before." When they sang, the assembled musicians followed songs like "Blue Suede Shoes" with the world premiere of "Cold Turkey," which had not yet been released to the public. After that everyone but John left the stage and Yoko climbed out of a large canvas bag that had been sitting to one side of the stage. Then they did a seventeen minute version of "Don't Worry Kyoko, Mummy's Only Looking for Her Hand in the Snow."

John thoroughly enjoyed playing live again. With the improvements that had been made in speaker and amplifier technology, he could finally be heard over the crowd. He was so happy with the experience that on the plane ride home he decided that he was going to tell the press that he was leaving the Beatles and forming his own band.

Klein convinced Lennon to hold off for awhile because he had just finished negotiating contracts for the Beatles with EMI and Capitol, but they had not yet been paid their advances. Allen suggested that John wait until the contracts were finalized before saying anything about the Beatles disbanding.

Still, John just couldn't wait to tell Paul. When he got back from Toronto Lennon set up a meeting at Apple. As soon as he arrived McCartney began telling the others about all his new ideas for Beatles projects. No matter what Paul said, John kept saying, "No, I don't want to do that," leading to a huge argument. Then Paul went into a Beatles pep talk, ending it by saying, "When everything is said and done, we're still the Beatles, aren't we?"

John couldn't take it anymore. He started screaming: "I ain't no Beatle! Don't you understand? It's over! Over! Can't you get that through your bloody head!" Then he stormed out of the building with Yoko. John was very angry, but he still refrained from announcing his imminent departure from the Beatles to the press.

Soon after that, Lennon began focusing on his peace campaign once again. This time he and Yoko produced a billboard campaign. They had billboards erected in twelve major cities around the world, with the following message: "War Is Over-If You want It-Happy Christmas, John and Yoko." They started the campaign off with a charity concert for the United Nations Children's Fund, held at the Lyceum Theater, in London. The day after the concert the couple began planning a free "peace concert" in Toronto. They held a press conference at the Ontario Science Center to announce that the peace concert would incorporate a worldwide "peace vote," in which the audience would vote for peace or war on a ballot. Then John and Yoko would give the ballots to the United Nations counsel.

In Montreal they had a meeting with Canadian Prime Minister, Pierre Trudeau. After the meeting John said of the Prime Minister, "If there were more leaders like Mr. Trudeau, the world would have peace."

Shortly after Christmas, John and Yoko flew to Aalborg, Denmark, to visit Tony Cox (Yoko's former second husband and Kyoko's father) Tony's second wife, Melinda, and Kyoko. They wanted to make peace with the Cox's at last. Tony had been rather reluctant to let the Lennon's see Kyoko since the accident in Scotland, in which she was injured. Cox was also aware of the couple's chemical habits and didn't want his daughter exposed to that sort of thing. But John and Yoko were determined to convince him of their good intentions so that he would allow Kyoko to return to Tittenhurst with them.

When they got to Aalborg, they soon discovered how opposed Tony was to the use of mind altering chemicals of any kind, including tobacco. He was vehement about keeping these things out of his house and away from Kyoko.

As it turned out, Cox was involved with a group called the "Harbingers," who proved to be some sort of cosmic commune. Hamrick and Leonard, who seemed to be important figures within the group, came over to hypnotize John and Yoko in order to help them quit smoking. They wanted to do something to sort of commemorate the event, so they all cut off their hair. It was very, very short; down to the scalp. John and Yoko saved the clippings of their own hair in plastic bags.

Not long after that, concert promoter John Brower flew to Aalborg to get the couple's official approval on plans for the upcoming peace concert. Brower and his associates were also asked to leave any and all chemical substances at the door before entering Tony's home.

Much to Brower and his entourage's surprise, they found John and Yoko in the kitchen with all of their hair cut off. Kyoko kept pulling at Brower's jacket and whispering, "I'm a girl, I'm a girl."

John and Yoko started reading over the promotional material for the concert and John came across a flyer that said, "Free (for one dollar) John Lennon Peace Festival in Toronto, July 3, 4 and 5, to celebrate the year 1 A.P. War is over if you want it."

John was very upset by this, "No! No! No! Free means free, man! Not one bloody dollar!"

Brower tried to explain some of the logistics of such an endeavor to the couple. He explained that it just wasn't feasible to set up a concert that was to be attended by hundreds of thousands of people, without some money to at least pay for things like sanitation. He also told John that a business called Karma Productions had already been set up to sell tickets.

That made John really angry. He refused to even have his name connected with the event if it was not 100% free.

Lennon then appointed Hamrick and Leonard, of the Harbingers, to deal with Karma Productions. They also came up with some Magic Alex sort of ideas, on the side. One really outlandish thing that they did was give press conferences in which they announced that flying saucers would appear at the concert as a featured event, and John and Yoko would arrive in an "air car" that ran on psychic energy. Somehow, the whole thing just never happened.

By 1970, John and Yoko had become involved in a wide variety of causes. At this point, John began to be seen as a subversive by the American government. The coup de grace ended up being a press conference to announce the opening of the Black House, a sort of black cultural center in Camden Town, sponsored by Michael Abdul Malik (better known as Michael X). He was a top leader in the Black Panther movement in London. Malik, John, and Yoko had become friends, and the couple had agreed to help raise money for Michael's cause. The press showed up for a ceremony on the roof of the Black House, where John and Yoko presented Michael X with the bags of hair that they had saved from their trip to see Tony Cox in Denmark. The hair was destined to be auctioned off at Sotheby's, and the proceeds would go to the Black Panthers. For the very first time in the history of any type of events connected with the Beatles, nothing about it appeared in the papers.

By 1970 Yoko had become pregnant again. It was a very difficult pregnancy and she had to be confined to bed. They started to argue a lot and it was beginning to really strain their relationship. Then, one morning, a book came in the mail. It was called The Primal Scream, Primal Therapy: The Cure for Neurosis. The author of the book, Arthur Janov, was a new age therapist in California practicing this technique.

Janov's theory was that the "primal scene," which occurs in everyone's life around the age of five, is the single most shattering moment of our lives. Since we repress negative emotion, almost from the time of birth, a patient must be taken back to the moment of his primal scene to both re-examine and re-experience the trauma in order to finally be able to release it. When the "primal state" is achieved, the session ends with the patient letting out all of their emotions with a scream that comes from those deep down feelings.

In the end, this therapy ended up being a big disappointment to John. Janov recognized this himself, when he first talked to John and Yoko on the phone. At that time, he told them to think long and carefully about what they were doing. If they did decide to go through with his treatment, Janov wanted them to write letters about their childhood, in order to figure out what they wanted to accomplish through primal therapy. The letters must have impressed Janov a great deal, because he temporarily left his practice and moved into Tittenhurst Park with John and Yoko.

When he arrived, Janov began by explaining to John and Yoko that they must remain in separate rooms and have no contact with each other for twenty-four hours prior to his arrival. He also told them that they could not watch TV, talk on the phone, or indulge in any chemical substances during this time. Then, when Janov arrived they could get straight to work. John would lie on his back in the middle of the floor, while Janov took him back through all the hurt and rejection of childhood. His screams could be heard throughout the house.

After working with them in their home for three weeks, he asked John and Yoko to come back with him to California to continue treatment. They agreed to go back with him and to take a four to six month course of intensive therapy at the Primal Institute in L.A. John and Yoko left the next day and rented a house in Beverly Hills for the duration of their stay. Soon after they got there, Yoko had another miscarriage. The couple was absolutely heartbroken once again, but they decided that the therapy might help. They spent two and a half days a week in treatment over the next three months.

Yoko never did totally accept Janov's methods; however, she did appreciate the fact that men using this technique learned how to cry and release their repressed emotions, which she thought was very useful. That part of the therapy was of tremendous benefit to Lennon. It really helped him to understand some of the feelings he was having and to get in touch with his rage. Yoko, on the other hand, was already very much in touch with these feelings and even incorporated some of the screams into her work on the stage and in recordings of her music. Still, they got along very well with each other until Janov brought a sixteen millimeter camera to one of their sessions and asked if he could film it. Of course, they feared that the tapes would leak out at some point and be embarrassing. John absolutely refused to be taped, saying, "I'm not going to be filmed, especially not rolling around on the floor screaming.

Janov became very angry and accused them of being "too big to be filmed." John and Yoko got very upset also. They simply did not want these private moments on tape. Soon after they had this disagreement, John and Yoko left the program.

John did get some benefit from the therapy, however; which is evident on the solo album that he made when he returned, called the Primal album. This work can only be described as a sort of musical exorcism. The song "Mother" is a perfect illustration of his venting emotions, with lyrics like, "You had me but I never had you" and "Mama don't go, Daddy come home." At the end of the song, the pain is quite evident in his voice. Most of the songs on that album make a very powerful statement. Lennon shows us a vulnerable side of himself that many people had never seen before.

Another problem arose for the Lennons in 1971, when Tony and Kyoko went into hiding. Yoko was determined to locate her daughter and Tony was determined to keep her away from the sort of life in the fast lane existence that the Lennon's led at that time. He ended up going into hiding with her because he didn't have the kind of money it would take to fight a court custody battle against someone with a name as big as John Lennon's.

John and Yoko hired a team of private detectives, who tracked Cox to the island of Majorca, off the coast of Spain. At that time, Cox was studying with the Maharishi Mahesh Yogi, just as the Beatles had done in 1969. The Lennon's quickly rented a plane and slipped onto the island unnoticed, with a colleague, Dan Richter. They checked into the Melia Mallorca Hotel and started their search for the girl. They soon learned that, while Tony was studying with the Maharishi, Kyoko was staying at a communal children's camp.

Once they had pinpointed Kyoko's location, John and Yoko didn't waste any time. They rushed over to the children's camp and kidnapped Kyoko in broad daylight. As the car screeched off, John and Yoko, fearful of roadblocks by police trying to recover the girl, laid down in the back of the car with Kyoko between them. Dan was the getaway driver. They got all the way back to the hotel before they discovered that Kyoko didn't have any shoes with her, so they sent Richter to buy some. By the time he reached the lobby, the police had surrounded the place.

A picture of John carrying a very frightened nine year old Kyoko over the threshold of the police station was splashed across the front of the tabloids the next day. Cox was very upset with the Lennons, needless to say. Instead of trying to talk to him about some sort of custody arrangement, they had attempted to kidnap the child. The couple was held at the station for fourteen hours and questioned about the attempted abduction. In the end, the judge allowed Kyoko to choose the person that she wanted to go with. Having lived with Tony for most of her life, she chose him.

Yoko was still unwilling to give up that easily. She told the press: "We will be back for her, wherever she is. ... How can you kidnap your own baby? I did what any mother would do."

The Lennons flew back to London to consult with their lawyers on the matter. They were advised to go to the Virgin Islands, where Tony and Yoko's divorce had been granted, to put in for a writ of custody there. Custody was, in fact, granted by this court, but by that time Tony had moved back to America with the child. This actually turned out to be to the Lennon's advantage because the custody writ could only be enforced in the United States or one of its territories. John and Yoko decided to move to New York in order to continue their search.

In 1973, the Lennon's bought an apartment at the Dakota, overlooking Central Park. It was one of the most desirable places to live on the Upper West Side, despite the fact that the movie *Rosemary's Baby* had been filmed there. Shortly after the Lennons moved there, the fact that they spent almost all their time together was getting on both their nerves. It started to have an impact on their relationship. After talking it over, John and Yoko decided that they needed to be apart for awhile. They mutually agreed that John should go to Los Angeles and make a record, taking with him their lovely twenty-three year old assistant, May Pang. That was the beginning of the adventure that would later become know as "the lost weekend."

May and John had first met each other during the making of the underground movie *Fly*. She was hired as an assistant and sent to a Chinese restaurant to collect hundreds of live flies for use in the film.

When Lennon arrived in Los Angeles, he started to hang out with Harry Nilson, Keith Moon, Ringo Starr, and Alice Cooper. The original plan had been to go out to California and cut a record with Phil Spector, featuring the songs that John loved the most. The title of the album would be *Rock and Roll*.

John switched to "Plan Two" when he got to L.A. and discovered the condition that Spector was in. At that time he was far more out of control than John had even imagined being. Lennon had expected to be able to work with Phil on this new project. Instead, he had to witness many of the frightening changes in Spector firsthand. His behavior had become bizarre. May Pang went with John when he met with Spector at his Beverly Hills home. When they arrived, Phil actually locked them up in the house and held them there for nine hours. It was a highly volatile time for everyone involved. But, if that wasn't bad enough, Spector was even worse in the studio. In

fact, he got so bad that one day Spector actually picked up a pistol and fired it into the ceiling of the control booth. Shortly after that, he disappeared with all the session tapes.

When John protested that he owned the tapes, he was told that because Spector had paid for the sessions personally, through Warner Brothers, that it was up to Lennon to get the tapes back. By this time Spector had really gone off the deep end, barricading himself in his house. There was a huge battle over the tapes. John grew really depressed and went on a terrible drinking binge that made all the papers. There was even a story in the British press about it. It seems that Lennon was thrown out of the Troubador nightclub, on Sunset Boulevard, for heckling the Smothers Brothers.

While watching the show John and Harry Nilsson had gotten really drunk on Brandy Alexanders and John kept totally disrupting the act with his wisecracks. Finally, he managed to stop the show completely and he and Harry were kicked out of the club. Then, on the way to the parking lot, Nilsson got into a shoving match with the manager of the club and a photographer, who was trying to get the incident on film. What he did get was a picture of Nilsson about to throw a punch, while John tried to hold him back. The picture also made the papers the next day.

After this incident, John decided that the two of them were getting into too much trouble and he asked Harry if he would like to make an album with him. He thought it might help them both to get a better perspective on their own lives. They rented a beach house in Malibu together and tried to get going. Unfortunately, the two had a notoriously bad influence on one another. John literally had to lock himself in his bedroom to keep from drinking too much. The pair finally did come up with an album called *Pussycats*, on RCA, but it didn't go over very well.

Meanwhile, back in New York City, Yoko was getting a blast of hostility from the rock press, who still blamed her for the breakup of the Beatles. Also, May Pang kept Yoko up to date on how things were going with John in L.A. Pang gave her regular reports on John's health and mental status and Yoko tried to help May to handle the situations that arose.

In August of 1974, John went back to New York. As soon as he arrived, John checked into a suite at New York's Regency hotel for awhile. After that he stayed with May Pang at her apartment until he could find a bigger place. Being away from all the partying, and back in New York, gave Lennon a burst of creative energy. He wrote all of the songs for his next album, *Walls and Bridges*, in one writing session. He recorded the album at the Record Plant with Klaus Voorman, Jim Keltner, and Nicky Hopkins. This was another effort that helped John to come to grips with his life. Critics and fans alike loved it and all that love gave John a real ego boost.

Then, the day before he started work on *Walls and Bridges*, his tapes were finally recovered from Phil Spector. Al Coury, the president of Capitol Records, paid Spector $94,000 for them, and it turned out to be mostly junk. John was only able to salvage four songs from that original mess. So he took it all back to the Record Plant, where he recorded ten more rock classics in five days, with the musicians that he had already gotten together for *Walls and Bridges*.

Somewhere around this time, Yoko called John and asked him over for tea. This happened three times. John brought a friend with him each time because he felt a little awkward around Yoko after everything that had gone on. The first time he came, he brought Harry Nilsson with him. The two had worked out their signals ahead of time. When it was time Harry would stand up and tell them that he had to leave for an appointment. Yoko walked him to the door, while John sat there hoping that Yoko would ask him to stay for awhile. Instead, she stood holding the door for him, while Harry waited in the elevator.

During the next visit, John looked wistfully out the windows over Central Park; he said, "I forgot how beautiful it was."

"Don't start that again," said Yoko with tears in her eyes. She had to send him away because otherwise she feared that she would break down and ask him to stay.

John and Yoko did get back together, at Elton John's concert on Thanksgiving of 1974, at Madison Square Garden. Elton had played and sung with John on "Whatever Gets You Through The Night." Elton subsequently recorded John's song "Lucy In The Sky With Diamonds" for one of his own albums, on which Lennon sang in the back-up chorus. It was during that recording session that Elton asked John if he would appear live with him if "Whatever Gets You Through The Night" hit number one. Lennon agreed because he didn't think it would get that high on the charts; but it did, so John kept his promise to appear.

When Yoko heard about the concert she called Tony King, who was working for Elton at the time, and told him she wanted to attend the concert but that she did not want John to know she was there. She requested a seat that allowed her to see the show but would keep her out of John's sight. This was arranged for her, and Tony led Yoko to her seat, right after the lights went down.

Just before the two entertainers were supposed to go on stage, two gift boxes filled with white gardenias were delivered to their dressing rooms. Both notes that were included, said, "Best of luck, all my love, Yoko." John rushed into Elton's dressing room to show him, saying: "Thank God Yoko's not here tonight. I couldn't go on I'd be so nervous." Elton only smiled, and they took the stage.

When Lennon walked onto the stage the crowd went wild for several minutes. In her box seat, Yoko burst into tears because she could see how much other people really loved him, as well as herself, and yet he was still alone.

When the show was over, Tony King took her backstage, knocked on Lennon's dressing room door and said, " I've got a surprise for you," and Yoko walked through the door. John was astonished, but that night was the beginning of a reconciliation for them.

While John didn't move back into the Dakota right away, it wasn't very long before he returned for good. By the time he got back, two months later, he had agreed to stop smoking, drinking, and drugging, and he promised to eat a healthy diet. When he arrived there he was clean and sober. He and Yoko went on a forty day liquid fast to cleanse their body of any harmful elements. After that, Yoko went to a Chinese acupuncturist who put both she and John on a diet of fish and rice, assuring Yoko that she would be able to get pregnant and have the baby this time. A few days later, she found out that she was.

At that point John had been planning to return to the studio, but his imminent fatherhood made him alter his plans a little. That was the beginning of John's "househusband" phase. Again, Yoko had to stay in bed, but was destined to have a much better outcome than she had with her other pregnancies with John.

It was during Yoko's pregnancy that a long-running battle John had with immigration was finally resolved. The Nixon White House was caught up in Watergate by this time and had already fallen. John started to attend all his hearings in person in order to fight for his U.S. citizenship. He even cut his hair and wore a tie to court. In June of 1975 John's attorneys lodged a suit against former U.S. Attorney General John Mitchell and former U.S. Attorney General Richard Kleindeins, charging that deportation actions the government had taken against Lennon were improper. Yoko went into premature labor. She went into convulsions and had to be rushed to the hospital, where the staff managed to keep her alive with blood transfusions. John did not leave her side for a moment through the whole ordeal.

After a very rough night, Yoko gave birth to Sean Ono Lennon on October 9, 1975, John's thirty-fifth birthday. John was so happy to finally have a baby with Yoko that he decided he would always be there for him. Elton John became Sean's godfather.

In April of 1976, John's father, Freddie Lennon, died. John had called the hospital to talk to him while he was ill and they talked for hours. Freddie had stomach cancer and was in a lot of pain, but was very glad to be hearing form his son. During these calls John tried to lighten the mood that hung over Freddie's hospital bed. He later told friends that he would have felt better about the whole situation, if he and his father had been able to see each other in person before he died. Apparently, that just wasn't meant to be.

John really loved New York City from the beginning. It was a chance for him to get a fresh start, a place where you could sometimes be anonymous if you wanted to be, even if you were John Lennon. The problem was that Lennon had never been one to try to blend into the background. In fact, shortly after meeting Jerry Rubin and Abbie Hoffman, John Lennon would become known as one of the most outspoken activists in the United States.

This is really where most of John's immigration troubles started. Hoffman and Rubin were labeled as subversives by the Nixon administration, and considered to be a direct threat to national security because of their political agenda.

Almost as soon as the Lennon's arrived in New York City, David Peel, another "subversive," actually threw a welcome to New York parade for the couple. Everyone involved was dancing through the streets of the city singing, "You also met an underground welcome to freaky town."

Not long after that, John and Yoko started hanging out at Max's Kansas City, a once super-hip club, patronized by such gifted artists as Andy Warhol. It had since turned into the home for underground rock. John started to practice there with a band called Elephants Memory.

With Rubin and Hoffman as role models John "came out" politically. In October he appeared at a protest on behalf of American Indian civil rights. In November he appeared at the Attica Relatives benefit at the Apollo Theater in Harlem, for the relatives of the men in the bloody prison riots. He wrote guest columns for underground Sundance magazine and went to Ann Arbor, Michigan, to appear at a John Sinclair rally. Sinclair, founder of the White Panthers, had been given ten years for selling two joints to an undercover cop.

Next, Lennon set out to take on the Nixon White House. Rubin and Hoffman were working on a plan for a demonstration, to be held at the Republican National Convention, in 1972. They wanted to sponsor a rock concert that would draw around 300,000 antiwar protesters and actually bring the convention to a stand-still. John Lennon would be the star attraction at that concert. They never actually pulled it off because word of the plan somehow leaked out and *Rolling Stone* published an article about it.

That was more than enough for the administration. The Nixon White House officially labeled Lennon a threat to national security and started looking for anything that they could use to deport him. By early 1972 the Senate Internal Security Subcommittee of the Judiciary Committee was doing a through investigation of Lennon. They even sent out a classified memo on the couple, listing all of John's activist causes and the names of the people that he associated with.

While all this was going on, John's immigration attorney filed for a six month extension on his non-immigration visa. It was granted at first, but then the memo started to pass through the political pipeline.

By March 6th, John's visa extension was canceled. The government gave the official reason as being the Lennon's arrest for marijuana in 1968. While the Lennon's knew that this wasn't the real reason for the cancellation, they didn't think that it had anything to do with their politics. They thought they were being asked to leave because, in January, they had given a concert at Alice Tully Hall without INS permission. They had no American work permits and were forced to perform from their seats, where Yoko conducted the band with an apple instead of a baton. John's attorneys appealed the case and applied for a temporary extension on his deportation date. The case against Yoko, who had no criminal record, was dropped, and John became its solitary focus.

Ironically, getting a permanent visa was supposed to be John and Yoko's primary concern. In order to get final custody of Kyoko, Yoko had to live in America. Even with everything else they were involved in, the couple hadn't given up their search for Kyoko. They hired more private detectives and found out that Tony had moved to Houston, Texas. He and Melinda moved there because she had grown up there. Since the Lennons had last seen him, Tony had become a born again Christian. He had also applied to Houston's Domestic Relations Court for permanent custody of his daughter.

John and Yoko heard about his plan and flew to Houston to face him in court. There, they presented the custody papers that they had obtained in the Virgin Islands. Judge Peter Salito considered the case very carefully. On the one hand, he had two world famous radicals as potential parents—who had been away from the child for most of her life. On the other hand, he had a set of conservative, Christian parents, with whom Kyoko had already lived for most of her life. He chose to overrule the Virgin Islands order and return custody to the Cox's. Shortly after that, Tony went into deep hiding with Kyoko. Yoko was unable to locate her again before she came of age. Since then, she has refused to see her mother.

The Republican National Convention came and went, with no interference by political activists. The one place that John was known to appear was at the One to One concert at Madison Square Garden, where he and Yoko helped raise one and a half million dollars to help mentally challenged children.

While John was busy taking care of Sean, Yoko started to take care of their business matters. Her first deal was a five million dollar settlement with Allen Klein. No doubt about it, she is a very sharp businesswoman. Around this time she made some very lucrative, if strange, investments. First, she bought up more apartments in the Dakota as they became available, then she opened Lennon's Music in an office on the ground floor. She had someone paint clouds on the ceiling of her office for a more tranquil effect.

Next, she purchased a three-hundred and sixteen acre farm in the Catskills of New York, along with homes in Japan, Oyster Bay, Long Island, and Palm Beach. She also began to invest in cattle, which turned out to be a very lucrative venture. One of the Lennon cows sold at auction for $250,000, a new record.

In the summer of 1980, John took a trip to Bermuda. He enjoyed it so much that he called Yoko and asked her to send Sean to be with him. One day while father and son were taking a walk through the Botanical Gardens, John spotted a gorgeous white flower called a "Double Fantasy," and it inspired him to write a song. He called Yoko and played it for her over the phone. Yoko, too, had written a song and she played it for him. John decided that it was time to make an album again, after nearly six years. Just before John's fortieth birthday, John and Yoko signed a contract with Geffen Records and they started producing the *Double Fantasy* album at the Record Plant.

The public was overjoyed that John was back and the couple did a series of interviews with top publications like *Newsweek*, *Playboy*, and *Esquire*. The album was very well received by critics and fans alike. John was on top of the world.

Just as it began to look as if John's life was almost exactly the way he wanted it, Mark David Chapman came into the picture.

While authors before me have chosen to spend a good deal of time discussing Chapman's life, I chose to give him no more perverse glory. What he did deserves no recognition. It is difficult, however, not to talk about the heinous crime that he committed against the peace movement and a large segment of humanity.

On Monday, December 8, 1980, Chapman arrived outside the Dakota early on in the day. When John and Yoko left for their recording session at 5 p.m., his limo picked them up at the curb, instead of inside the security gates of the building. After all, John had always been safe walking the streets of New York before, and always stopped to sign autographs when he had the time. In fact, he signed a copy of *Double Fantasy* for Chapman before going to the Record Plant. Another fan actually got a picture of Lennon signing Chapman's album, an image that made some of the papers later.

The couple returned home at around 11:00 p.m. The security gates were still open so the limo pulled to the curb once again. John and Yoko got out and started to walk toward the building when a voice called out, "Mr. Lennon?"

John tried to see who was speaking to him from the darkness, but he never had time to reply. Chapman shot him five times in cold blood. John never had a chance.

Yoko didn't realize that John had been shot until he fell down on the floor of the Dakota security office.

After the police had been called, Jay Hastings, the doorman at the Dakota, went out to see if he could catch a glimpse of the gunman. To his horror, Chapman still stood in front of the building, calmly reading from his copy of *Catcher in the Rye*.

"Do you know what you just did?" Hastings asked.

"I just shot John Lennon." Chapman said calmly. (Brown and Gaines 1983, 436)

By this time Yoko was hysterical. She started screaming and wasn't able to calm down until the police arrived. They took John to Roosevelt Hospital in the back of their police cruiser, because they feared he wouldn't survive until the ambulance arrived.

Yoko followed in another cruiser, whispering over and over again to herself, "It's not true, tell me its not true."

When they got him to the emergency room the staff worked over him for half an hour, but it was too late...

Apparently, Mark David Chapman seems to think that he was able to take John Lennon away from us. He was not. No one can ever take away the kind of things that Lennon gave to the world.

Promotional Items

The poster from the press kit.

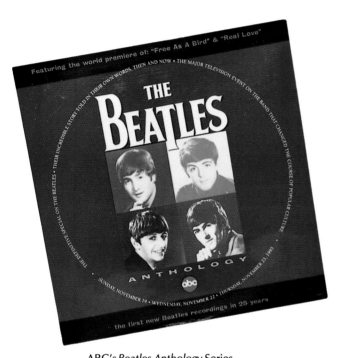

ABC's *Beatles Anthology* Series press kit, which was sent out to locally affiliated stations for promotional purposes. The next two shots show the kit opened up and the poster that came with the other press kit material. Value: E: $60 NM: $65.

Inside view of the press kit.

1996 Promotional Box, which was sold separately with the first Anthology video set. Apple Corps Ltd. Under exclusive license to EMI Records Ltd. Printed in USA, Apple-Capitol Video. Distributed by Turner Home Entertainment. Value for promo box: E: $30 NM: $35. Value for the first video set: E: $140 NM: $160.

Same 1996 promo box shown opened up. The videos fit into the compartment in the center of the open box.

The second part of the Anthology Series videos, along with the corresponding eight volume laser disc set. Value for the videos: E: $140 NM: $160. Value for the laser disc set: E: $220 NM: $230.

Record store p.o.p. (an album size card) for *Anthology 1*, 1995. Under exclusive license from Apple Corps Ltd. Value: E: $15 NM: $20.

This Anthology three-ring binder was a promotional giveaway for radio stations. This makes them fairly limited. Value: E: $70 NM: $75.

Framed *Anthology 2* 1996 litho, Apple Corps Ltd. Licensed by Determined Productions, 1993, U.K. Value: E: $225 NM: $250.

Record store p.o.p. for *Anthology 2*, 1996. Value: E: $15 NM: $20.

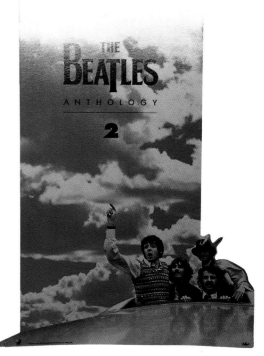

Anthology 2 countertop display, for record stores. Apple Corps. Ltd., 1996. Value: E: $25 NM: $30.

Record store p.o.p. for *Anthology 3*, 1996. Value: E: $15 NM: $20.

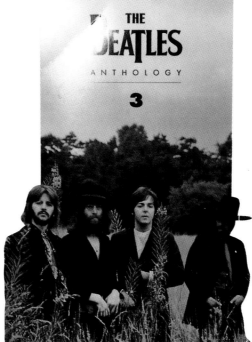

Anthology 3 countertop display that was sent out to stores as a promotional album. Apple Corps Ltd., 1996. Value: E: $25 NM: $30.

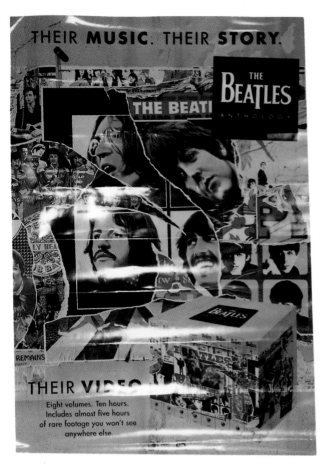

Anthology 3 poster, 1996, Apple Corps Inc. Ltd. Value: E: $15 NM: $18.

The back of the *Anthology 3* poster.

These are the boxes that go with the standee. They are valued separately. Value for the set of three: E: $90 NM: $100.

This Anthology Series standee was also a promo item for record stores. It measures 35" wide by 65" long. Value: E: $200 NM: $225.

Anthology Series Part I and II *Request* magazines. These were put out as promotional material for the Anthology series. They are loaded with fascinating facts about the Beatles. Value for each: E: $10 NM: $15.

"Real Love" countertop display that held "Real Love" and "Free As A Bird" cassette singles. It measures 8 1/4" x 12", 1996, Apple Corps Ltd. Printed in USA. Value for display: E: $20 NM: $25. Value for cassette singles: E: $5 NM: $7.

The Beatles Anthology wallet. Made of hemp by the Hempstead Co./Apple Corps Ltd. Value: E: $12 NM: $15.

"Real Love" countertop display that held "Real Love" 45 rpm single. Value: $5 NM: $7.

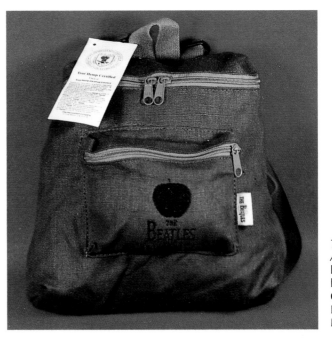

The Beatles Anthology school bag. Made of hemp by the Hempstead Co./Apple Corps Ltd. Value: E: $35 NM: $40.

The Beatles Anthology Plexiglas apple-shaped ornament. Value: E: $3 NM: $5.

Anthology Series CD wallet by Roundhouse Inc. Value: E: $12 NM: $15.

The Beatles Anthology promotional CD that was given out to local radio stations in west Texas. It is marked "Promotional" and "Not For Sale." Value: E: $20 NM: $25.

Anthology Buttons, set of fourteen, 1995. The buttons are 1 3/8" in diameter. Capitol Records Inc. Value for the set of fourteen: E: $40 NM: $50.

This 3" "Ask Me About The Beatles Anthology Video" button is a promotional item. Value: E: $5 NM: $7.

The 2" "I Heard It First!" The Beatles Anthology II, Beatlefest '96 button was purchased at the Chicago Beatlefest that year. Value: E: $3 NM: $5.

"The Beatles Anthology" gift boxes. They came with an Anthology T-shirt, four photo cards (one of each Beatle), a paperweight, and a special limited edition certificate, #1194 of 5000. Apple Corps Ltd. Value: E: $65 NM: $75.

"Real Love" gift boxes. They come with everything seen here. Value: E: $65 NM: $75.

New Memorabilia

"Beatle City" was an exhibit brought over from Liverpool to three major U.S. cities, for a limited time. The exhibit provided highlights of career milestones, a brief history of each Beatle, early photos of the Quarrymen, and the Silver Beatles, early hand bills, and posters left over from Beatles gigs, Cavern Club photos, memorabilia, and many more items, too numerous to mention. Value is for everything shown: E: $40 NM: $45.

This is the front of a bronze coin bought at Beatle City in Liverpool in 1985. Value: E: $25 NM: $30.

The back of the bronze coin from Beatle City.

Beatlemania program with two ticket stubs. This was a stage show that was as close as some people ever came to a live Beatles performance. Value for program: E: $12 NM: $15. Value per ticket stub: E: $3 NM: $5.

The Cavern

Export pilsner, The Cavern beer, from the new The Cavern in Liverpool. The old one was torn down years ago to make room for a parking lot. Value: E: $12 NM: $15.

Leather book mark from "The Beatles Shop" in Liverpool. Value: E: $4 NM: $6.

A piece of carpet left over from the remodeling job on the new Cavern Club in Liverpool. This particular piece of carpet is owned by Kathy Childers, who plays guitar with City Zoo, an up and coming band out of Seattle. The piece of carpet measures 19" in length and 10" at its widest point. Value: E: $80 NM: $100.

Clocks, Coin Holder, Color Book

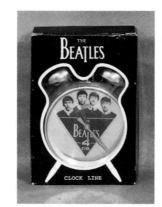

"The Beatles" alarm clock, Apple Corps Ltd., 1988. Value with box: E: $75 NM: $85.

1987 Beatles clock put out by Apple Corps Ltd. and sold at "The Beatles Shop" in Liverpool. Value: E: $35 NM: $40.

"The Beatles" coin holder from "The Beatles Shop" in Liverpool. Value: E: $8 NM: $10.

Beatle City Colouring Book. © Beatle City 1984. Value: E: $20 NM: $25.

A sample of some of the pictures in the *Beatle City Colouring Book.*

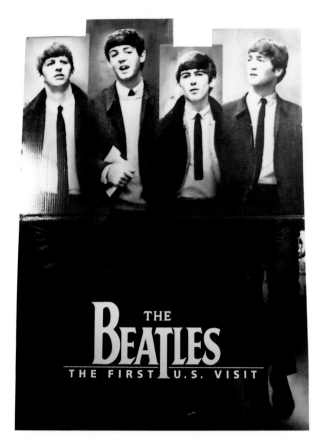

John, Paul, George, and Ringo: Beatles Russian Nesting Dolls with their names painted at the base of each doll. Value: E: $100 NM: $150.

"The Beatles, The First U.S. Visit" standee. This was a promotional item sent out to record stores. MPI Home Video promo. Value: E: $140 NM: $150.

Five Beatles Russian Nesting Dolls: John, Paul, George, Ringo, and Brian Epstein, the Beatles first manager. Value: E: $100 NM: $150.

Sgt. Pepper's style Russian Nesting Dolls with the Union Jack. Value: E: $100 NM: $150.

The following soft sculpture dolls were purchased at "The Beatles Shop" in Liverpool. These two dolls are George and Ringo. Value per doll: E: $8 NM: $10.

John and Paul soft sculpture dolls. Value per doll: E: $8 NM: $10.

George and Ringo soft sculpture Sgt. Pepper's dolls. Value for each: E: $12 NM: $15.

John and Paul soft sculpture
Sgt. Pepper's dolls. Value per
doll: E: $12 NM: $15.

George and Ringo soft
sculpture dolls in black and
blue. Value for each: E: $8
NM: $10.

John and Paul soft sculpture dolls
in black and blue. Value for each:
E: $8 NM: $10.

Drum Head and Sticks

Drum sticks. Value: E: $10 NM: $12.

Sgt. Pepper's Drum Head, custom painted for Dennis Dailey. Value: E: $40 NM: $50.

Figurines

Pan Am flight to the USA commemorative lead figure of the Fabs on the steps of the plane. Value: E: $65 NM: $70.

"Free As a Bird" lead figure, with John Lennon portrayed in ghostly white. Value: E: $65 NM: $70.

Shea Stadium, Flushing, Queens, New York City: lead figures of the Beatles on stage. Value: E: $65 NM: $70.

"The Beatles" pocket flashlight from "The Beatles Shop" in Liverpool. Value: E: $8 NM: $10.

Fab Four bust of the group. Recent vintage. Value: E: $55 NM: $60.

Box of fudge from "The Beatles Shop". Value: E: $12 NM: $15.

Greeting Cards

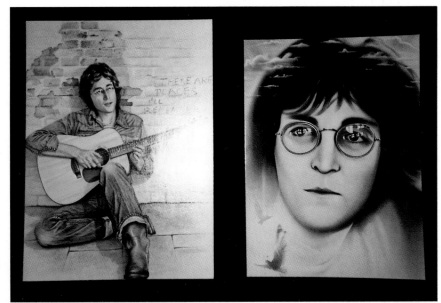

Two John Lennon, Beatlegraphics greeting cards. Value per each: E: $3 NM: $5.

Set of five Beatlegraphics greeting cards. Value for set: E: $20 NM: $25.

Set of five Beatlegraphics greeting cards. The values for all of the sets of five Beatlegraphics cards will be the same.

Five more Beatlegraphics greeting cards.

Another five Beatlegraphics cards.

Five Beatlegraphics cards.

Four Beatlegraphics greeting cards. Value for set: E: $15 NM: $20.

Four Beatlegrphics greeting cards. Value for each: E: $3 NM: $5.

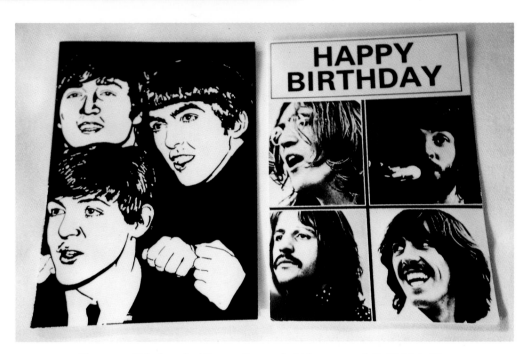

Close-up of black and white greeting cards. Value per card: E: $3 NM: $5.

Three postcards from Liverpool. Value per card: E: $3 NM: $5.

Beatles hair, gag gift. Made in 1983 by Maden Jest Inc. Value: E: $15 NM: $18.

Magnets, Matches, and Mouse Pads

Sgt. Pepper's and Revolver mouse pads for your p.c. Value per pad: E: $10 NM: $15.

Legends of the Fridge Magnet by Polar of Canada. Value: E: $12 NM: $15.

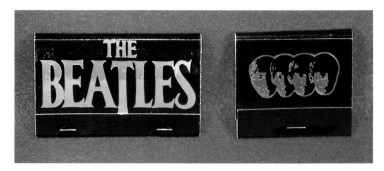

Books of Beatles matches from "The Beatles Shop". Value large: E: $2 NM: $4. Value small: E: $1 NM: $2.

Mouse pads with the pictures used in the Anthology Series. Value for each: E: $8 NM: $10.

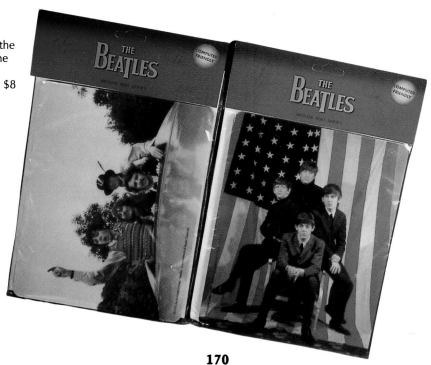

Drum shaped mouse pads with "The Beatles" and *Sgt. Pepper's Lonely Hearts Club Band*. Value for each: E: $8 NM: $10.

Music Boxes

Abbey Road and *Sgt. Pepper's* Bell Jars, put out by the Franklin Mint. A limited edition Beatles Product © 1995. Apple Corps Ltd. Value: E: $90 NM: $100.

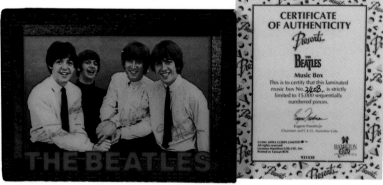

"The Beatles" Enesco music box, 1991. Comes with a certificate of authenticity. Value: E: $25 NM: $30.

Help! and *Magical Mystery Tour* Bell Jars. Same description as "Abbey Road" and "Sgt. Pepper's" Bell Jars. Value: E: $90 NM: $100.

"Beatles '65" Bell Jar. Same value and description as the other jars.

Enesco, individual Beatle music boxes with an album cover and Beatle figure on each box. Value is for the set of four: E: $100 NM: $105.

Ornaments, Phone Card, and Pillows

Avedon photo Christmas ornaments. Value: E: $20 NM: $25.

Set of four Beatles Christmas ornaments. Value: E: $20 NM: $25.

Abbey Road phone card by Omitel. Value: E: $3 NM: $5.

Beatles Silk Pillow. Measures 20" x 20". Apple Corps Ltd. Value: E: $45 NM: $50.

Signs/Standees

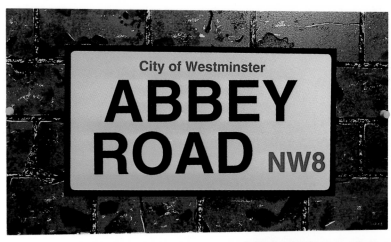

"Abbey Road" street signs, made of cardboard. Value: E: $5 NM: $7.

Cardboard street signs representing streets of Liverpool. Value per sign: E: $5 NM: $7.

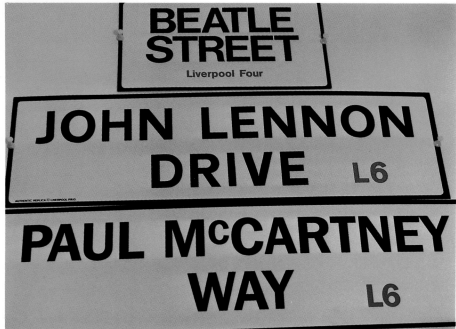

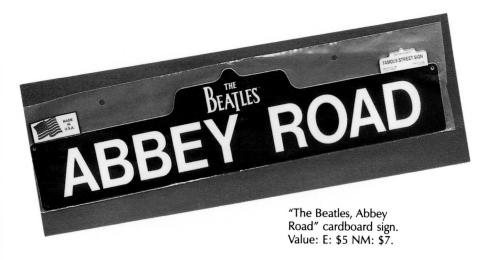

"The Beatles, Abbey Road" cardboard sign. Value: E: $5 NM: $7.

Thimbles/Tickets

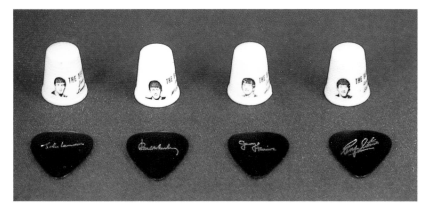

Unauthorized thimbles and guitar picks, one for each Beatle. Value for the set of four thimbles: E: $15 NM: $20. Value for the set of four picks: E: $10 NM: $12.

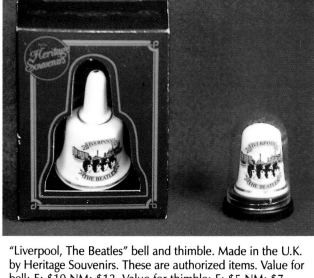

"Liverpool, The Beatles" bell and thimble. Made in the U.K. by Heritage Souvenirs. These are authorized items. Value for bell: E: $10 NM: $12. Value for thimble: E: $5 NM: $7.

An original Shea Stadium ticket with a reproduction poster and a certificate of authenticity signed by Sid Bernstein. Value: E: $80 NM: $85.

This is the signed certificate of authenticity.

Eight reproduction back-stage passes in a frame. No markings. Value with frame: E: $55 NM: $60.

Videos/Wallets

The Beatles Cartoons volume one. Value: E: $15 NM: $20.

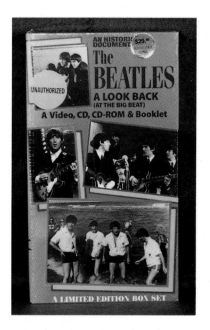

Beatles CD Rom *A Look Back*. Big BCD, M.I.L. Multimedia, LLc with a bonus booklet. This product is unauthorized. Value: E: $15 NM: $20.

"The Beatles" leather wallet, billfold, and a comb with a case. Value for the set: E: $25 NM: $30.

Bibliography

Augsburger, Jeff, Marty Eck, and Rick Rann. *The Beatles Memorabilia Price Guide*. Antique Trader Books, 3rd ed., 1997.

Bacon, David & Norman Maslov. *The Beatles England*. Press Book, 1982.

Brown, Peter & Steven Gaines. *The Love You Make*. New York: McGraw-Hill Book Co., 1983.

Carr, Roy & Tony Tyler. *The Beatles, An Illustrated Record*. New York: Harmony Books, A Division of Crown Publishers Inc.

Clayson, Alan. *Ringo Starr, Straight Man Or Joker*. New York: Paragon House, 1991.

Clayton J., B. Ezrin, J. Lennon, & A. Moore. *Julian Lennon's Help Yourself* CD. Charisma Music Pub. Inc., Virgin Music Inc., 1991.

Coleman, Ray. *Lennon*. McGraw-Hill Book Co., 1984.

Corbin, Carole Lynn. *John Lennon, An Impact Biography*. New York, London: Franklin Waltz, 1982.

Crawford, Barbara, Lamon, Hollis, & Michael Stern. *The Beatles, A Reference and Value Guide*. Collectors Books, Schroeder Publishing, 1994.

Dailey, Dennis. Personal interview. CONDAI @ NS.NQUE.COM.

Egan, Sam & Andrew Solt. *Imagine*. New York: Macmillan Publishing Co., 1988. By Warner Bros., Yoko Ono & Sarah Lazin.

Guiliano, Geoffrey. *Blackbird*. New York: Dutton, Penguin Books, 1991, Something Fishy Productions Ltd.

Guiliano, Geoffrey. *Dark Horse*. Skyboot Productions Ltd., 1989.

Guiliano, Geoffrey. *The Lost Beatles Interviews*. New York: Penguin Books, 1994.

Gutman, David & Elizabeth Thompson. *The Lennon Companion; Twenty-five Years of Comment*. London: The Macmillan Press Ltd.

Harrison, George. *I, Me, Mine*. New York: Simon and Schuster, Inc.

Kaye, Elizabeth. "Here Comes The Son." *Rolling Stone*, Issue #449, June 6, 1985.

Lennon, Pauline. *Daddy Come Home*. London: Angus and Robertson, 1990.

McCabe, Peter & Robert D. Schonfield. New York: Simon and Schuster Inc.

Norman, Phillip. *Shout!* New York: MJF Books, 1981.

Patterson, R. Gary. *The Walrus Was Paul, The Great Beatle Death Clues of 1969*. Dowling Press, Inc., 1986.

Taylor, Derek. *It Was Twenty Years Ago Today*. New York: Simon and Schuster Inc.

Twist, Cynthia. *A Twist of Lennon*. New York: Avon Books, 1978.

Website-Julian Lennon: In His Own Words"; excerpts from *Express* newspapers Ltd. From *Instant Karma*, issue #3, April-May of 1982.

Website-Lennon, Julian-juliansonrise

Website-Lennon, Julian-julianhelpinterview

Website-Lennon, Sean-seanspeaksup

Website-McWilliams, Courtney, www.beatles-collectibles.com. For lots more information and fun facts, join us on our website. We can help you find those hard to find items as well as well as helping you to preview and sell your own Beatles product line.

Website-Ono, Yoko-yointerviews32

Website-Ono, Yoko-Yoko on Ryko: Austin Chronicle

Index